IMAGES
of America

MOUNT PLEASANT
THE FRIENDLY TOWN

IMAGES
of America

MOUNT PLEASANT
THE FRIENDLY TOWN

Mary-Julia C. Royall

ARCADIA
PUBLISHING

ISBN 978-0-7385-0690-6

Published by Arcadia Publishing
Charleston, South Carolina

Printed in the United States of America

Library of Congress Catalog Card Number: 2001087923

For all general information contact Arcadia Publishing at:
Telephone 843-853-2070
Fax 843-853-0044
E-mail sales@arcadiapublishing.com
For customer service and orders:
Toll-Free 1-888-313-2665

Visit us on the Internet at www.arcadiapublishing.com

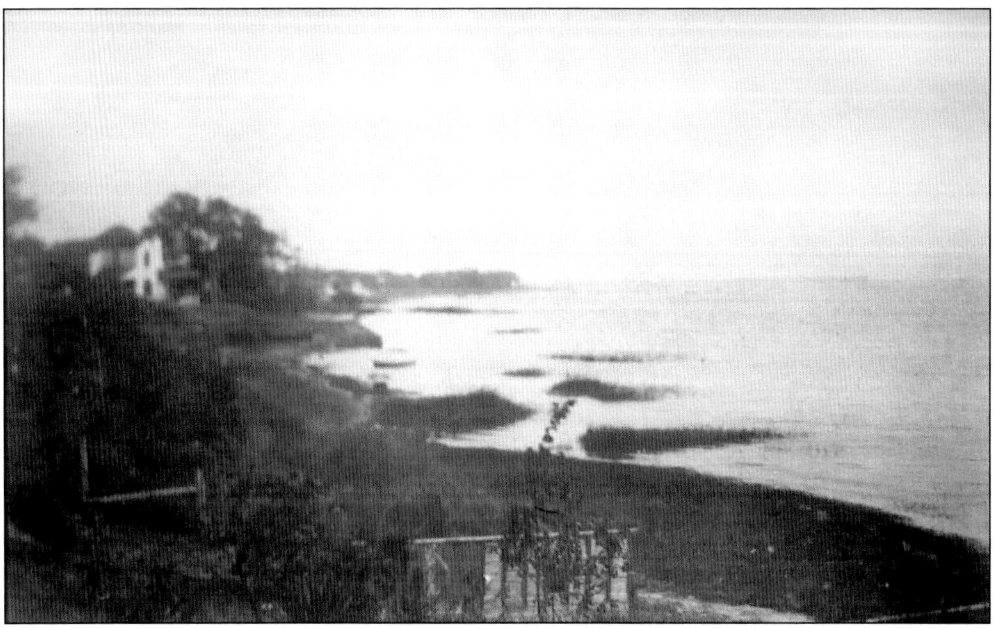

Mount Pleasant's shoreline in the 1930s was peaceful and quiet, but the little town would soon awaken.

Contents

ACKNOWLEDGMENTS

In order to give the reader a sense of community found in Mount Pleasant beginning in 1937, images have been selected that illustrate why it can be called the "Friendly Town." Mount Pleasant is fortunate in having two excellent authors who recorded its history. Petrona Royall McIver's *History of Mount Pleasant* and Anne King Gregorie's *Christ Church, a Plantation Parish (1706–1959)* contain valuable information.

Other sources include newspaper articles from the *Moultrie News*, *The East Cooper Pilot*, and the Charleston *Post and Courier*. Booklets published in the town include the 1939 Directory, 1944 World War II souvenir booklet, the 1987 Bicentennial Program, various maps, and the 1784 plat of Haddrell's Point Plantation from A.L. Lofton. The scrapbooks of Robert L. Coleman and Julia W. McIver, photograph albums of Jervey D. and Lee Royall, and Moultrie High School Annuals were also consulted.

Photographs have been loaned by many friends, including Gertrude King Appleby, Louise Boyd, Emily Lucas Burn, Robert L. Coleman, Kenneth Donaldson, Lou Edens, Marie M. Gleaton, Thomas Gleaton, Patti LaLone, Trisha R. Leach, Otis Pickett III, Anne B. Royall, Julia Royall-Kahin, Sarah McIver Townsend, Jack Ward, Bobbie N. Auld, Sarah R. Hamlin, and Eleise T. Farmer. The contemporary photographs were taken by the author.

The title was suggested by the late Eleanora Edmondston Bryant, who loved the little town. The book is dedicated to her memory. Many thanks to everyone, including editor Laura Daniels for her patience.

Introduction

Mount Pleasant: The Friendly Town begins in 1937 where *Mount Pleasant: The Victorian Village* ended. The progress that Mount Pleasant had hoped for at the end of its first century of incorporation has materialized, as we shall see as the story unfolds.

To understand the beginnings and growth of the little town, a retrospective look is needed. The five little English villages on Charleston harbor were all incorporated into a Town of Mount Pleasant during the 19th century: Mount Pleasant and Greenwich (pronounced Grin'itch) in 1837, Hilliardsville in 1858, and finally Lucasville and the Ferry Tract in 1872. Adjoining the boundaries of these little hamlets was Haddrell's Point Plantation of 471 acres of the 18th century. The earliest grant of 2,340 acres had been given to Surveyor General Florentia O'Sullivan in 1680.

The East Cooper area developed simultaneously with Charleston. Grants of land were given between Shem Creek and the Wando River, as well as along the harbor.

The Church Act of 1706 established ten areas along the coast called parishes, each with its own church. This was Christ Church Parish bounded by the Atlantic Ocean, the Wando River, and Awendaw Creek. Although it was an Anglican Parish by law, Dissenters were allowed and came early from England and New England. With this background, the story of *The Friendly Town* begins.

The story of the town's growth will be approached from various angles. The first chapter explains that progress is beginning with new organizations at work. "The Emerging Town" deals with the government, mayors, the municipal buildings, the fire department, waterworks, post office, library, and bank. Probably the most important addition to the community was the development of a medical center for the East Cooper area.

The town has never been an industrial center. In the early days, a basket factory and a cannery were located here. The ferry took businessmen to Charleston to work and students to the high schools. Stores were located here and there; some with living quarters upstairs. Eventually Pitt Street became the business center and Shem Creek the maritime.

With first mention in 1827 of a village church, as population grew, several denominations built churches. As time went on expansion followed. Some denominations moved to new locations; some stayed but added more adequate facilities.

Education has been important since 1809. New schools were built when facilities were outgrown. A high school was organized in 1940 using the facility on Pitt Street when the Academy moved. African Americans were educated at Laing, which began in 1866.

Chapter seven deals with people and what they did in the era following the Great Depression through World War II up to the present. Space limitations will not permit an in-depth study. Customs change with the passing of time. The focus will be on some the reader may have forgotten.

"Arts, Crafts, and Entertainment" highlights performances by local actors, concerts by opera stars, art shows, writers, newspapers, and television stations here. The town is seen as a friendly community with much local participation.

Children are an important factor in picturing this pleasant place. The "Memories" chapter may remind readers of happy events in their own lives.

Events in World War II affecting the little town will be mentioned. Travels of two local boys show the far-flung theaters of the war. And tribute is paid to the four who did not return. The town sponsored a celebration 50 years after the war was over to remind the citizens of what freedom means.

Bridges are a part of everyday life in Mount Pleasant. During the war years, one burned and one was broken.

Brief mention is made of the 1975 arrival of the World War II aircraft carrier, the *Yorktown*, and the development of the Patriots Point Maritime complex. This subject would merit a book of its own. It was named by Col. D.D. Nicholson Jr. without an apostrophe. As he said "It was that patriots would be attracted to and applaud a complex dedicated to commemorating naval and maritime lore." Many important events happened in this area.

In 1987 the town celebrated its 150th anniversary of incorporation. Many events were scheduled in celebration.

The final section pictures some of the destruction of Hurricane Hugo in 1989. Our area looked like a bombed-out war zone, but with a great deal of assistance from far and wide, recovery came. A beautiful Christmas snow covered the devastation, and with spring came renewal. Although the landscape will never be the same in our lifetime with the loss of many majestic trees, people are resilient. As Robert Browning wrote in his poem "Pippa Passes," "God's in His heaven, all's right with the world."

One

Progress Begins

The little Town of Mount Pleasant had celebrated its centennial in 1937 and was looking forward to growth because it was no longer isolated. The Cooper River bridge in 1929 had linked it with cities to the north and to the south. Recovering from the Great Depression, and hopeful of development, a Junior Chamber of Commerce was organized July 28, 1937, with Francis F Coleman as president, Courtenay G. Freeman as vice president, and Guy Eghbert Thompson as secretary-treasurer. Ten men were on the board of directors. Also, an East Charleston County Development Board was formed with S.A. Guilds as president-treasurer, Mayor W.L. Erckmann as vice president, and Pierre Mazyck as the managing director. Their slogan was "Come to Mount Pleasant and Live." Truly, its second century opened on an optimistic note.

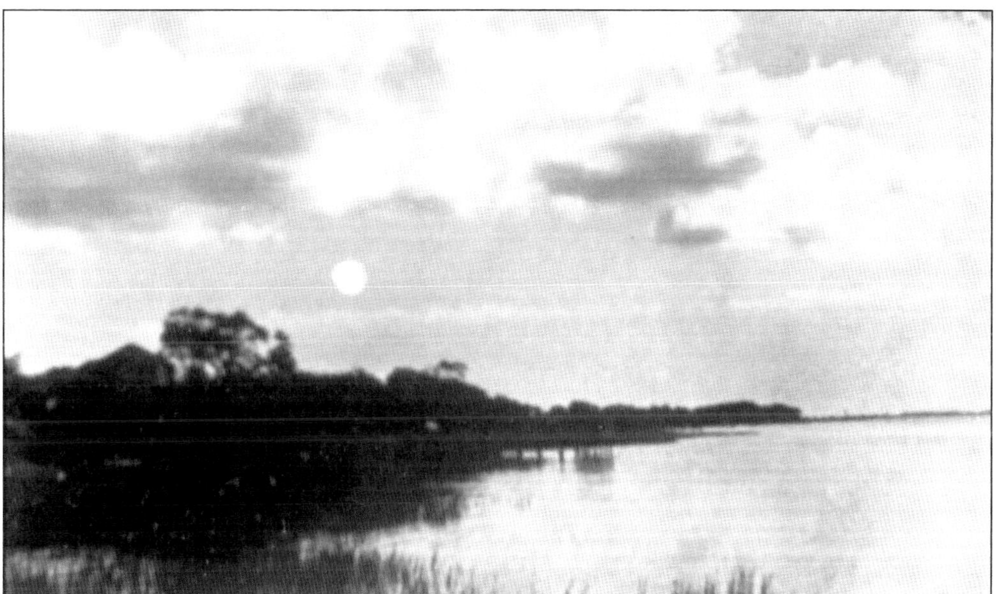

In 1937, Mount Pleasant had electricity, water, and plenty of opportunities. As in the photograph, its sun was rising.

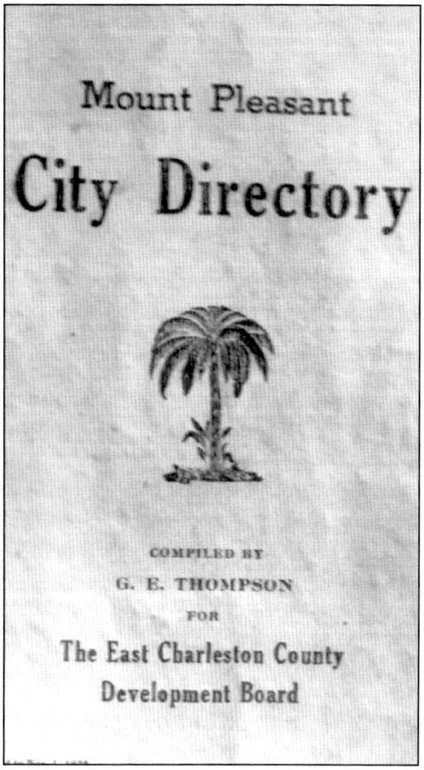

In 1939 a city directory of 24 pages was compiled by G.E. Thompson for the East Charleston County Development Board. The term East Cooper came into usage later. Of the 64 display advertisements, many came from Charleston. There were 378 entries, basically households, of names, addresses, and telephone numbers of only four digits. Not every household had a telephone, however, and Charleston was long distance.

The commercial section listings included grocers, garages, service stations,an oil company, a motor express office, beauty parlors, a barber shop, dry cleaners, a pharmacy, a bowling alley, a boat building company, a printing company, an ice company, a beer garden, a poultry and fish house, a school, a post office, waterworks, and a gift shop. It would be some years before Mount Pleasant would have a bank. The advertisement by Simmons Brothers Grocery was a full page and included a map of the town that indicated his store was at the bend where Church Street meets Pitt Street. Thompson wrote glowingly of advantages of this part of Charleston County, highlighting residence, industry, agriculture, and vacation areas to entice visitors to come. His hope for growth materialized.

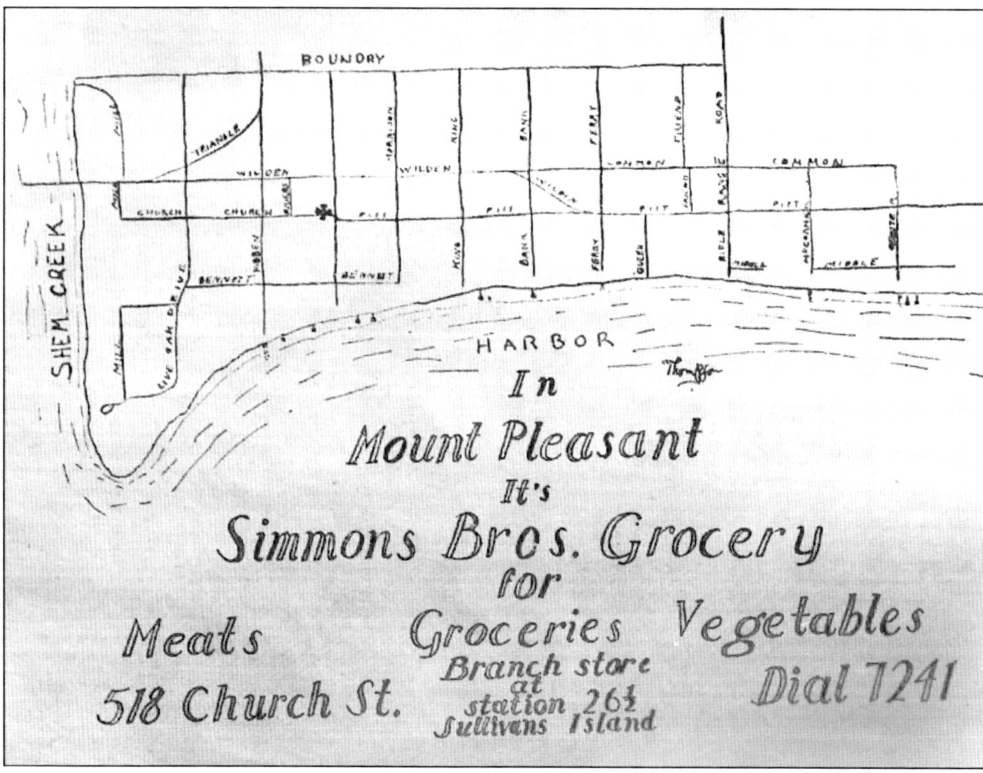

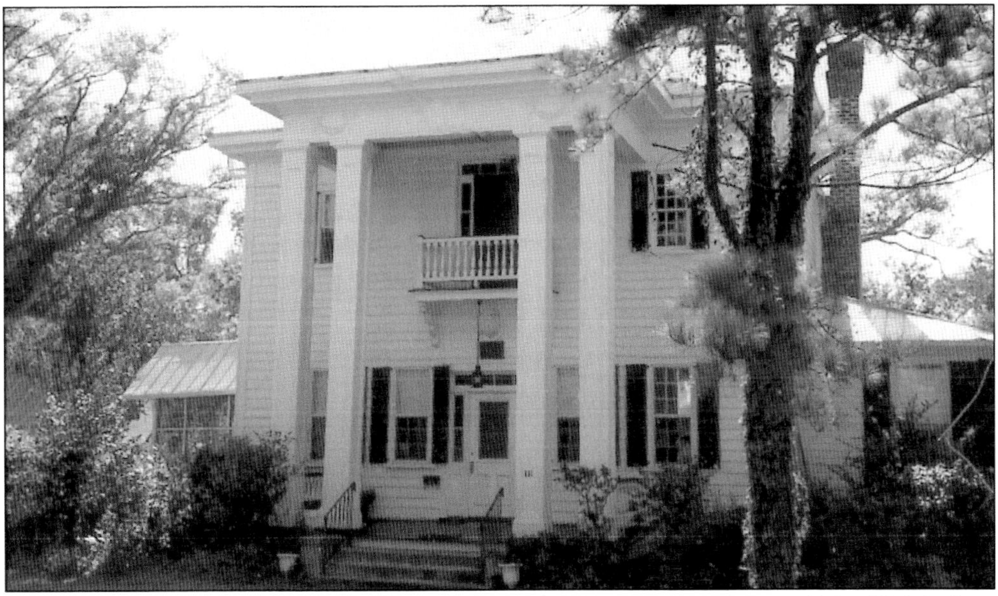

The historical overview in the directory was written by Mrs. W.W. McIver and Mrs. W. Moultrie Moore, both outstanding citizens of the town. Mrs. McIver had compiled the list of historical sites for the brochure when the Cooper River Bridge opened in 1929, and she was the author of the *History of Mount Pleasant* (1960 and 1970). Mrs. Moore was a school trustee for whom the Jennie Moore Elementary School was named. Many places of interest that they noted are still familiar today. Mrs. McIver lived at 111 Hibben Street, the Jacob Motte/Hibben house, which is said to be the oldest house in Mount Pleasant, built c. 1754. It is pictured here.

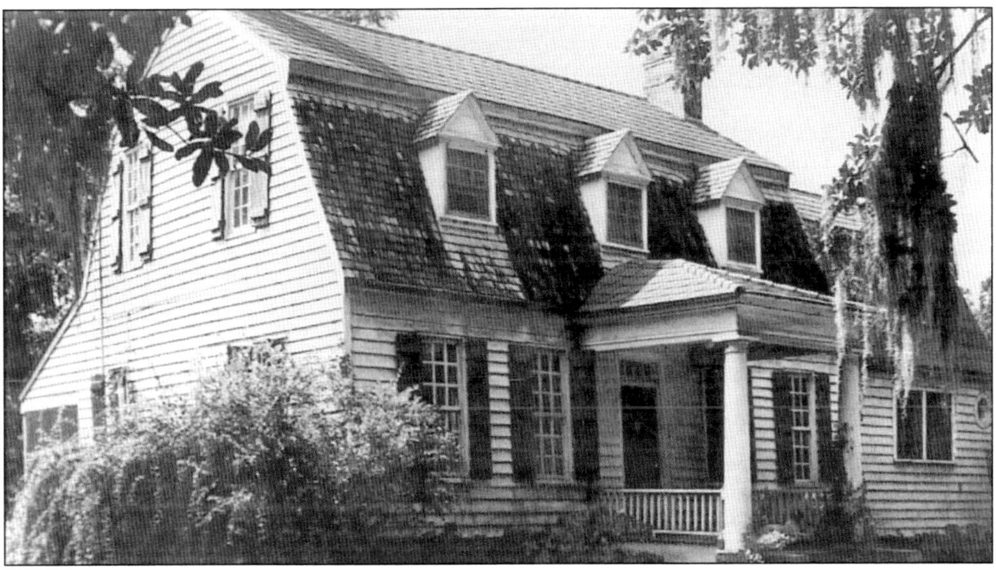

Most of the places listed in 1939 are extant—Christ Church, the parish church; Snee Farm; Boone Hall with its live oak avenue and large pecan grove; the Confederate breastworks, which extended from Boone Hall to Copahee Sound, built to protect the little town from Union troops; and many lesser known places. Oakland Plantation house is one of the oldest houses in Christ Church Parish. It was formerly known as Youghal (Yôl) and was built by a Dutch sea captain, c. 1740. In the image here the Dutch influence is apparent.

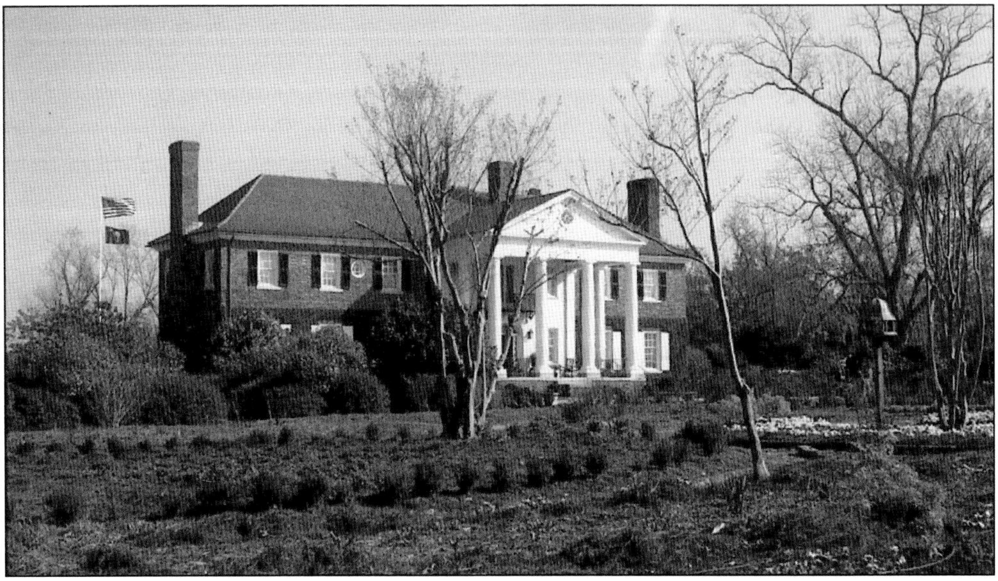

The ladies mentioned many other historic sites in the parish, including the sweetgrass basket weavers and the cemetery at Wappetaw Church on 15 mile landing road. Revolutionary War camping grounds and barracks were noted over toward Sullivan's Island, and it is said that the tabby material of the barracks was used to pave the roads. Later research has noted that the first sea battle of the Revolution was fought off Hog Island (now Patriots Point), with victory for the Americans. Pictured here, Boone Hall is among the newer plantation houses. It was built of bricks made there and replaced a previous house in the 1930s. The gardens are outlined with brick in the pattern of butterfly wings. The outbuildings are original, as are the ones at Oakland.

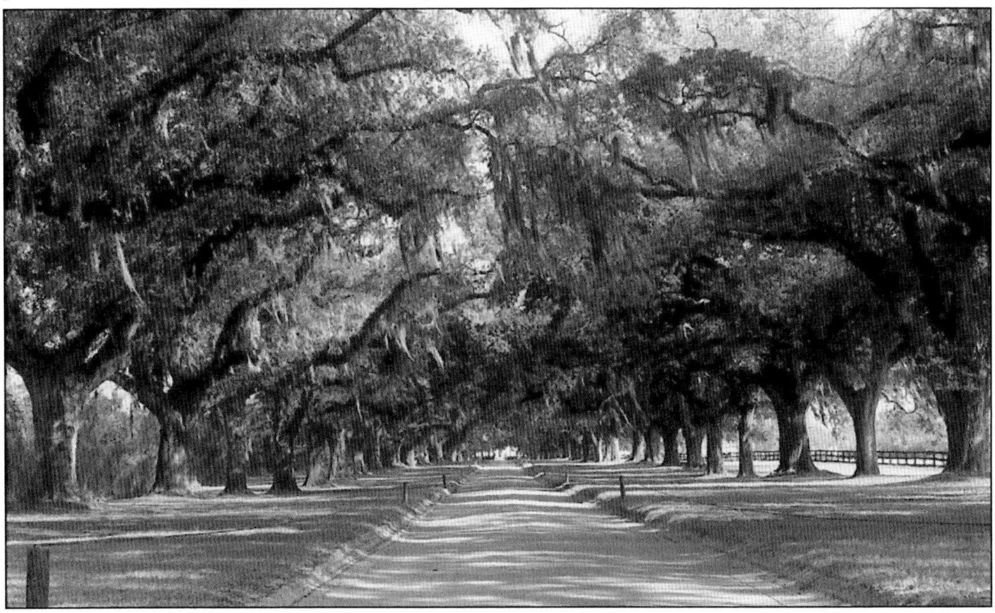

Avenues of oaks appeal to tourists today as they did in G.E. Thompson's day. Probably the oldest is at Oakland, dating from the 18th century. Boone Hall's (seen here) is also notable. The one leading to the Pinckney Site begins at the Highway 17 North entrance to Snee Farm. A lesser known avenue is in Hobcaw. Others that once were here have fallen victim to progress.

Two

THE EMERGING TOWN

In this section growth is traced through people and places as the little village grew into a town. William L. Erckmann served as mayor from 1934 until 1946. During his term the waterworks facility was completed in 1935, the town celebrated its centennial of incorporation in 1937, and the East Charleston County Development Board was organized. When Francis F. Coleman took office in 1946, the population numbered about 1,500. Annexations were begun. Various streets were renamed to honor previous mayors: Boundary became Simmons (Yonge Simmons), part of Rifle Range Road became McCants (T.G. McCants), and Commons Street was changed to Royall (Robert V. Royall). Later part of Highway 17 became Coleman Boulevard (Francis F. Coleman), a portion of Mathis Ferry Road became Magrath (pronounced "McGraw") Darby, and Highway 17 Bypass honored Johnnie Dodds. In 1960 G.M. "Groggy" Darby Jr. became mayor followed by John J. "Johnnie" Dodds in 1976. Richard "Dick" Jones took office in 1984. Upon his resignation, William "Billy" Mills served as mayor pro tem.

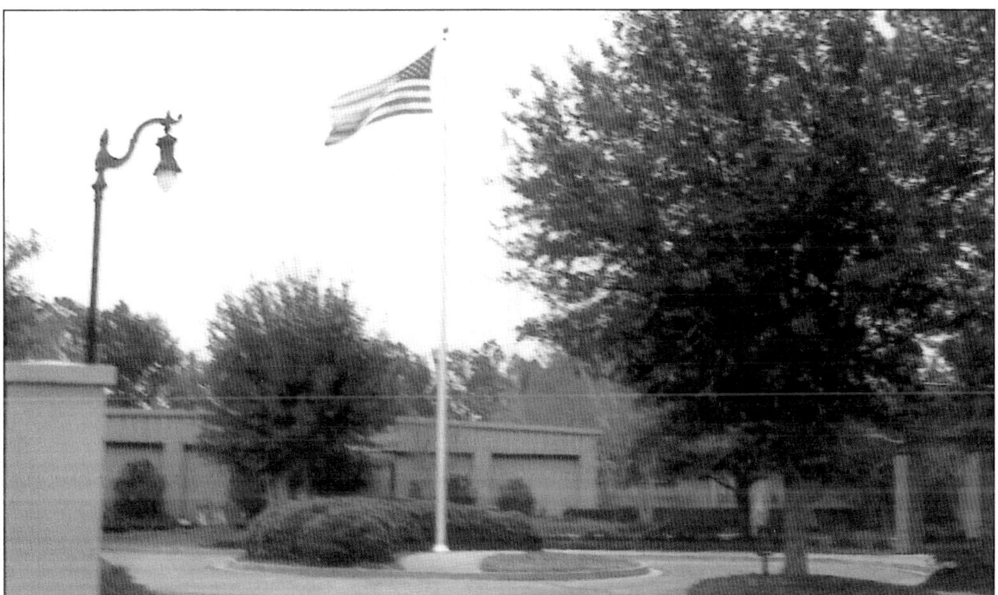

Cheryl Novak Woods (later Flowers) became the next mayor. Soon the town numbered 35,000 and was the eighth-largest incorporated area in South Carolina. The town offices expanded into the vacant East Cooper Private School facilities which are shown above. Harry Hallman Jr. serves as the present mayor.

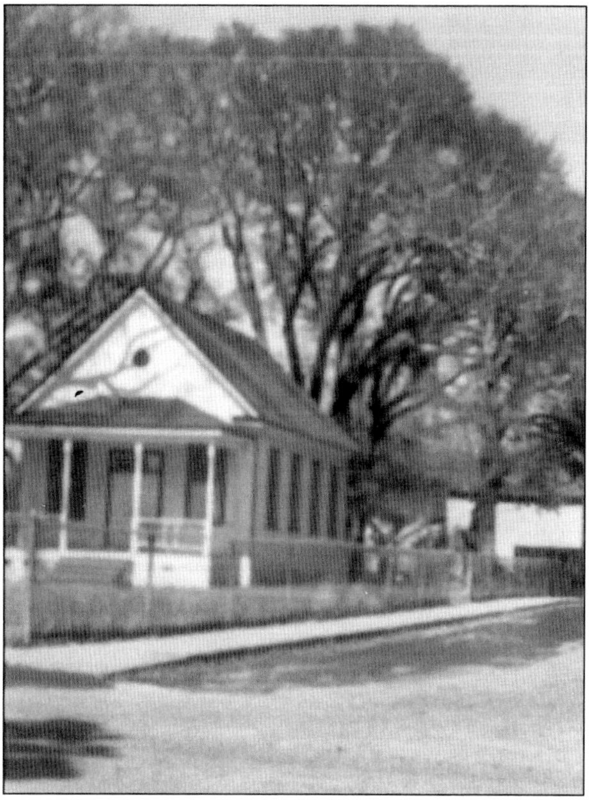

As the town grew, more space was needed for the town hall, police station, and fire department. The original town hall was moved in 1957 from Pitt near Bank Streets to the Miriam Brown playground, then to its present location on Bank Street where it serves as a sub-police station.

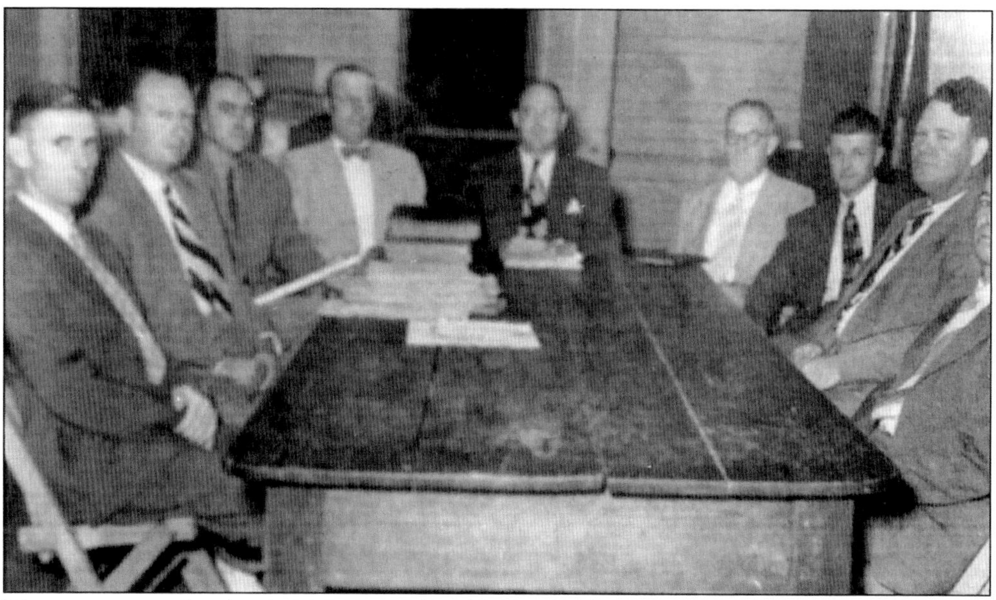

The town council is shown meeting in the old town hall in 1948. Francis F. Coleman was the mayor. Later the old Berkeley County Courthouse was renovated for the town hall. Then after the Hurricane Hugo damaged the building in 1989, the municipal offices and police department moved to the vacant East Cooper Private School property.

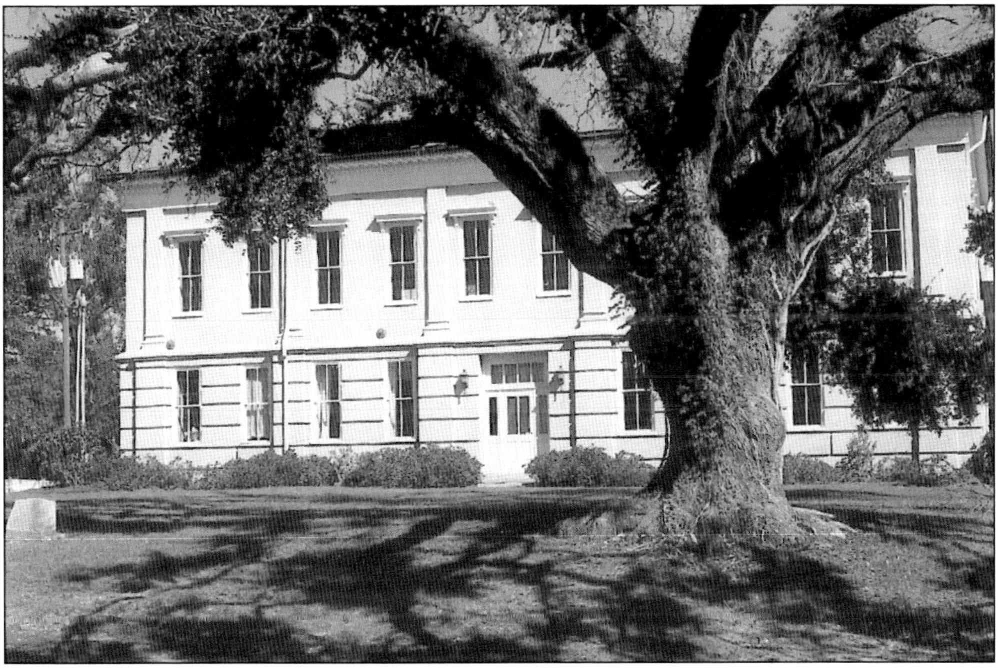

One of the most beautiful buildings in Mount Pleasant is the Darby Building on Pitt and King Streets. It was built in 1884 for the Berkeley County Courthouse, was used by the Lutheran Seminary, and then by the Baptist Church, with various other short-term tenants interspersed. It is now a part of the Town of Mount Pleasant's Recreation Department. When the town bought it in 1974 it was used as town hall until devastated by the 1989 hurricane. A museum was considered as a possible use for part of it, but this has never materialized. The granite marker in the left of the picture is a time capsule placed there at the sesquicentennial.

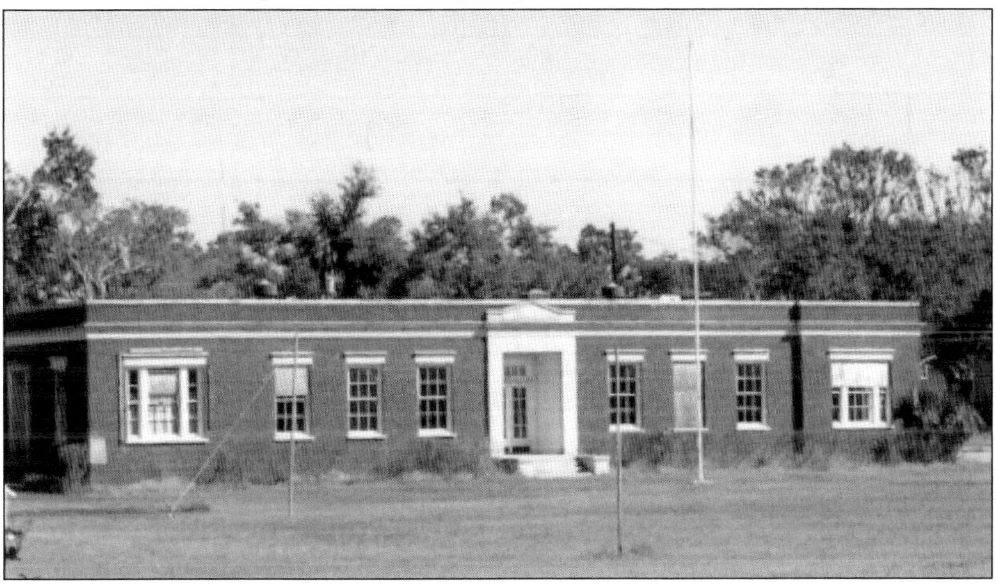

The brick municipal building in the block now called Edwards Park had been constructed during Mayor Darby's term. It housed certain offices, as well as police and fire departments. It was completely demolished by the hurricane.

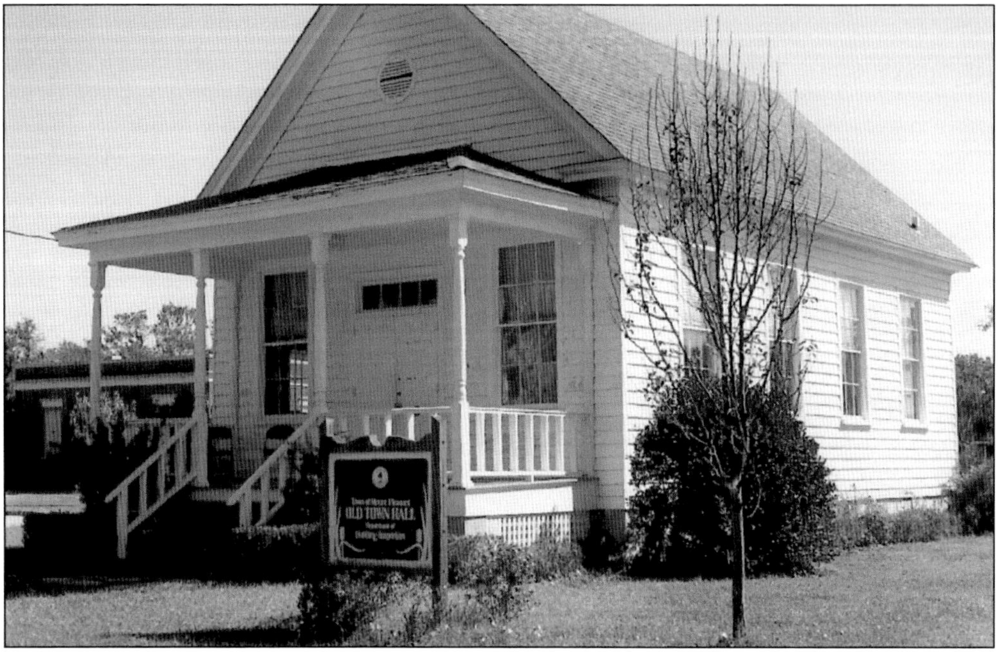

Edwards Park, bounded by Pitt, Bank, Royall, and Ferry Streets, contains two permanent buildings. The park was named in 1991 in honor of James B. Edwards, a local dentist who became Governor, Secretary of the Department of Energy, and then President of the Medical University of South Carolina. The old town hall building is now located at the foot of Carr Street on Bank Street.

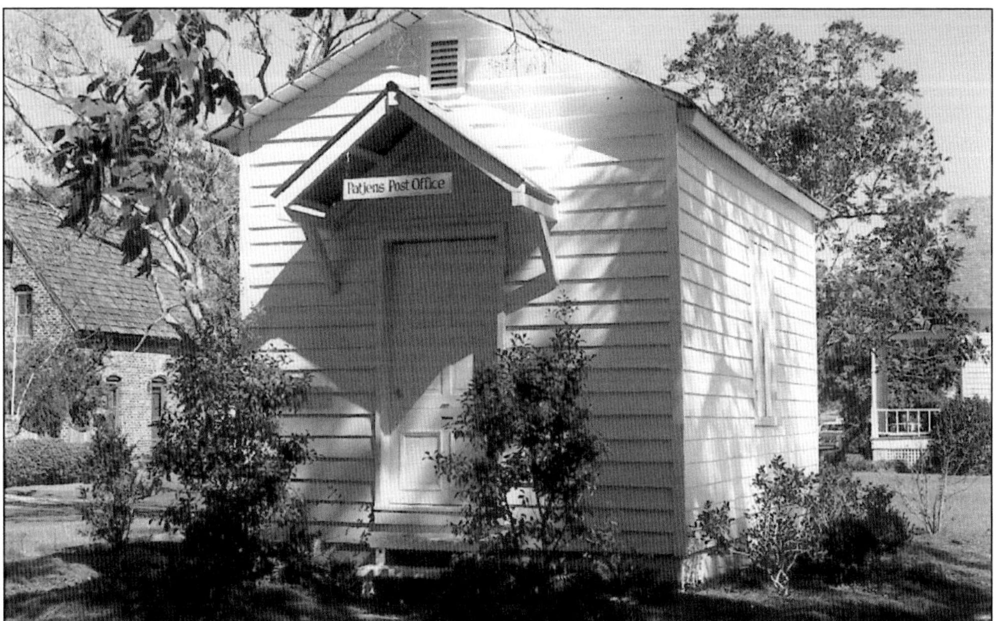

The smaller building on the corner of Pitt and Bank Streets was a post office in Mr. Andreas Patjens's yard on Church Street. The Patjens (Pat'jens) family was one the German families in the town in the 1800s.

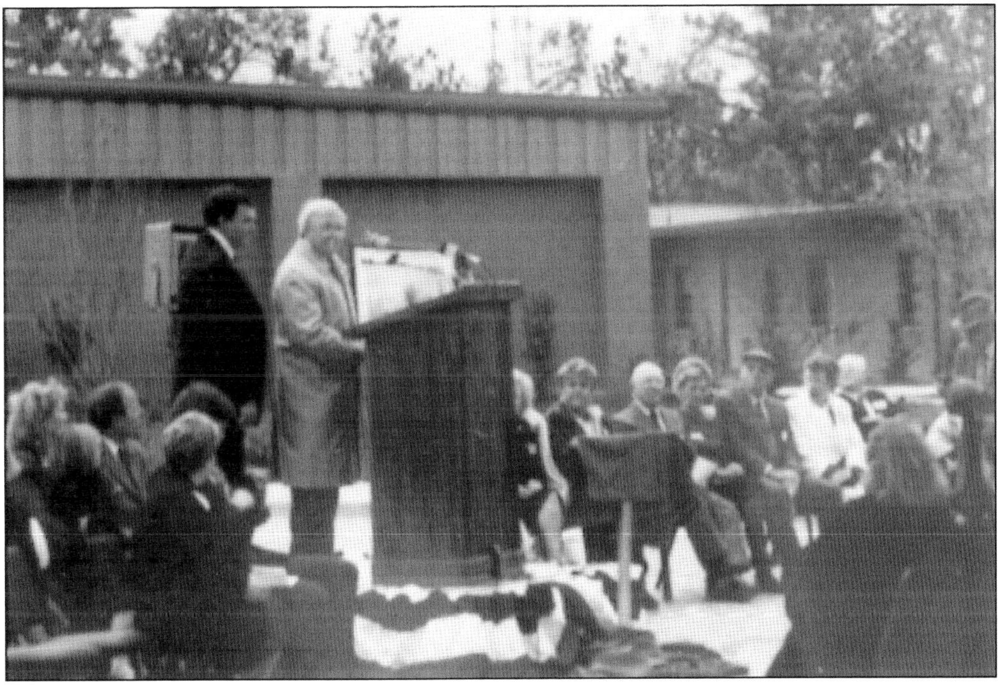

The Municipal Complex of today is housed in the renovated East Cooper Private School, which had been closed for some years. It was dedicated in a ceremony January 20, 1991, at which time various other buildings, streets, and parks were named or renamed.

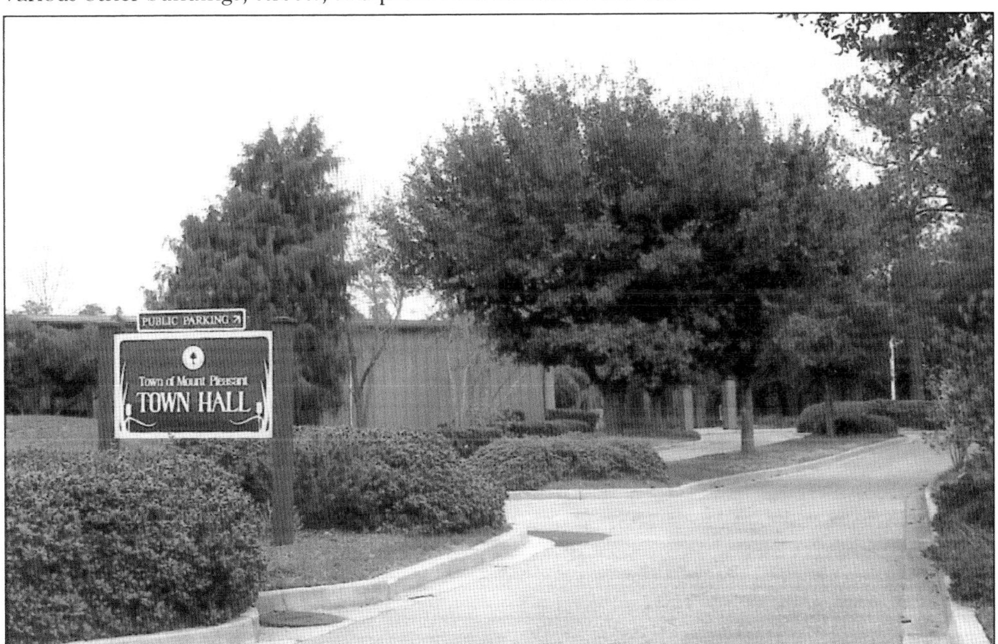

A more recent update and expansion has been completed. The various municipal departments and the police station are housed here on Ann Edwards Lane. This short street off Houston Northcutt Boulevard was named in honor of Mrs. James B. Edwards for her contribution to the town.

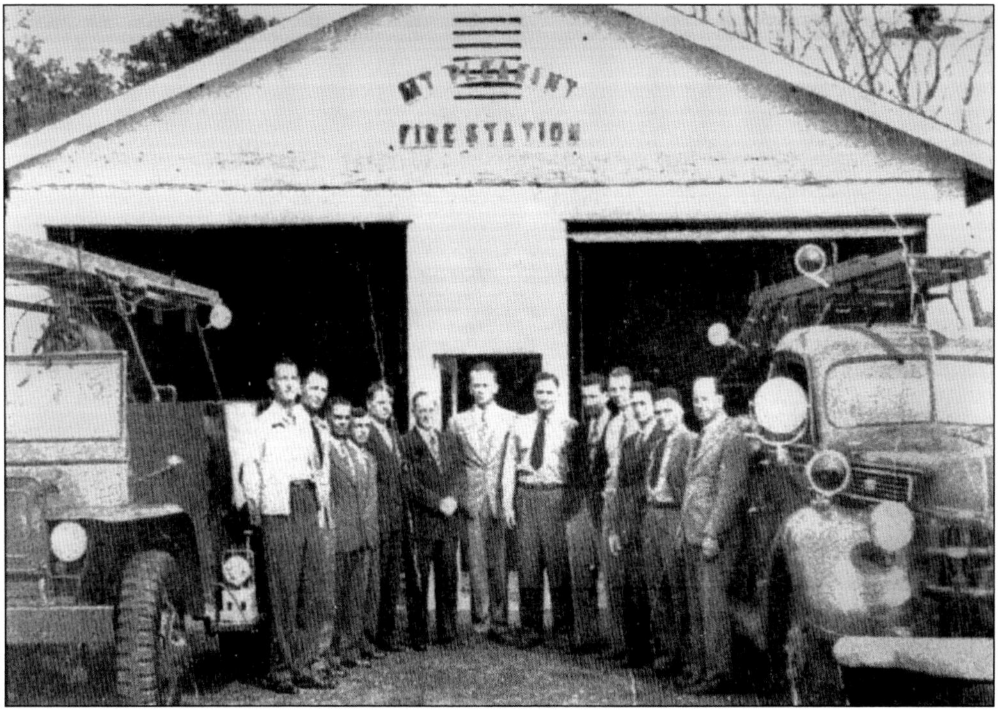

The fire department was manned by volunteers when it was located adjacent to the town hall on Pitt Street as seen here. The Mount Pleasant Volunteer Fire Department had officially been formed in 1928. In 1930 a model-A fire truck was purchased. In 1941 a Ford truck chassis formed the basis for the next piece of equipment. War surplus provided the next unit.

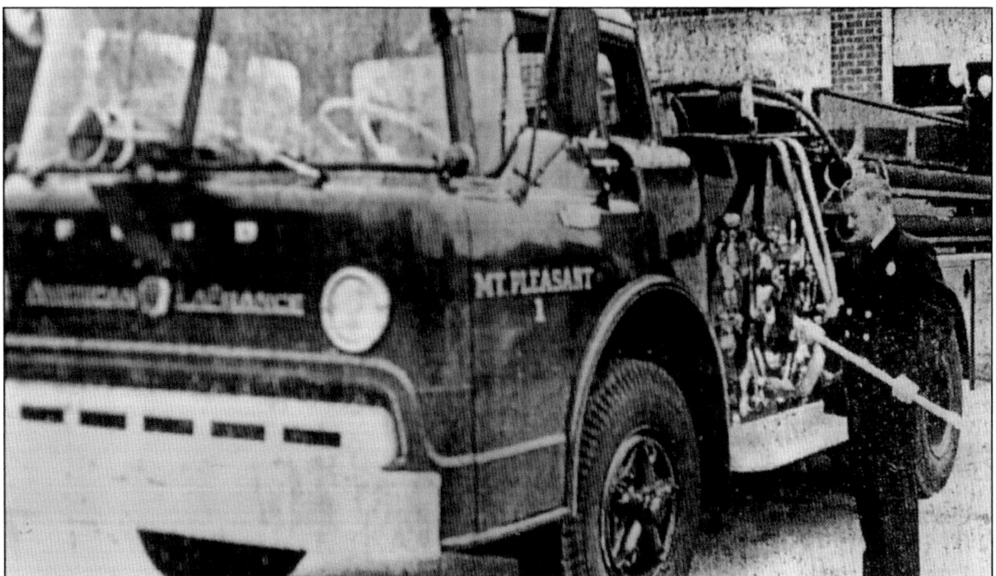

In 1966 a brand new fire truck was purchased for $17,000. This made three vehicles used by the department and housed in the new town government building on Royall near Bank. This building was completely destroyed by the 1989 hurricane. Now fire departments are located strategically throughout the incorporated area.

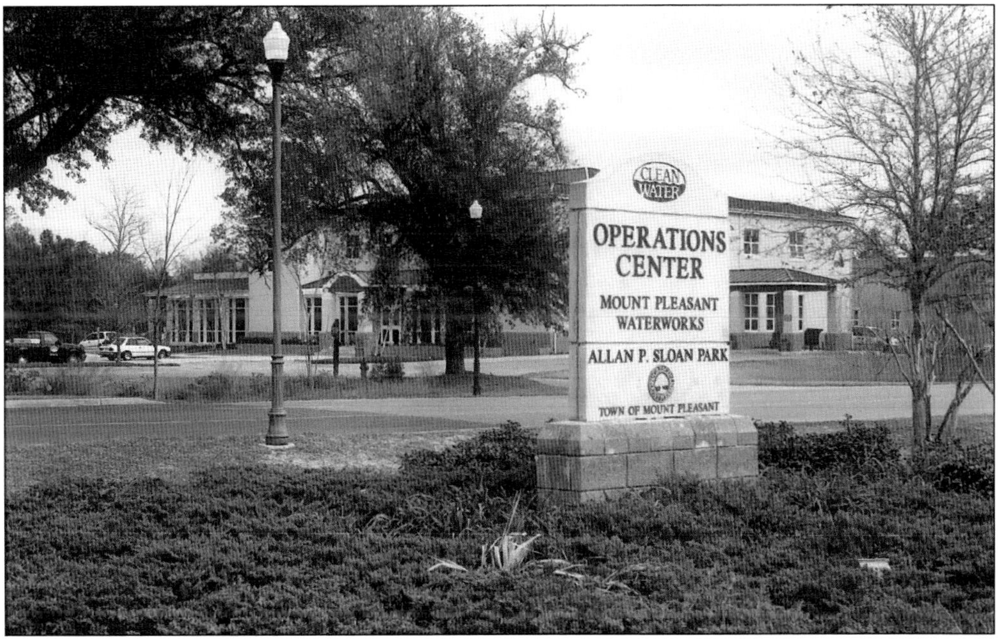

In 1935 Mount Pleasant had a waterworks system in operation, and by 1942, a sewerage system. From a small pumping station the waterworks expanded with standing tanks supplied by deep wells. In the 1970s the Bulls Bay Waterworks System became a reality, serving the outlying areas that depended on wells and septic tanks. It was governed by a board of commissioners appointed by the governor. After a few years the two systems merged. The Operations Center on Rifle Range Road is a modern facility housing the business-end of the system.

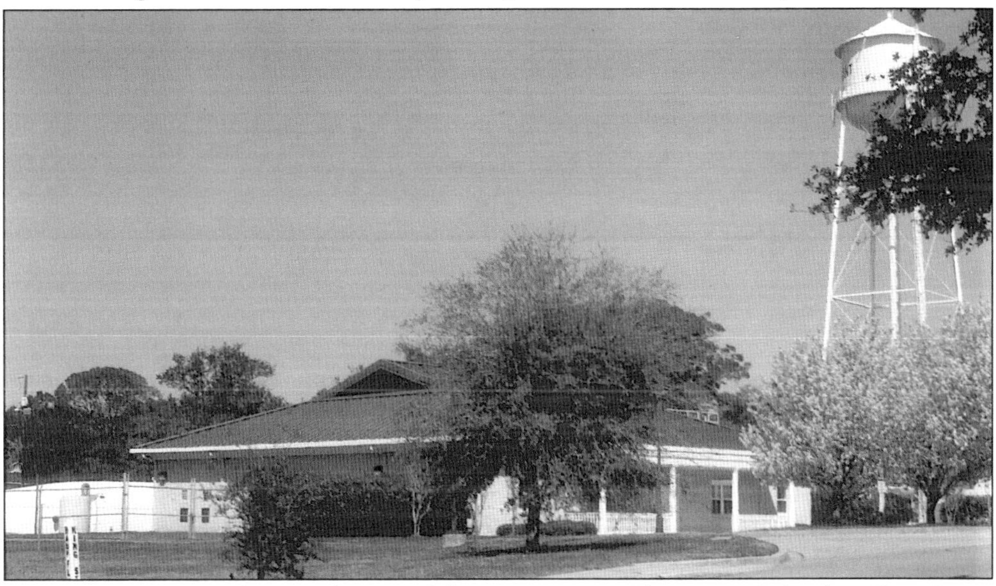

The reverse osmosis plant on the site of the vacant Laing Elementary School on King Street utilizes advanced technology to provide good-tasting water, which Mount Pleasant really never had. Water from this plant is mixed with water from the deep wells aquifer. "Osmo," a water drop, is used in publicity along with the "Clean Water" logo. The tank on the right of the picture is from the 1935 era.

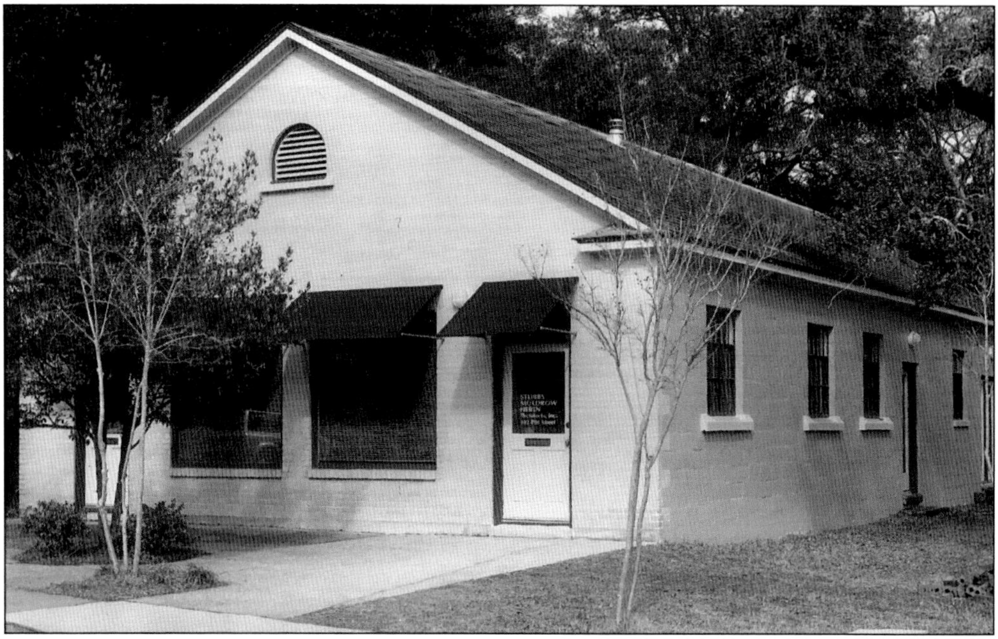

Mount Pleasant's post office has been housed in several buildings. On October 15, 1946 it opened in the concrete block structure across Pitt Street from its previous location in the little frame building where the Pickett Building now stands. Renovations by subsequent owners have updated it. The glass block windows have been replaced and attractive awnings added. Home mail delivery began in 1953.

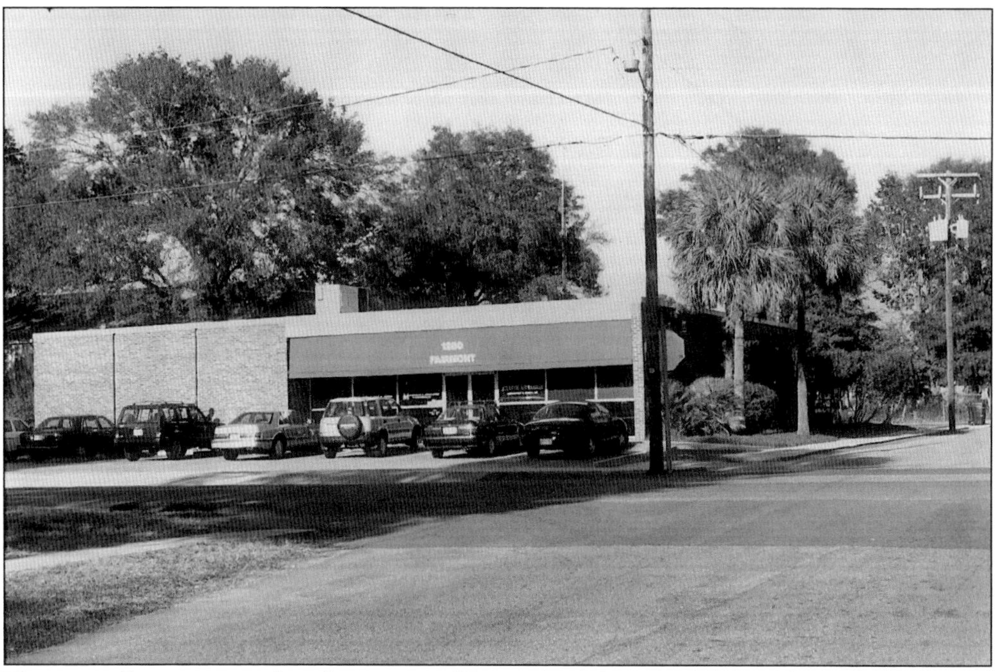

The post office was moved to the corner of Fairmont and King Streets in the 1960s when the Pitt Street facility became too small. After some years, for the same reason, it was moved to Johnnie Dodds Boulevard, where it is today.

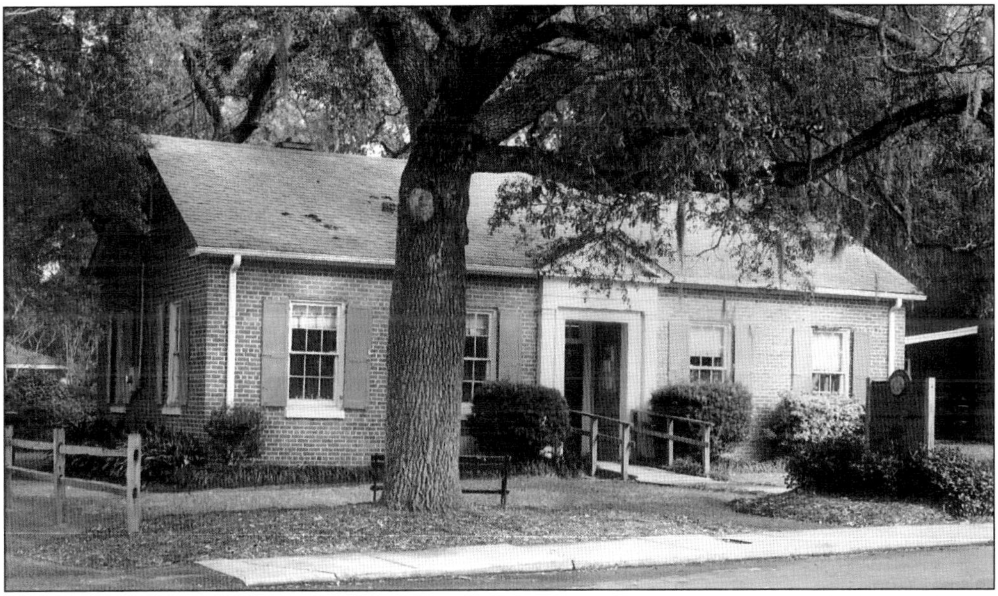

The library on Whilden Street was the first building constructed expressly for a library. Various organizations had libraries previously, which the public could use. There was even a little building on the corner of Church and Hibben Streets, which served as a library. This new facility opened August 2, 1948, with Mrs. Julian T. Melchers as librarian. It cost $15,000. When the Charleston County Library system built the Regional Library on Mathis Ferry Road, the possibility existed that this library would be closed, but public reaction decreed otherwise. Patrons of all ages use it, including children who delight in the story hours. The Village Library epitomizes the Friendly Town.

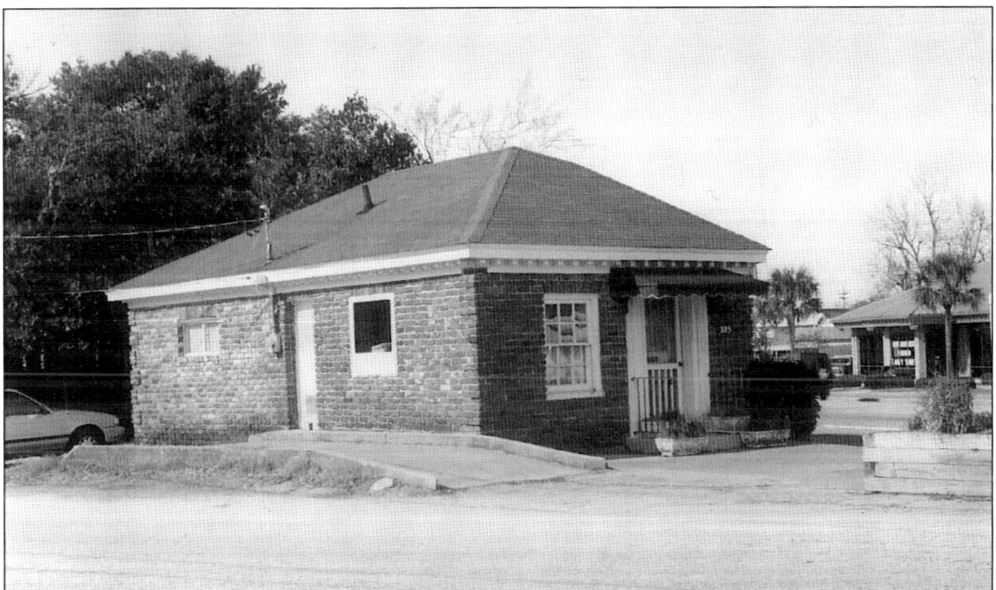

The first bank in Mount Pleasant was housed in this building at the intersection of Hibben Street and Coleman Boulevard. It was a branch of the South Carolina National Bank, which is now Wachovia. Before 1956, banking had to be done in Charleston.

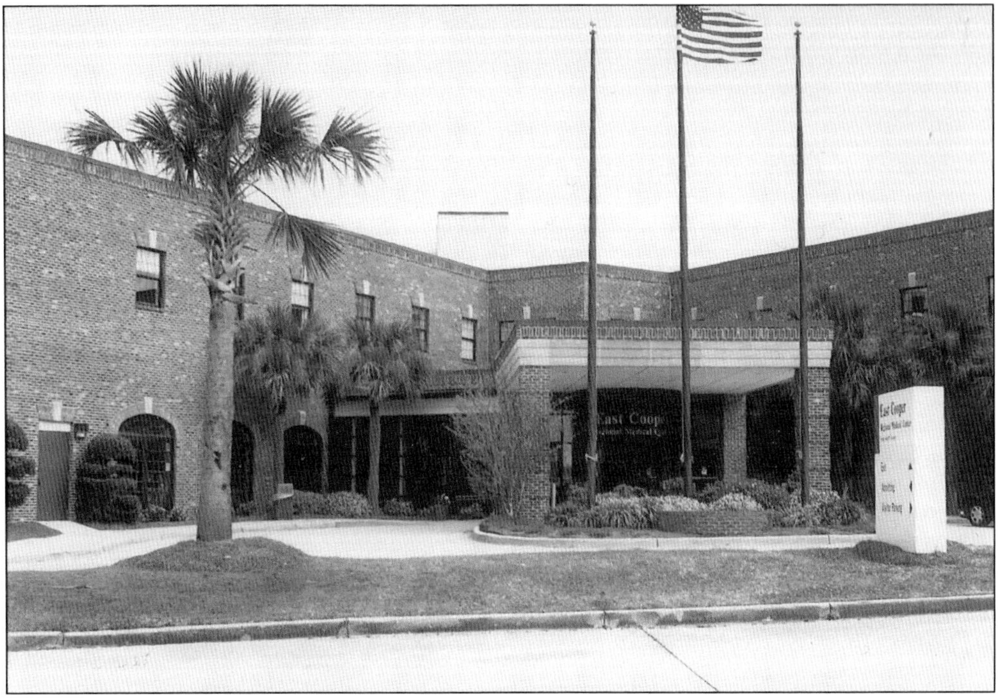

In 1986, the East Cooper Regional Medical Center became a reality. No longer would Mount Pleasant citizens have to go to Charleston for hospitalization. Immediately following the opening of the hospital, physicians' offices have literally surrounded it. Nursing homes, convalescent centers, and retirement complexes are clustered nearby.

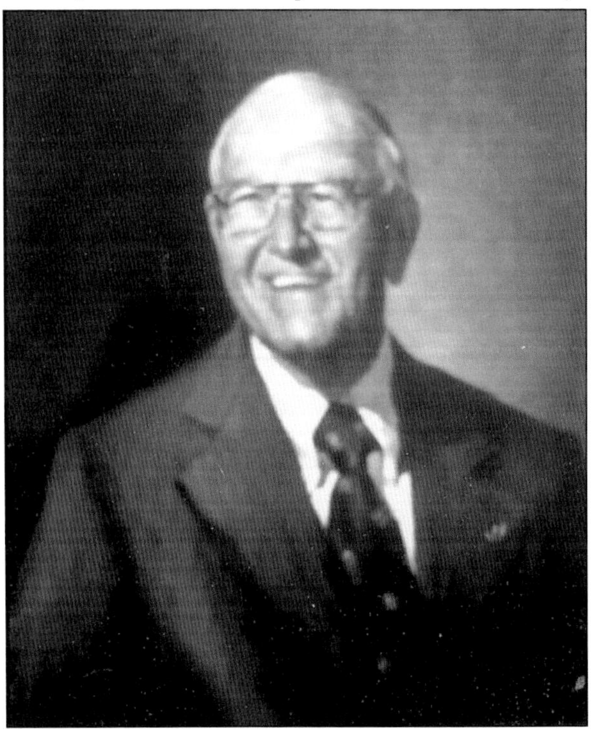

John J. "Johnnie" Dodds, whose portrait hangs just inside the hospital near the information desk, was the mayor at the time the hospital was being constructed. His work in getting the facility located in Mount Pleasant was invaluable.

A view across the harbor from Mount Pleasant shows how Morris Island lighthouse once was surrounded by trees and had a sizable house for the keeper and his family. Surrounded by water now, the light is all that is left as erosion has taken its toll. It no longer serves as a beacon to mariners. In the 1960s a lighthouse was constructed on Sullivan's Island to guide the ships into the harbor.

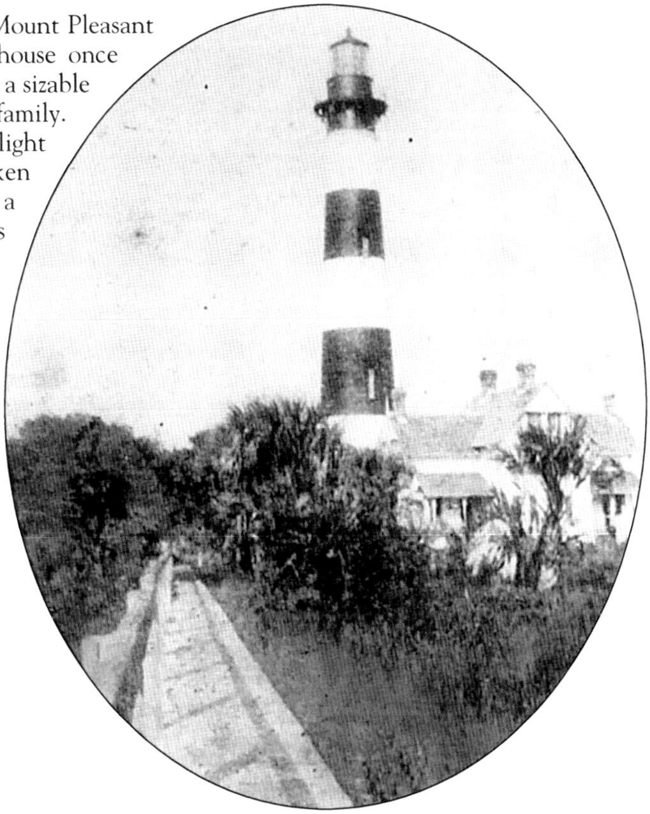

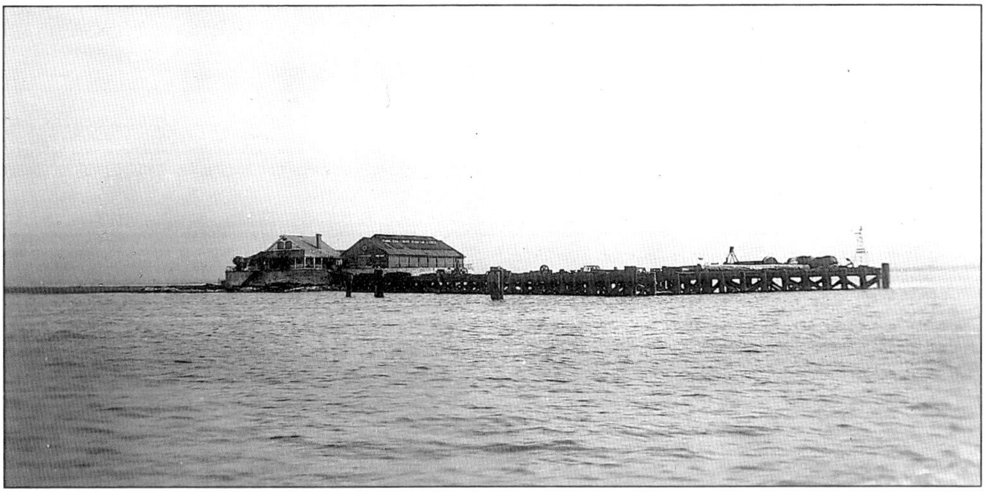

Castle Pinckney, seen to the right of Morris Island Light, has served as many things during its 200-year existence. E.P. McClellan Jr. recounts his childhood living there in the 1930s in *Ghosts of Castle Pinckney*. Erosion destroyed Morris Island while fire consumed Castle Pinckney's buildings. Once called Schute's Folly it is reverting to nature. The word folly describes a place of low-growing shrubs and trees. Schute was an early owner. Names have a way of being corrupted. For instance, I'On became Iron when referring to the swamp. Rathall (Rath-all) was turned into Rat Hall. Hog Island was not named for wild animals. All three were family names of English origin with local connections.

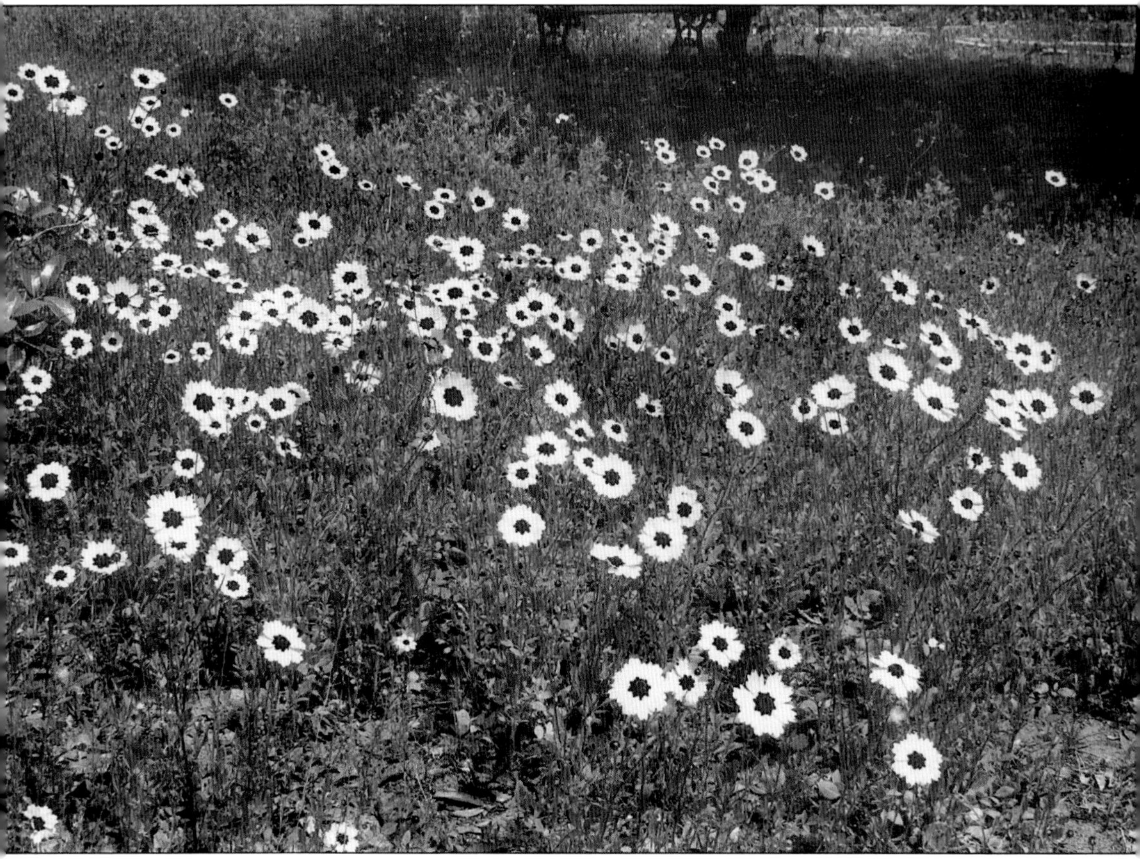

Long before landscaping with wildflowers became popular, Mount Pleasant had a profusion of them all around the town. Going to pick wild violets in the early spring was quite an adventure, and they grew naturally in moist places. Black-eyed Susans filled vacant lots with their brilliant orange-yellow petals around brown centers. Phlox appeared with the "Susies" in shades of pink and lavender. Our native cactus, the opuntia or prickly pear, added its clear yellow, waterlily-like blossoms in summer. Nature's landscaping contributed much to the beauty of the Friendly Town and to the enjoyment of children gathering the wild flowers. Even white clover blossoms could be fashioned into garlands. The tempo of living was peaceful before World War II.

Three

SHEM CREEK

Shem Creek has played an important role in the life of the East Cooper area. The name may have been derived from an Indian word; old maps show the word "Shemee." Shem Creek served as the north boundary of the Ferry Lands tract, Lucasville, and Haddrell's Plantation, but it also provided a means of transportation, recreation, and a source of food. (Until 1929, when the Cooper River bridge opened, travel to Charleston was by water with ferries running regularly.) Commercial shrimping developed in the early 1930s with the Magwood family playing an important role. The number and the size of the trawlers increased, but by the end of the century, the number was decreasing. Deep-sea fishing boats continue to dock on the creek but the prime business is the seafood restaurants. In the 1950s Mount Pleasant had only two, the Fork and the Lorelei. Now they line the creek. Pleasure boats even bring passengers there for meals.

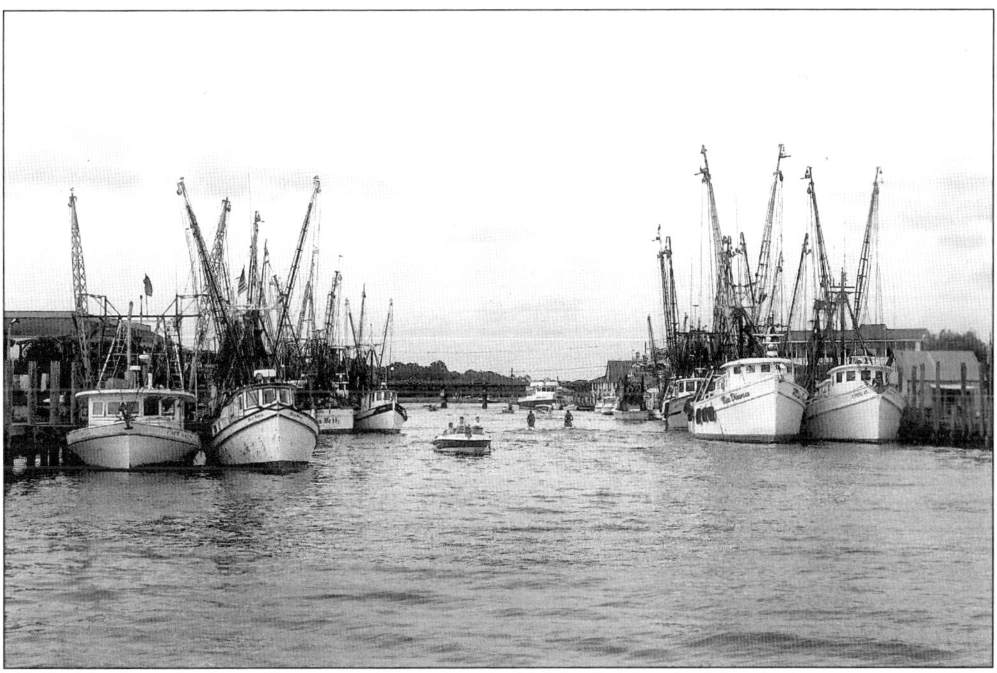

The creek is shown here in the heyday of shrimping. It is 90 feet wide in places with a depth of ten feet. Some of the trawlers are Texas rigged.

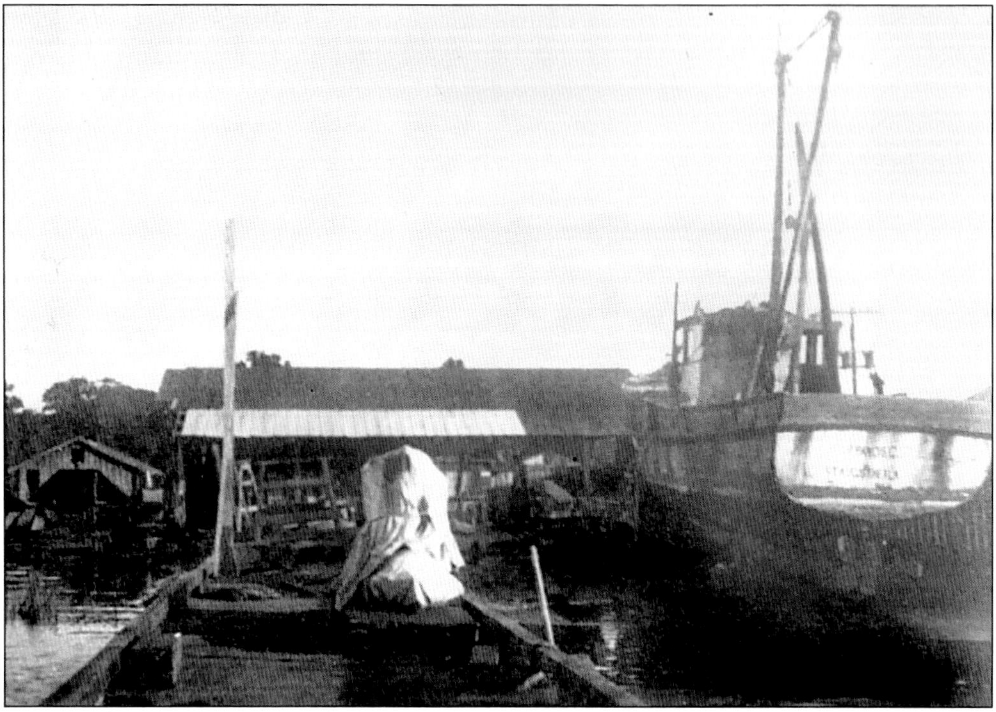

It was only natural, given its location on the harbor, that a boatyard was located on Shem Creek from early days. The Mount Pleasant Boat Building Company was the last. Beginning when E.O. Hall ran the boatyard, and continuing with the Darbys, Charlie North worked 67 years on the creek. He retired in 1964 at the age of 81. Employees were loyal in those days. The industry meant a great deal to the little town. Gone, now, is the sound of the whistle at noon and at quitting time, so regular that people used it to set their clocks. Gone, too, is the squealing sound of the marine railway as boats were pulled out of the water at high tide on moonlit nights for repairs. Santa and his reindeer no longer decorate the roof of the shop at Christmas. In their stead are beautiful homes.

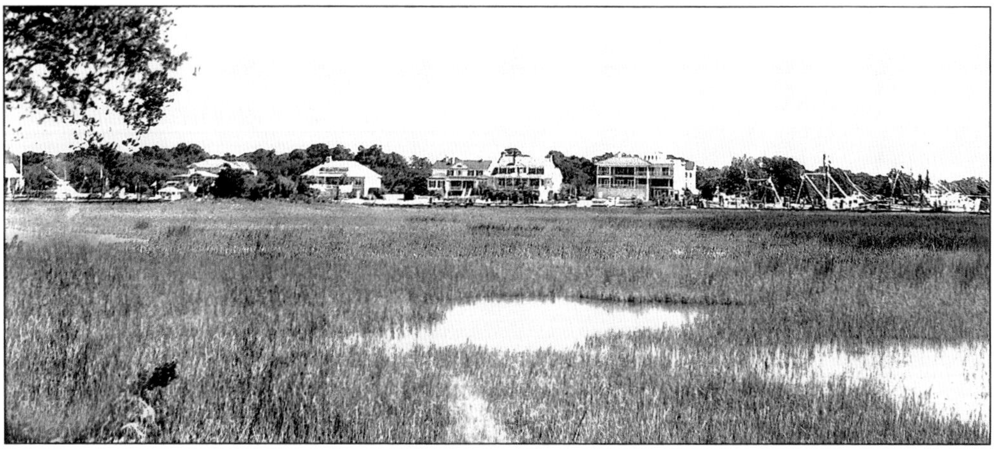

By 1990 the boat building property was divided into 12 building lots and magnificent houses are being built there. Wharf Street, which bisected the property, was relocated to the end which still gives the town access to deep water. Documentation of President Washington's 1791 Southern tour indicates he was rowed across from here to Charleston.

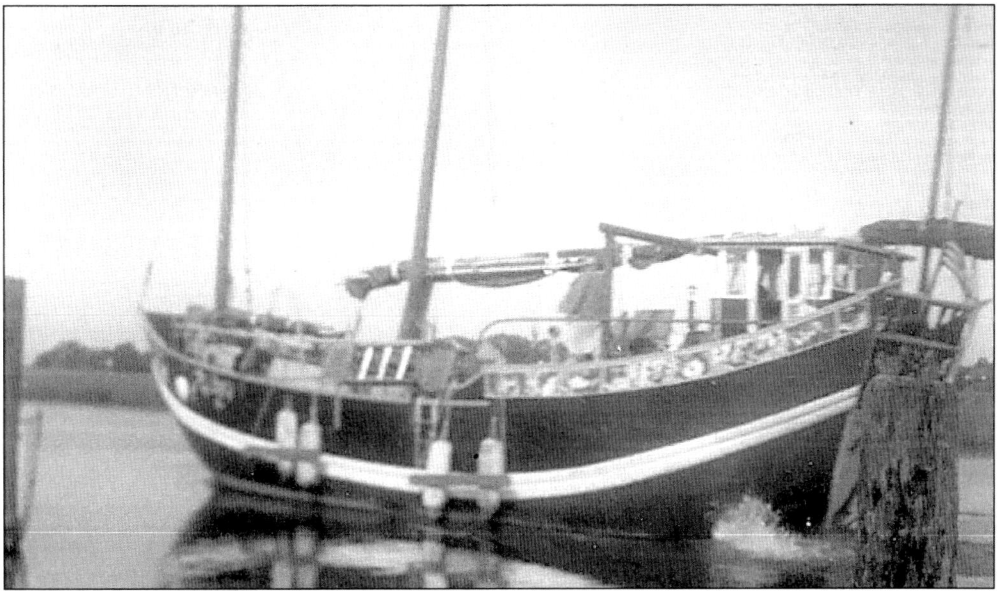

In addition to the usual pleasure boats that anchor in Shem Creek, boats from far away places occasionally anchor here. This Chinese Junk was a marvel to the eyes. It was painted bright colors and had sails, although an auxiliary motor was available. The deck was made of teak, and much carving adorned the boat. This visit took place in the 1960s.

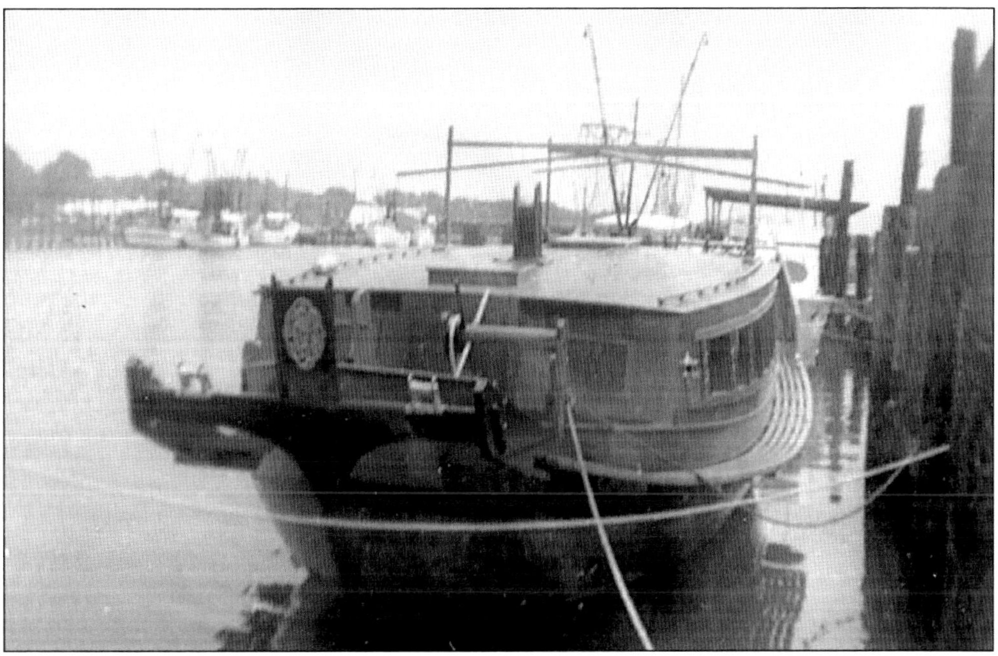

Another unusual looking boat that came in the creek was this, a variant of a junk, probably ten years after the other one. For many years residents kept their pleasure boats on the creek ready to go whenever time and tide suited. Boats coming down the Intracoastal Waterway frequently docked here on their way to Florida. Sometimes the owners came to church and friendships were formed. Year after year a tiny sailboat called the *Sea Gull* tied up at the boatyard as Robert and Anne Rose sailed from Massachusetts to Florida.

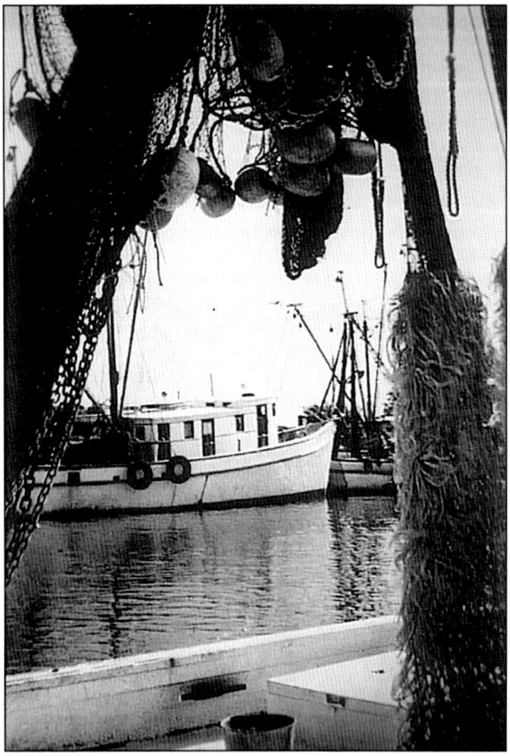

A trawler framed by nets on another boat is quite picturesque. The life is not easy, the days are long, and the work strenuous. As a student at Clemson University, Tommy Gleaton, a local young man, documented a day in the life of a commercial shrimper. The image is from the cover of his booklet, written in 1971.

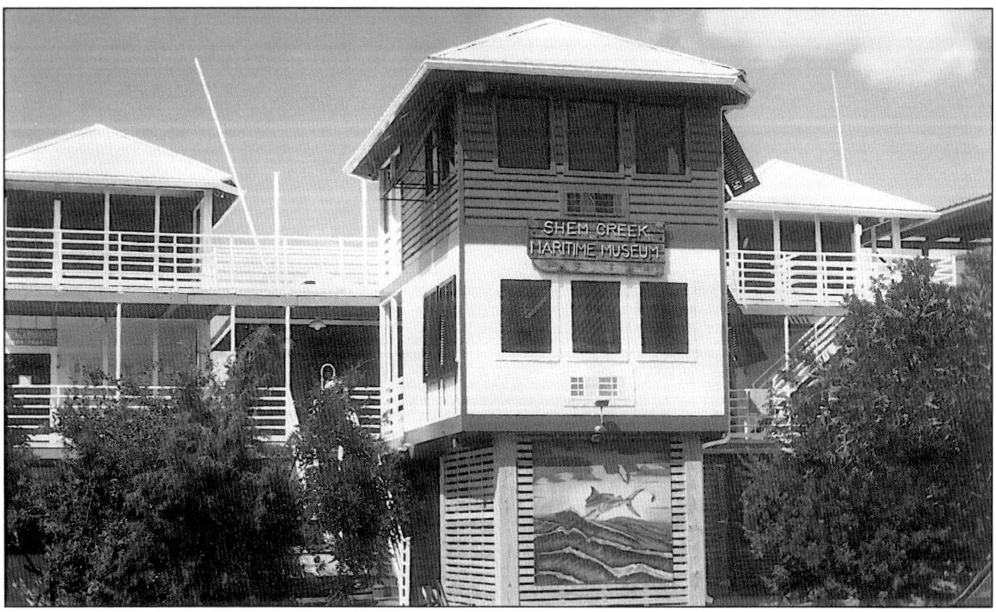

In the 1990s the Shem Creek Maritime Museum was located on Shem Creek. It utilized cabana rooms moved from a closed restaurant. Exhibits were located both inside the second-floor room and on ground level. They included the story of shrimping and the many facets of life on the creek, including dug-out canoe days, industries on the creek, and many pieces of maritime artifacts. Businesses now utilize the space. The mural on the downstairs level was painted by Mark Woodward.

Mark Woodward, artist/sculptor located in the Common, was commissioned by museum owner Lou Edens to do a larger-than-life representation of Capt. C.A. Magwood Jr. in 1995. Captain "Junior" was a member of the family long engaged in the shrimping industry. His fleet of orange-masted trawlers has been a familiar sight on Shem Creek for many years.

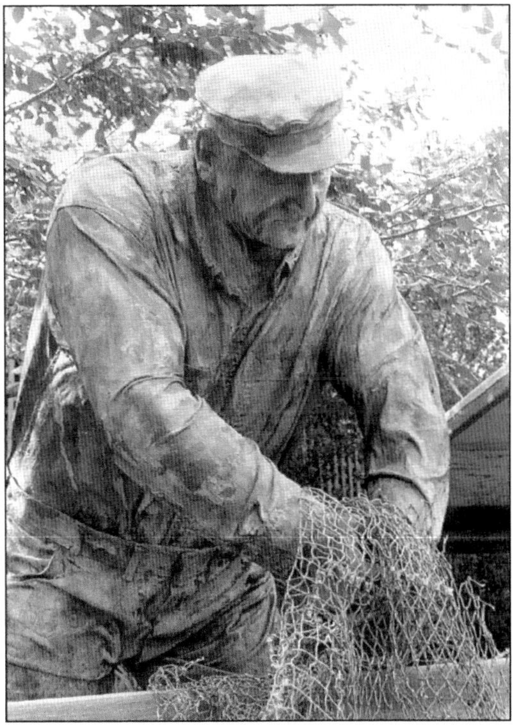

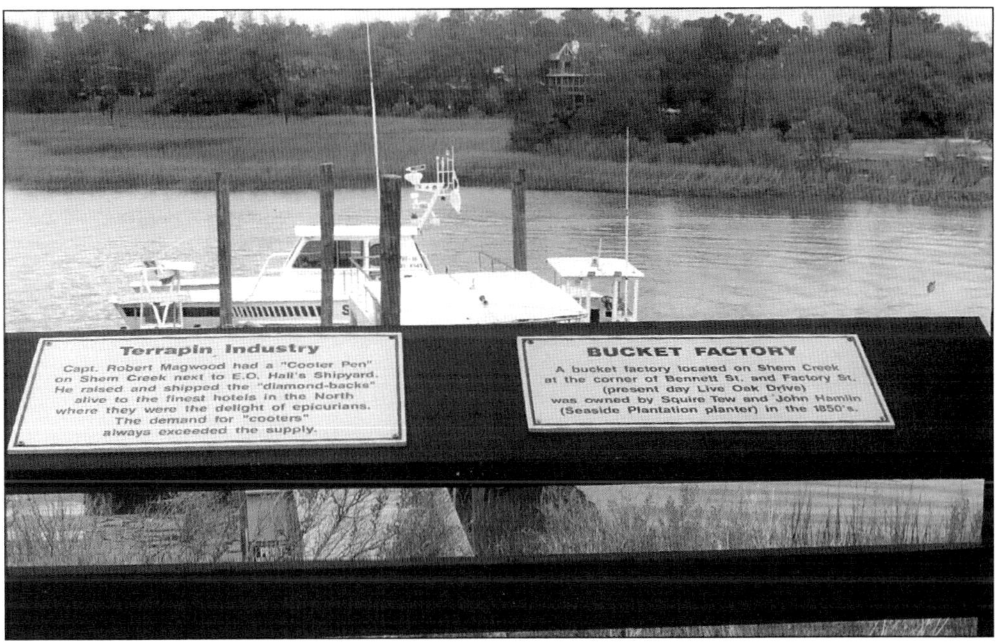

A view from the upper deck of the Maritime Museum shows a peaceful scene of Shem Creek. The story panels tell about the Terrapin Industry and the Bucket Factory, both long gone from the creek. Across the creek, almost opposite, is the remnant of a once-thriving farming operation. The Nix farm extended from Shem Creek over to the Wando River. Produce was carried from the fields to a shed at the end of this causeway to be loaded on barges and carried to Charleston where it was sent to New York. The fields are housing developments now.

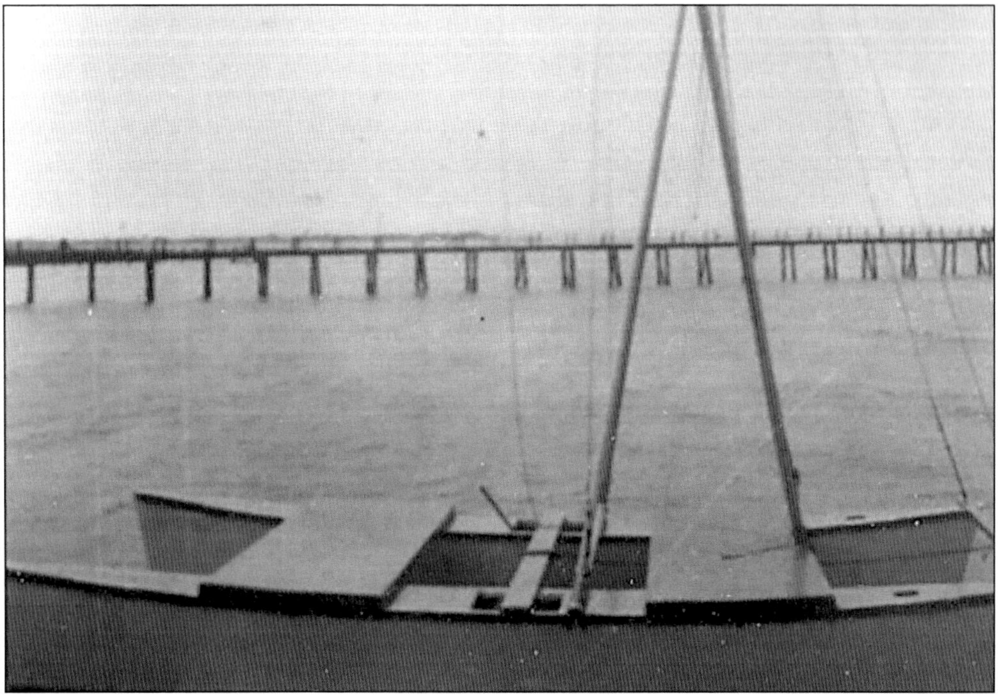

In 1949 Malcolm Donaldson, a retired electrical engineer, built the first catamaran in Mount Pleasant. It had 24-foot hulls and was fast. His idea came from *Popular Mechanics* magazine.

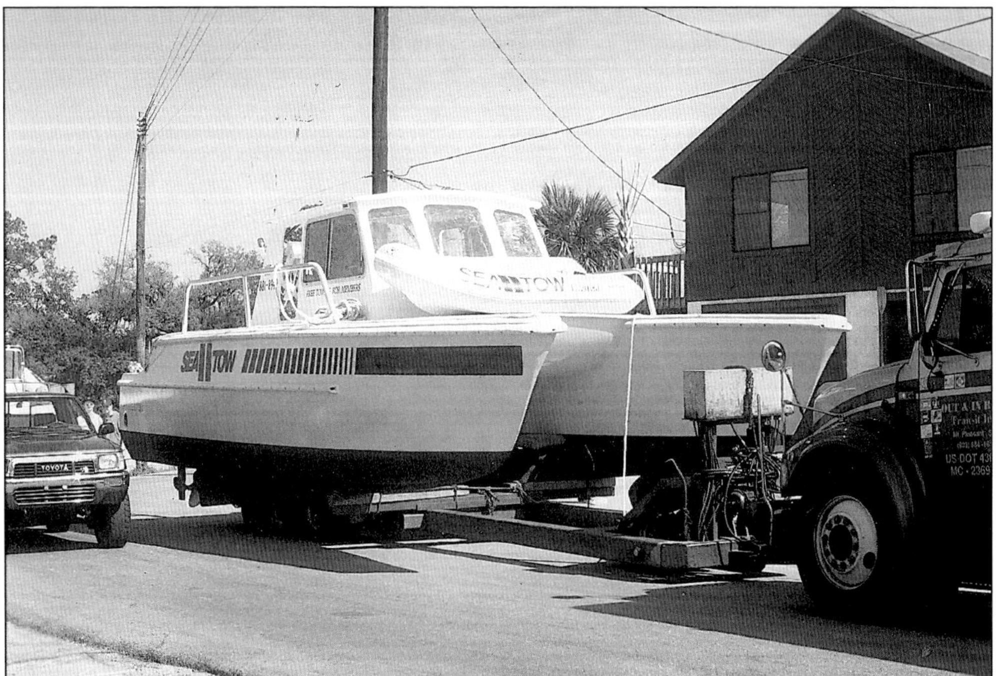

Almost 50 years later, Jamie Edens constructed a catamaran using contemporary materials. It was built to assist boats in distress and was slightly longer than the first one. Here it is ready for launch.

Four

PITT STREET

From 1937 through the next two decades, the business district of the little town was concentrated on Pitt Street in the block between Venning and Morrison Streets. The post office, dry goods store, hardware store, grocery, barber shop, dress shop, and drug store were here, as were the doctors' and the dentist's offices. A trip to Pitt Street on an errand most likely included a bit of socializing along the way since everyone in town knew everyone else. In the years before World War II life was most leisurely. One could shop in the morning for the midday meal, stop by the post office to pick up the mail, and chat with friends along the way. When business was slow some of the merchants would gather in front of the grocery store to discuss the affairs of the nation. However, on Wednesday afternoons, the stores were closed, then a long-standing custom. At Christmastime in the 1950s and 1960s, the store windows were painted with seasonal scenes by local artist Taffy Stratton. Little carolers, manger scenes, shepherds, and kings decorated the storefront windows, creating a Dickens-like atmosphere. The large cedar tree in front of the post office served as the town's Christmas tree and was lighted at the end of the parade. With the coming of supermarkets and malls, Pitt Street ceased to be the center of the shopping district. Offices moved into the old store buildings while an inn is located in the hardware store. The drug store remains, as do the barber shop and the pediatrician's office.

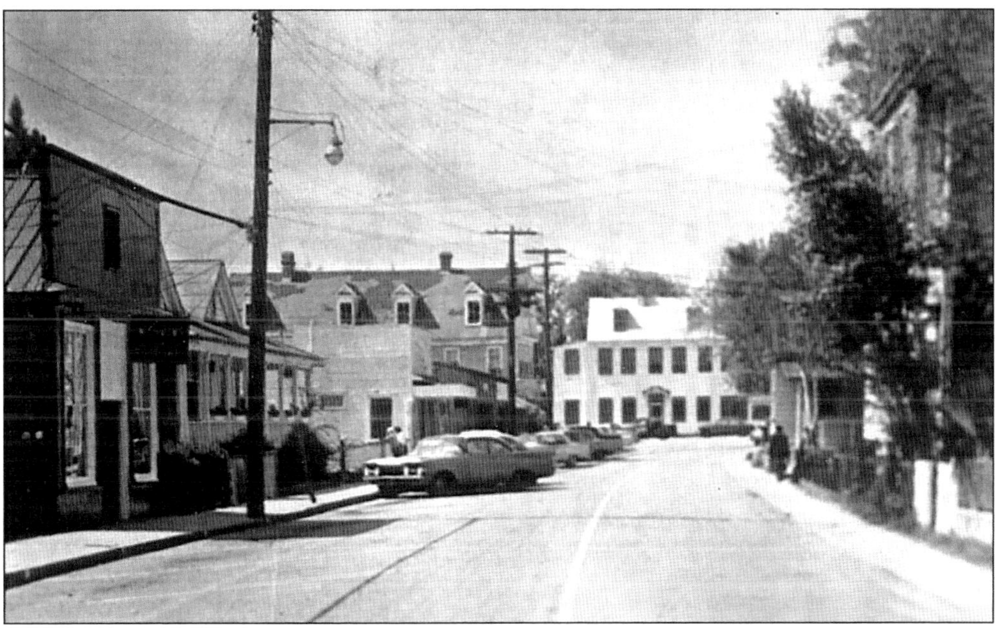

A picture postcard shows the business block of Pitt Street in the 1950s.

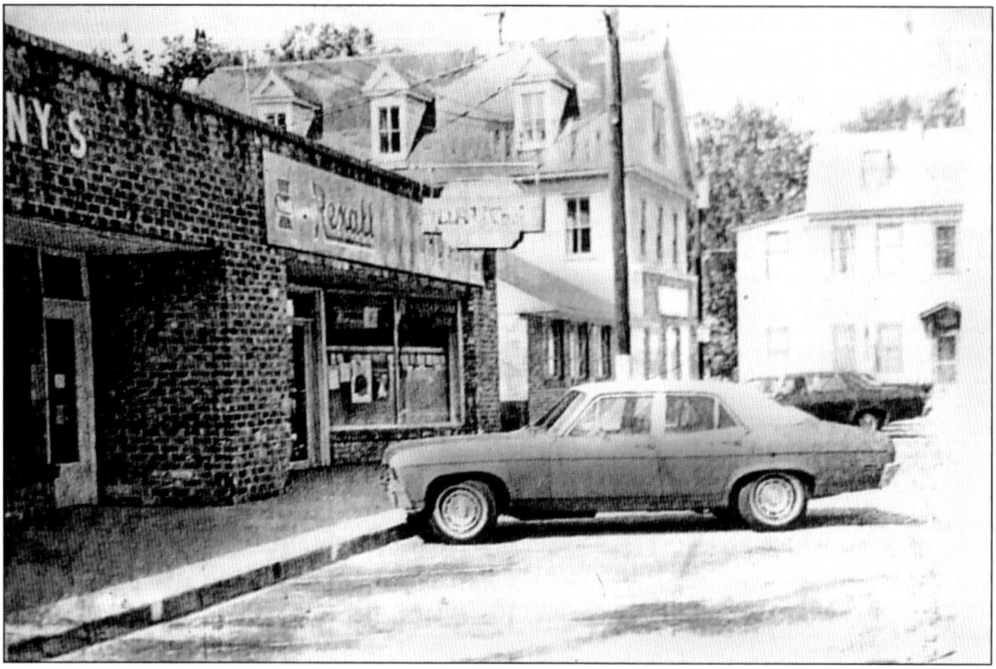

Dr. "Waddie" Zeigler started Pitt Street Pharmacy and soda fountain in 1938, but it has been in its present location since 1956. Should a person need a prescription filled after hours or on the weekend, "Doc" would oblige. He died years ago, but the pharmacy continues—although no longer in the Rexall chain. The drygoods store next door, run by Kenny Donaldson, closed. He had opened it in 1946 when he returned from World War II. At the far right in the picture is the dentist's office. Coleman Hardware (now Guilds Inn) is in the center.

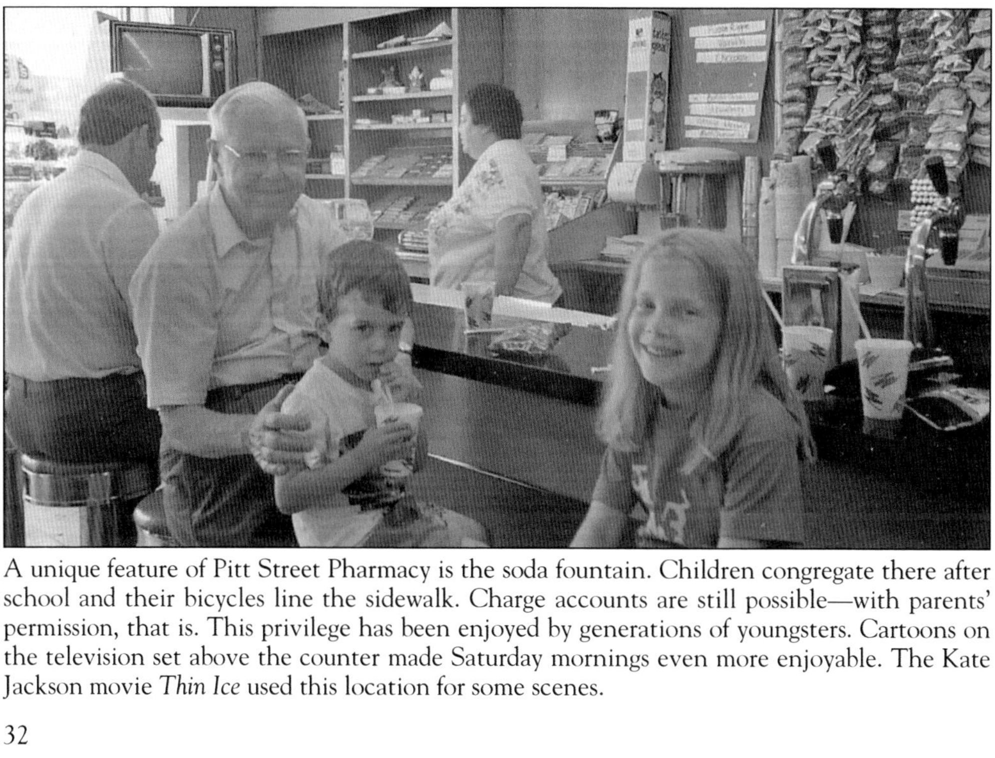

A unique feature of Pitt Street Pharmacy is the soda fountain. Children congregate there after school and their bicycles line the sidewalk. Charge accounts are still possible—with parents' permission, that is. This privilege has been enjoyed by generations of youngsters. Cartoons on the television set above the counter made Saturday mornings even more enjoyable. The Kate Jackson movie *Thin Ice* used this location for some scenes.

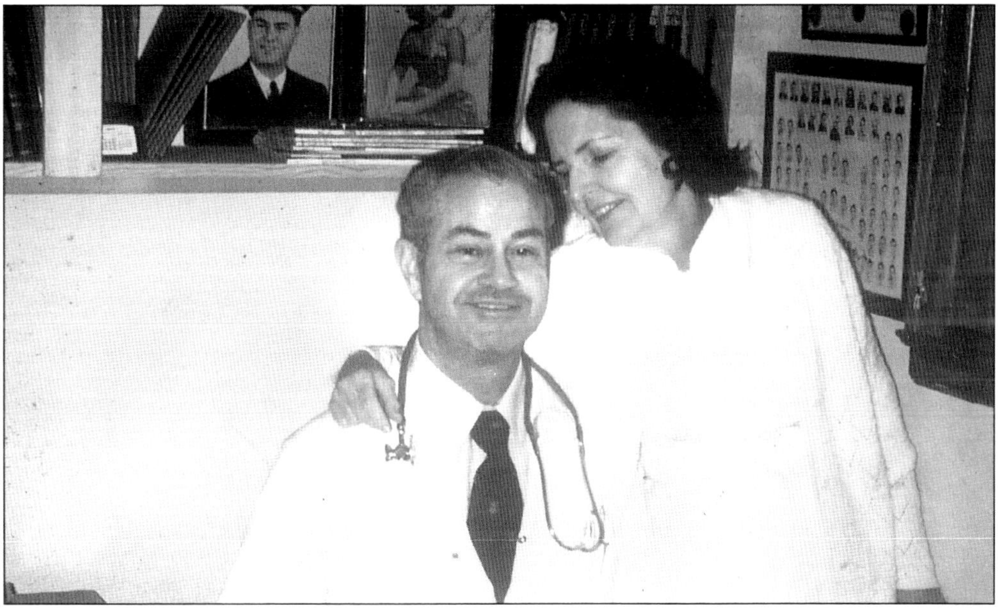

At 109 Pitt Street, next to the pharmacy, was the doctor's office. Here Dr. Otis Pickett Jr. treated old and young, black and white, rich and poor. In the earlier years of his practice, house calls took him all over the area. After a Naval tour of duty, he returned to the town and the people he loved, and who loved him in return. All the while he was honing his skill at diagnosing illnesses. For a while pediatrician James G. Ward Jr. shared the office until he moved down to 121 Pitt Street. The stability of Dr. Pickett's office staff gave further reassurance to the patients. His wife, Ruth, was indeed his helpmate.

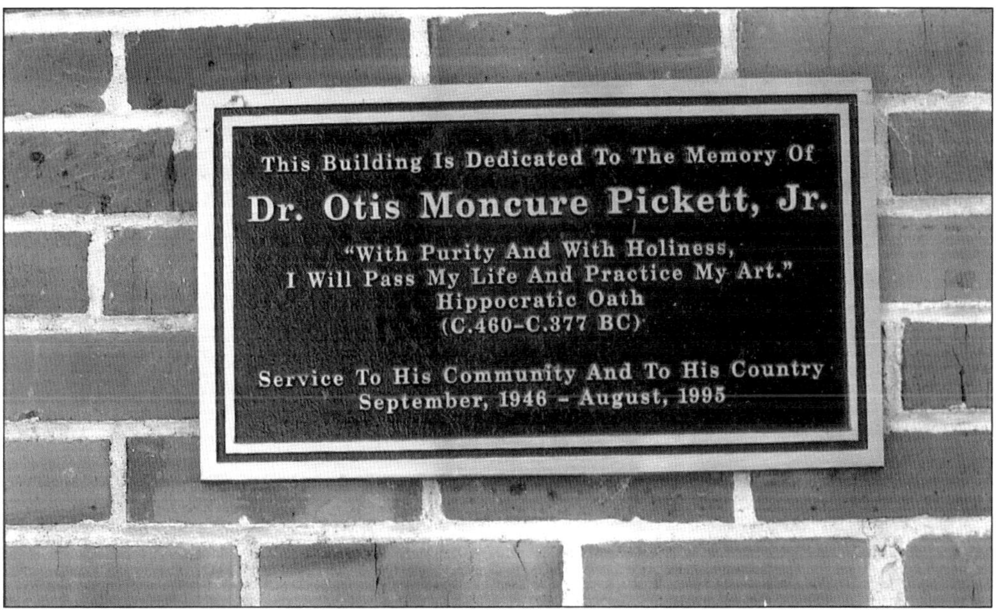

Dr. Pickett was honored by the governor with the Order of the Palmetto and by his alma mater, the Medical University of South Carolina, as Doctor of the Year. After his death the building where his office was for so many years was dedicated to his memory in an impressive ceremony on March 23, 1996.

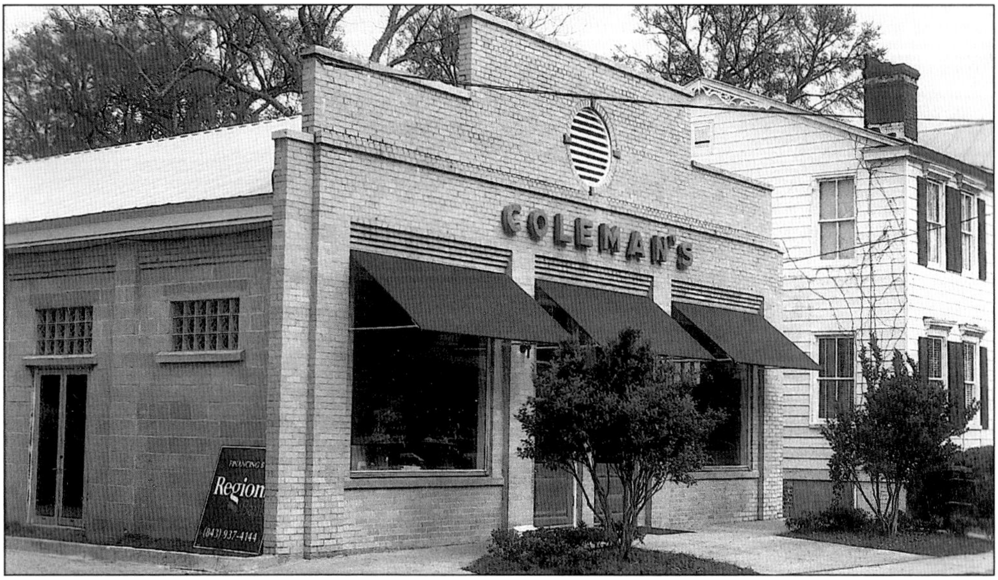

In the earlier years, vegetables were peddled door-to-door by the people who grew them using a horse and wagon, then by a truck. Several individually owned grocery stores served the townspeople with food. Coleman's was one of the last, and it closed in 1971. Mr. Bertie made the early morning trip to the markets in Charleston for fresh produce and meat. The store offered delivery service. In fact, "Cheese" Porcher not only delivered the order, but would put it on the kitchen shelves for the customer.

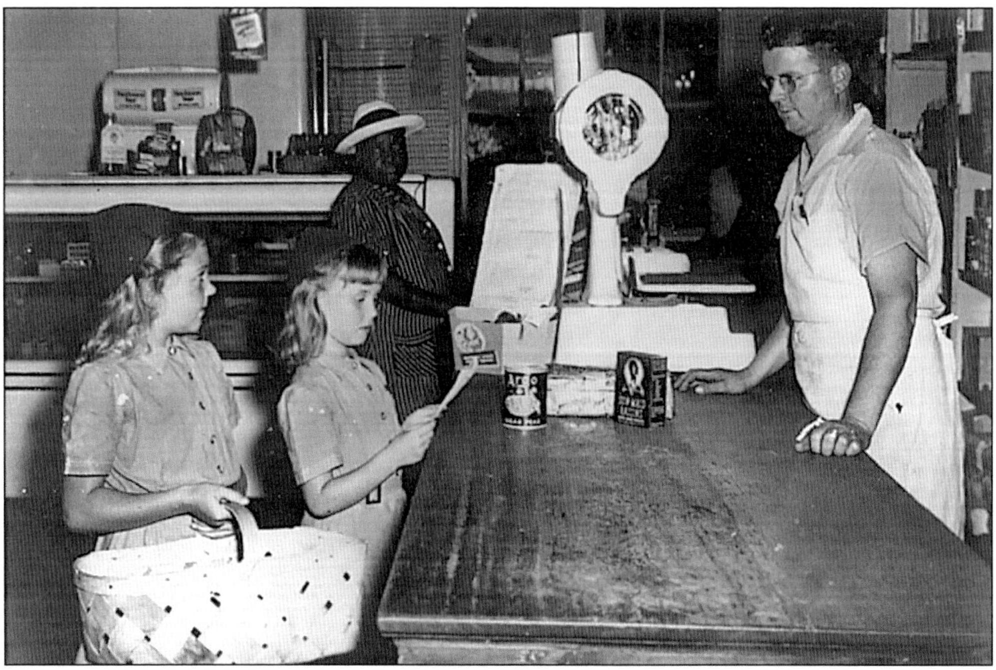
Here Hasell serves Scouts as they check off their shopping list while Isabelle Weathers looks on. The time is the mid-1940s. In that era brown paper wrapping tied with string secured the items purchased. (Plastic bags would come later.) Many items were bought in bulk and weighed out for each customer. Apples came in barrels, but bread was now sliced and wrapped at the bakery.

Across the street from the grocery, in the corner building was Coleman's Hardware Store. The building had begun as a grocery years before. Coleman's stocked every sort of hardware, kitchenware, seed for planting, and advice for the asking all under the watchful eye of the animals on the wall. Robert, a skilled taxidermist, had mounted them. Mr. Wesley's memory was remarkable. At an advanced age he could still recite long poems by Longfellow he had learned as a child at the academy.

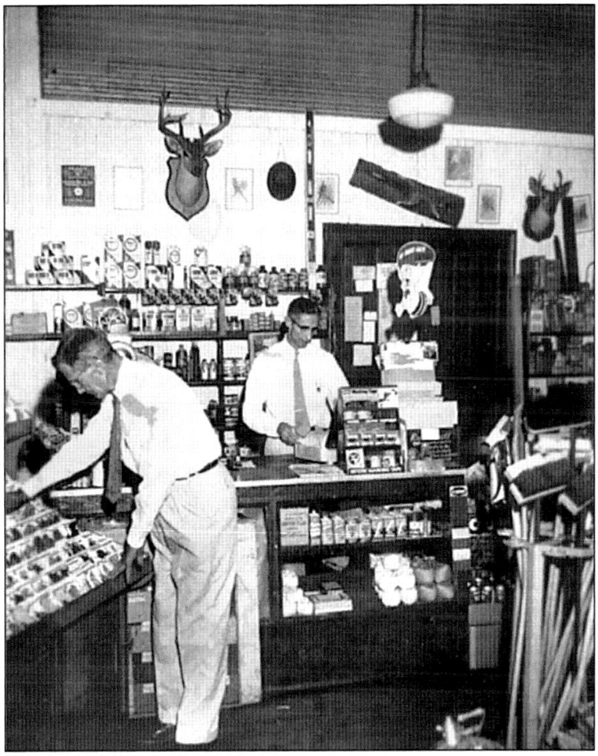

The hardware store, in addition to regular merchandise, also supplied repairs. Saws could be sharpened, as could scissors. Birdseed was sold by the pound, except during the summer, because Mr. Wesley believed that the birds had plenty of wild seed to eat then.

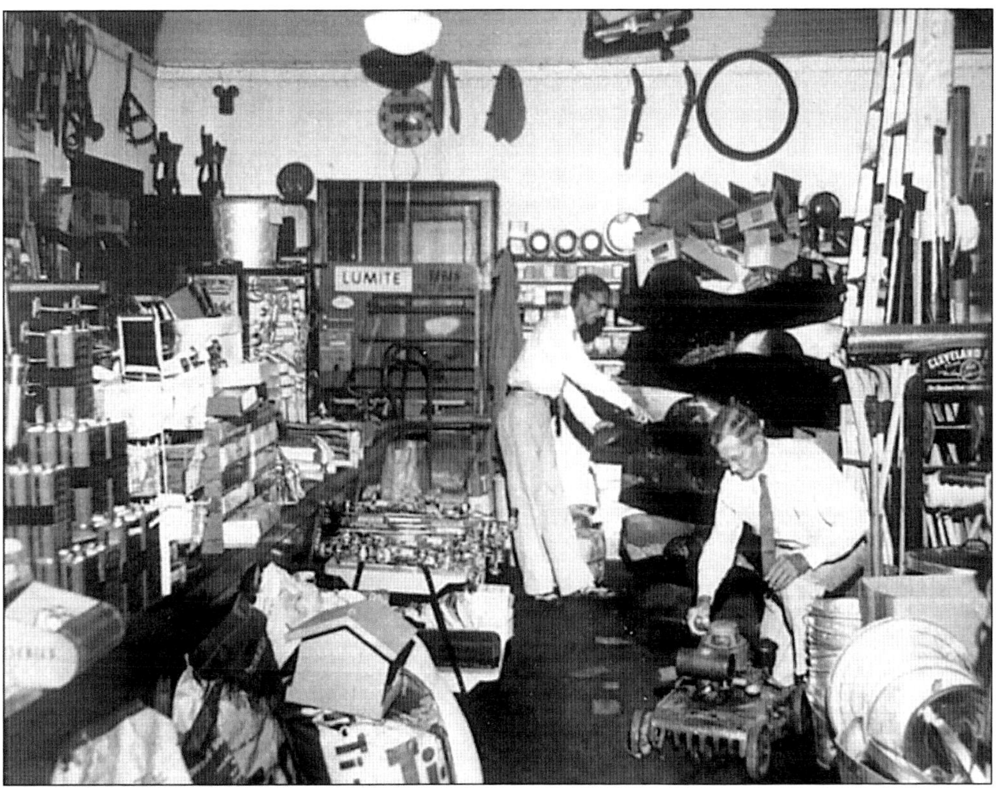

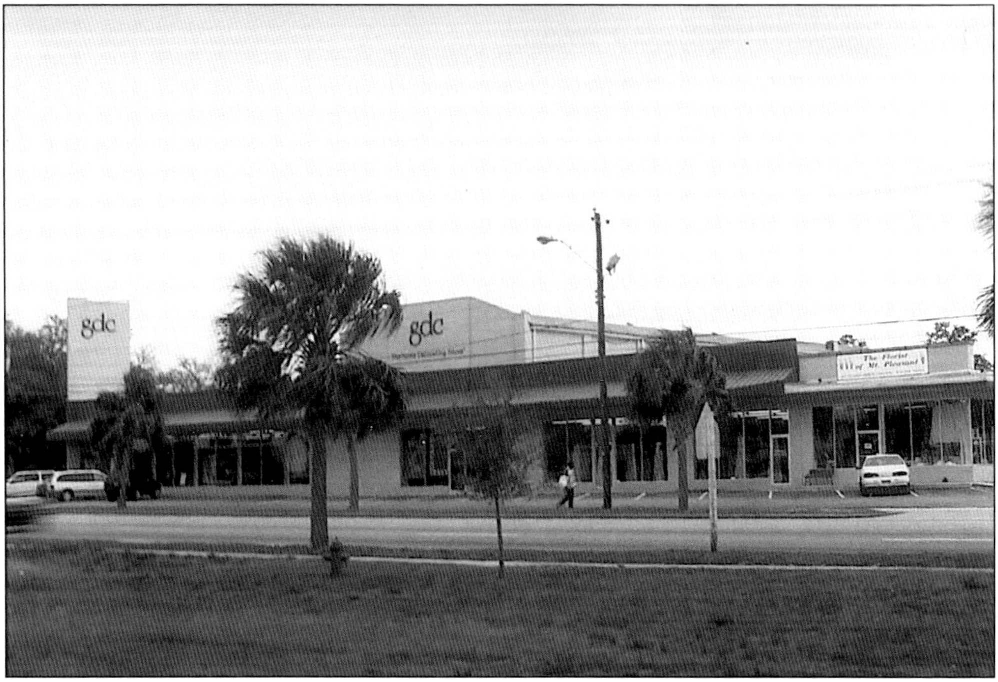

Grocery stores that were connected to chains began appearing in the little town. Piggly Wiggly at the Sea Island Shopping Center was owned and operated by the Langley family. The first shopping center was on the corner of Coleman and Fairmont Streets. Big Star, which became Colonial, had Tom Rivers as manager and was located at the end where GDC is now. A movie theatre was in the center. It had a short life span because about the time it opened people were getting their own television sets, and preferred to stay home and watch TV. A drug store, Western Auto, and Krispy Kreme donut shop completed the complex. The donut shop continued for many years with a group who came every morning for coffee—the best in town, made with water from a deep well on the property.

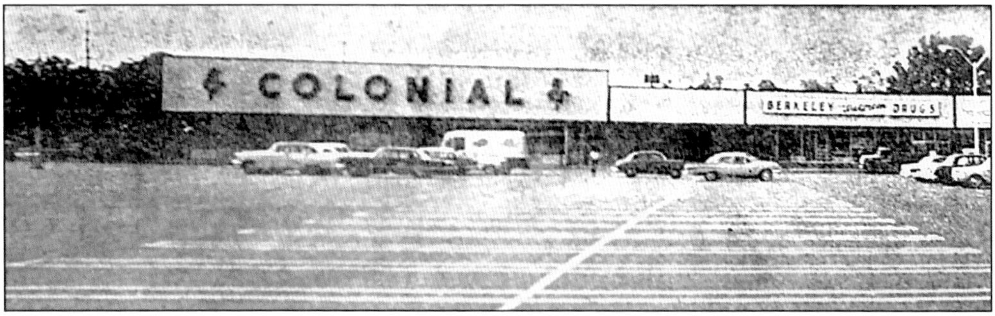

In 1963, Moultrie Shopping Center opened on Coleman and Simmons, across the street from Moultrie High School. It was anchored by Colonial on one end and Grants on the other. With over 25,000 people between the bridge and McClellanville, it was hoped that the center would draw many customers. Among the shops were a barber shop and a beauty shop, a fabric shop, a dry cleaners, a drug store, and a do-it-yourself laundry. Several of these had moved from across the street. Since then, strip malls and plazas have proliferated throughout the area.

Five

CHURCHES

Grants of land had been given to various people in the late 1600s, and in 1706 the Church Act established the Anglican religion in the English colony. Ten parishes were laid out, each having its own Anglican Church. Geographically Mount Pleasant was in the area called Christ Church Parish, bounded by the Atlantic Ocean, the Wando River, and Awendaw Creek. However, Dissenters soon became a dominant force. One of these groups from New England arrived around 1699 and established a Congregational church at the headwaters of the Wando River. Only the cemetery of Old Wappetaw remains.

Christ Church, the parish church, was located on the King's Highway, which probably began as an Indian trail and then became a stagecoach road between Charleston and Georgetown. Although no king ever traveled it, the first president, George Washington, did in 1791 on his Southern Tour. Eventually it was known as the Old Georgetown Road, then Route 40, and now Highway 17 North.

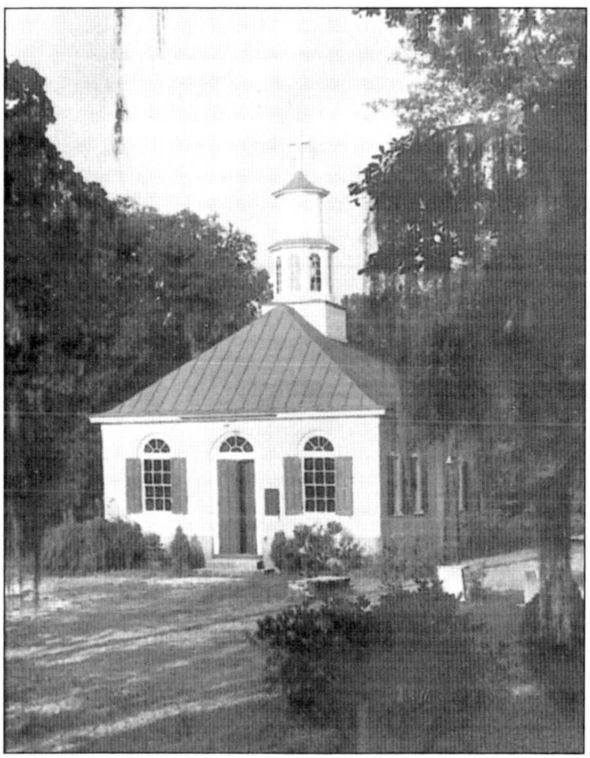

Christ Church dates from 1726. The Vestry House is older. For years it was known locally as Six Mile Church because of its distance from the town's waterfront. In recent years Christ Church has experienced a resurgence because of the population growth nearby. A bequest from a school teacher has been used to erect the handsome ironwork fence around the property. Restoration work has been done on the old sanctuary, an endowment for upkeep of the cemetery has been established. A new sanctuary situated behind the little church has been built.

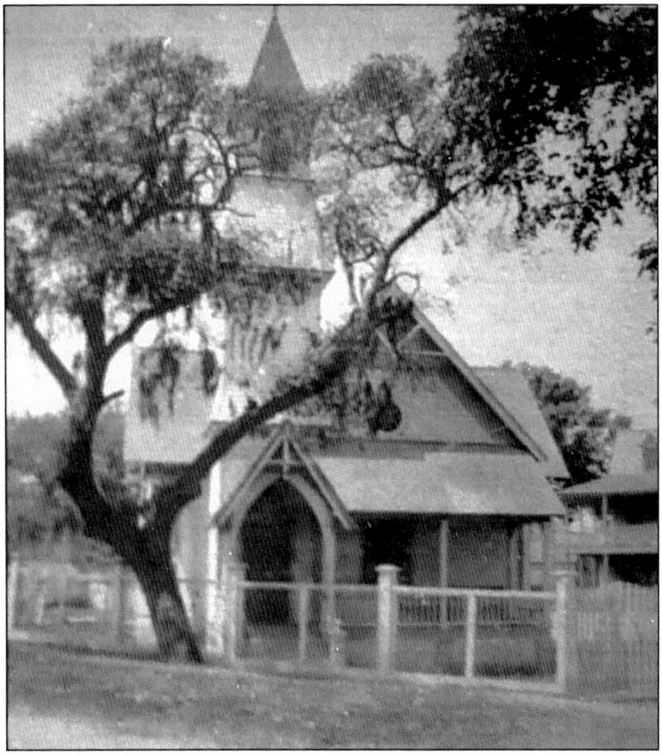

The name Hibben United Methodist Church honors the founder of the town. When James Hibben was dividing his Mount Pleasant plantation into 35 building lots, it is said that he gave one to each of the various denominations and to the school. From 1809 until the mid-1900s change was slow. Then expansion seen in the town was reflected in the churches. Hibben Methodist Church was practically destroyed during the Civil War but was rebuilt on its original site about 1901. This building on the corner of Hibben and Bennett Streets is currently used by the Seventh Day Adventist congregation.

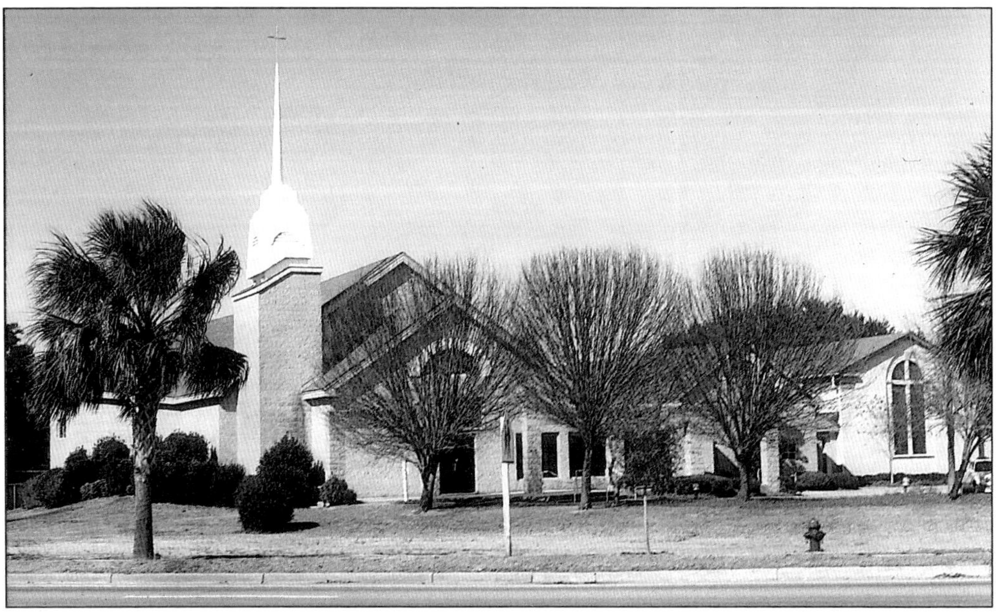

In 1955 the Methodist congregation having outgrown its facilities bought a highly visible location on Coleman Boulevard and Vincent Drive. Starting in 1959 with a multipurpose auditorium and classrooms, they have expanded over the years, including a new sanctuary in 1984 and recently with additional educational facilities. Two programs sponsored by the church to assist families devastated by the 1989 hurricane, Habitat for Humanity and East Cooper Community Outreach (ECCO), continue to serve the area.

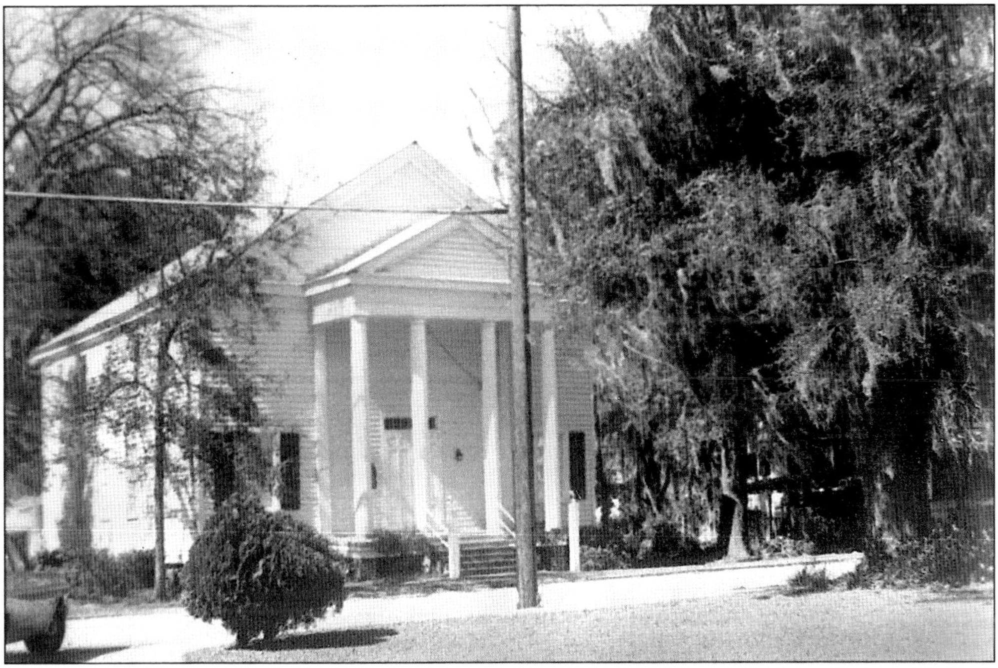

Mount Pleasant Presbyterian Church chose to stay on the same corner of Hibben and Church Streets. This historic (1854) building on Lot 50 in Lucasville has three Sunday morning services to accommodate its growing congregation. To commemorate its tricentennial, a history has been compiled, beginning with its roots in Old Wappetaw Church in 1699.

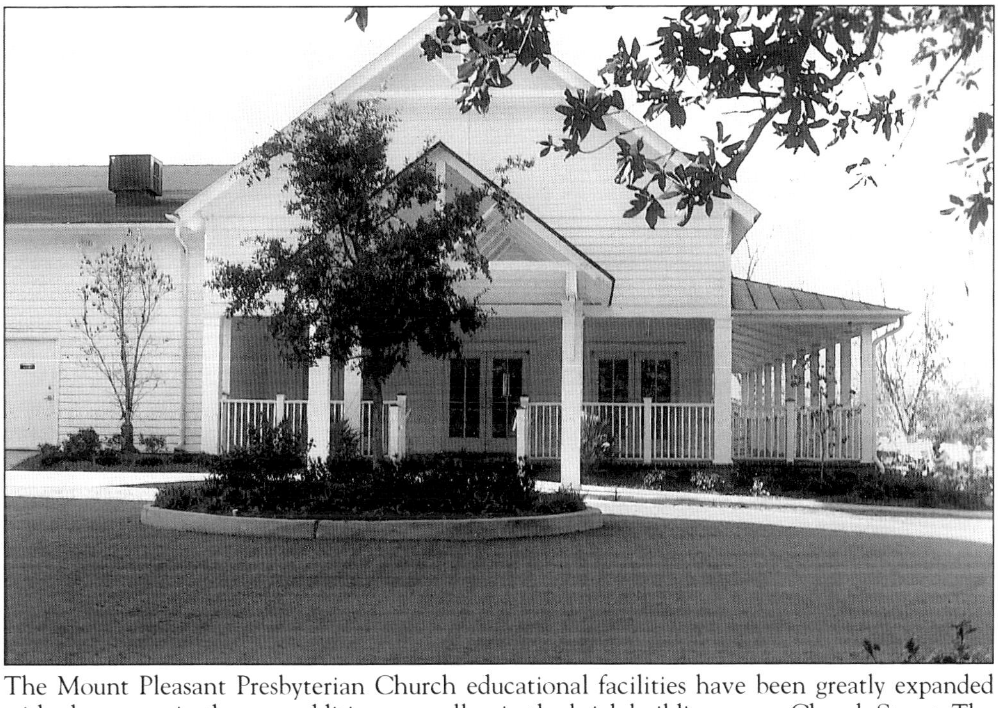

The Mount Pleasant Presbyterian Church educational facilities have been greatly expanded with classrooms in the new additions as well as in the brick building across Church Street. The new buildings reflect the angle of the church rooflines.

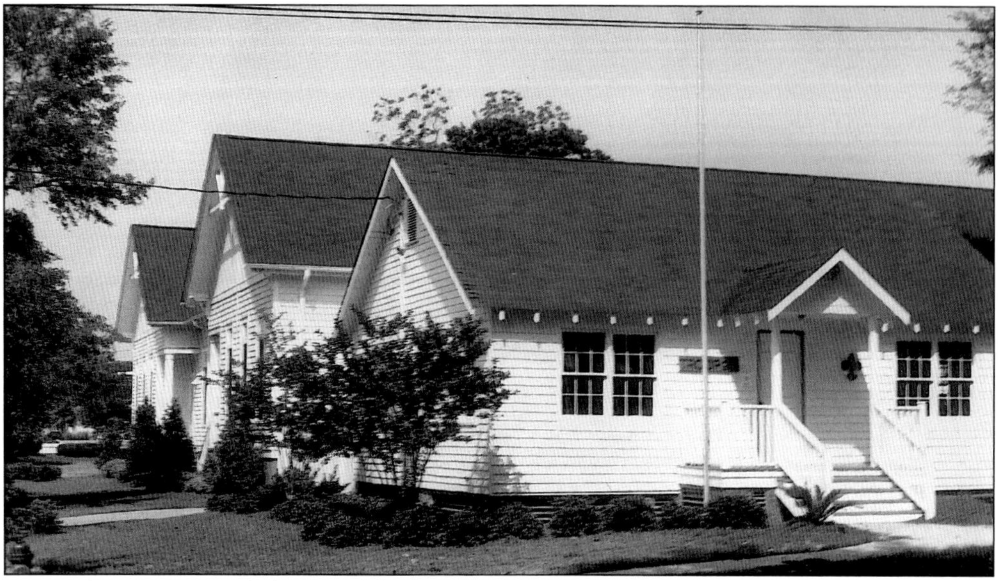

Outreach programs include a weekday kindergarten, and Mothers Morning Out. There is an active Scouting program, which has its own building on the corner of Live Oak and Church Streets. Troop 20 has produced 53 Eagle Scouts since 1970. The Scout hut is the first building in this image and the Scout emblem is by the side of the door. The building had been a residence before the church bought the property.

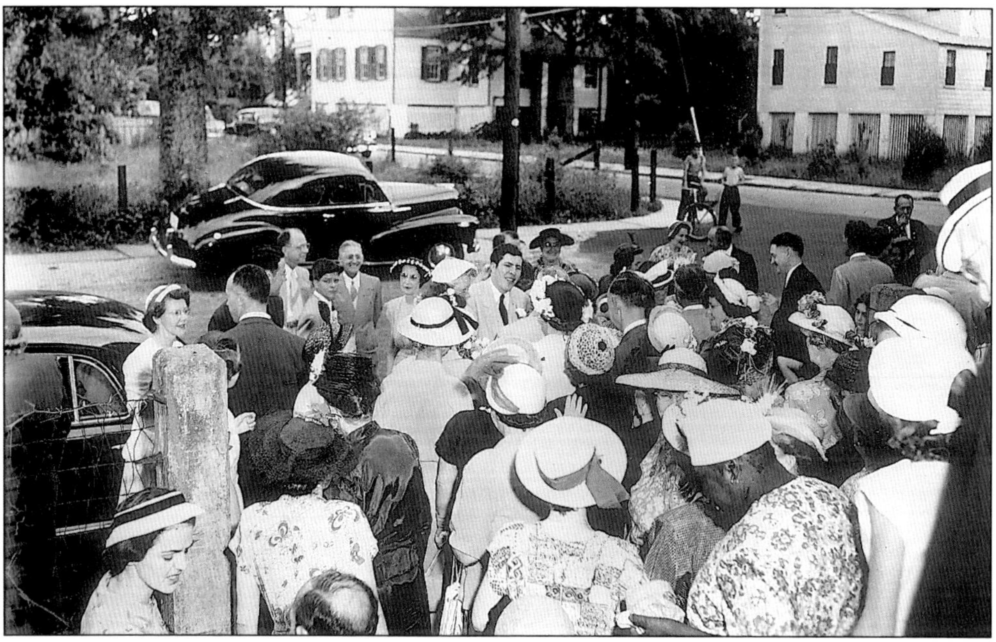

Certainly one of the happiest occasions in the history of Mount Pleasant Presbyterian Church was the wedding in 1950 between the church's first full-time minister, Rev. T.W. Horton Jr., and Miss Sue Royall. The congregation and townspeople filled the church. Early records indicate a village church about 1827 with the present building having been erected some 27 years later. In 1870 the congregation was officially accepted by the Presbytery and served by part-time pastors until 1949.

St. Andrew's Episcopal Church on the corner of Whilden and Venning Streets was organized as a chapel of Christ Church, the Parish Church some six miles away, for the members who lived in the town. The original building (1835) was soon too small and was sold to the Masonic Lodge which still uses it. In 1857 the present building was erected. The architect was Edward B. White, who designed a number of Charleston churches.

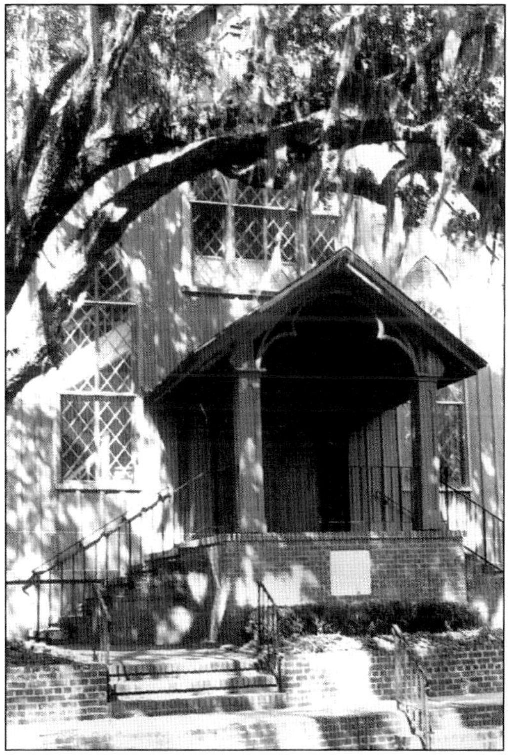

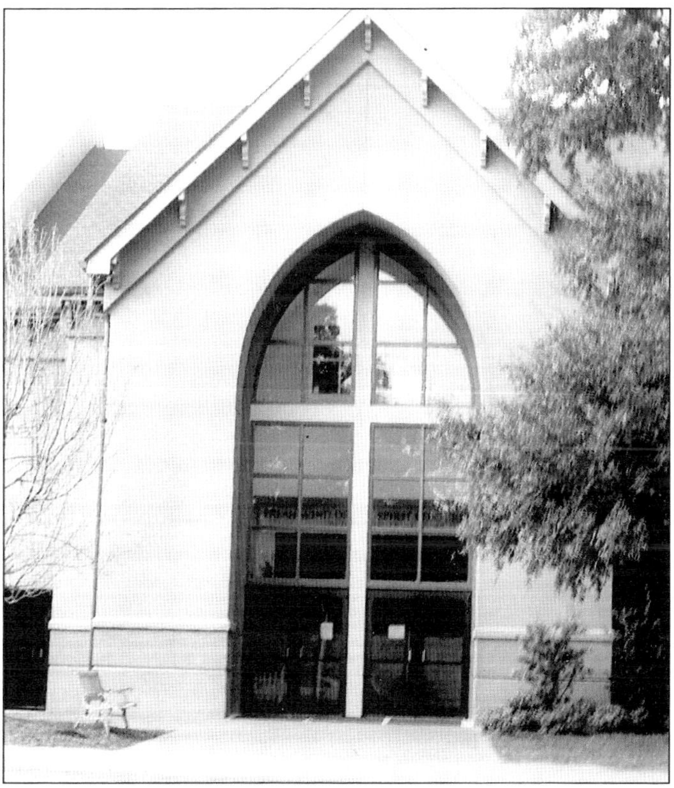

As the congregation grew, the 1857 building was enlarged, and then in the 1990s a large Ministry Center was constructed on Venning Street.

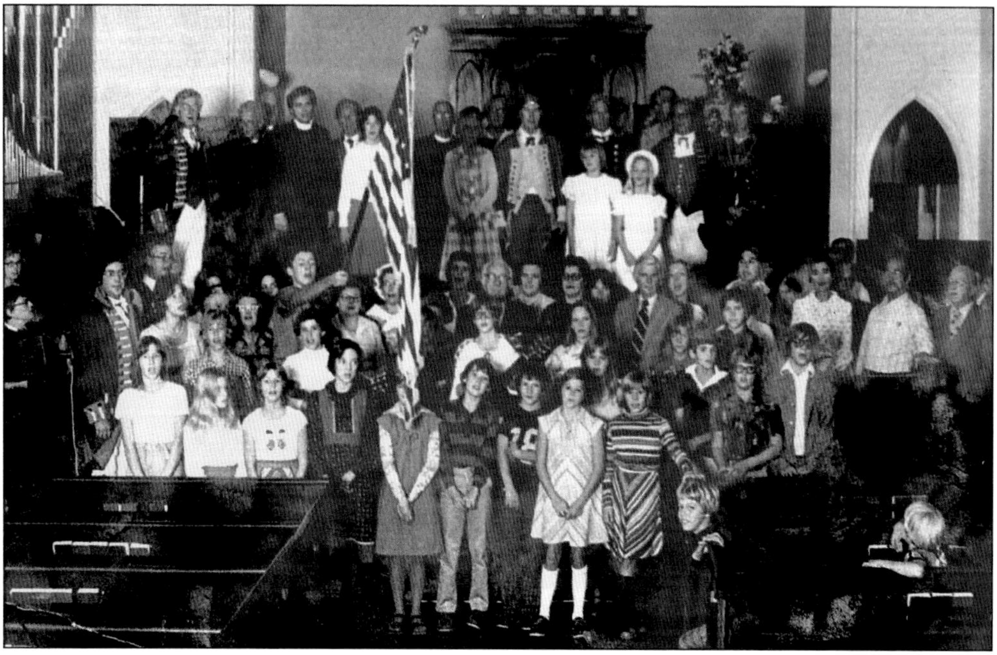

In 1985, St. Andrew's celebrated its sesquicentennial with a pageant depicting the church's history. As the image indicates, the pageant included a large cast of characters. A written history was also compiled at this time.

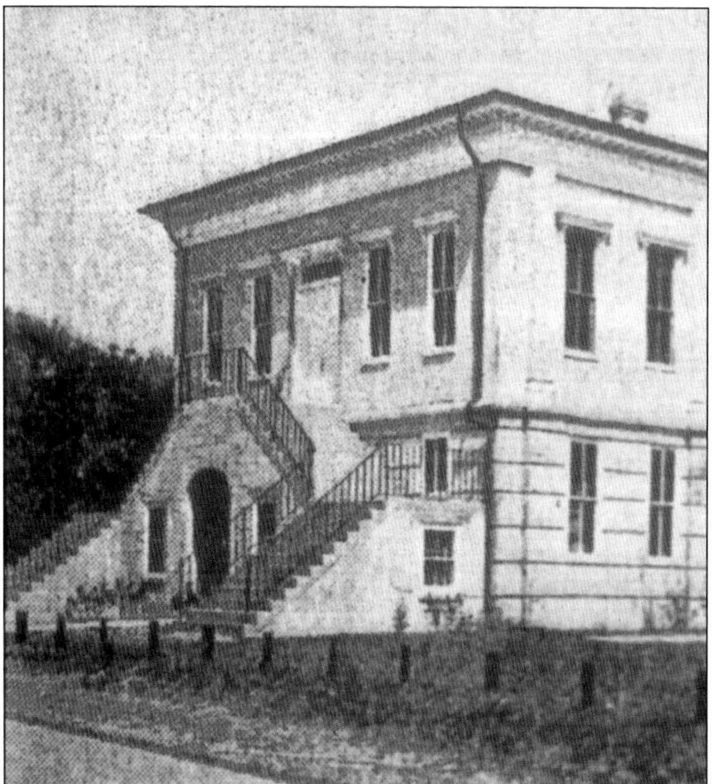

The First Baptist Church had its beginnings on Church Street in the 1870s. After that facility burned, the congregation bought the old Berkeley County Courthouse at Pitt and King Streets and began worshipping there about 1919.

The communion silver inscribed "Mt. Pleasant Baptist Church, 1871" was found by an early member's granddaughter almost 100 years after it had been stored in the attic following the 1877 fire. She returned it to the church, now known as First Baptist Church.

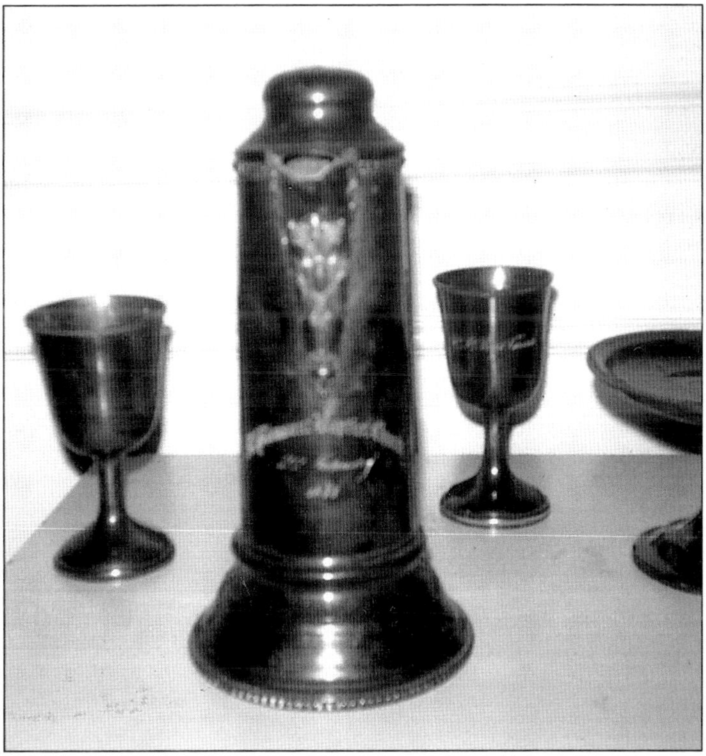

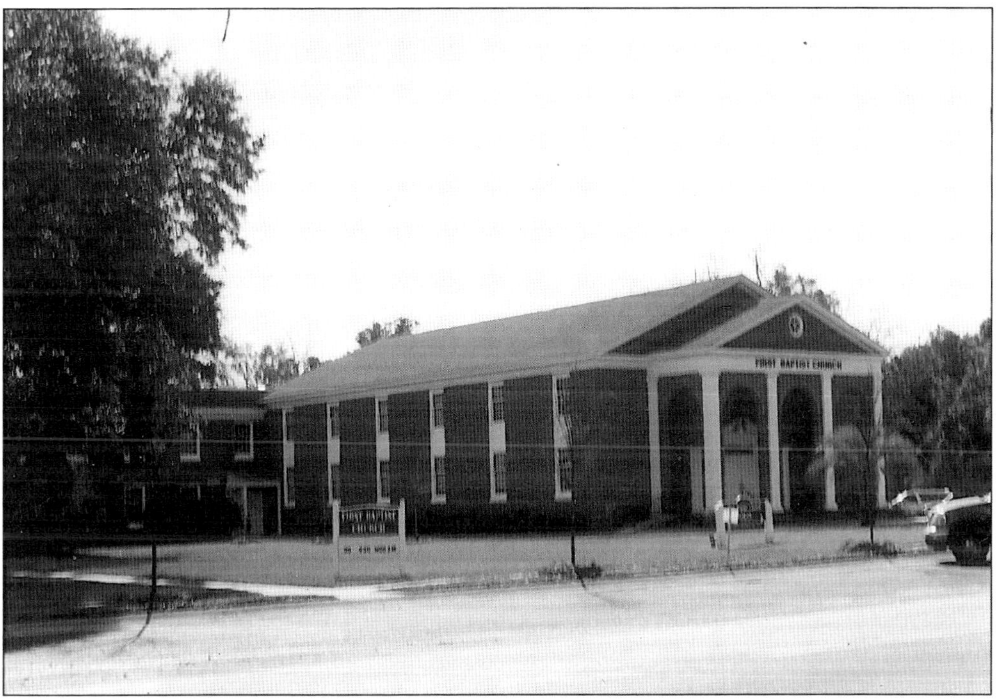

A much larger sanctuary, located on McCants Drive, was dedicated on March 15, 1964, by the First Baptist Church congregation. Then, in 1987, they dedicated their new Christian Life Center. The church also has a weekday school, which utilizes their facilities during the week.

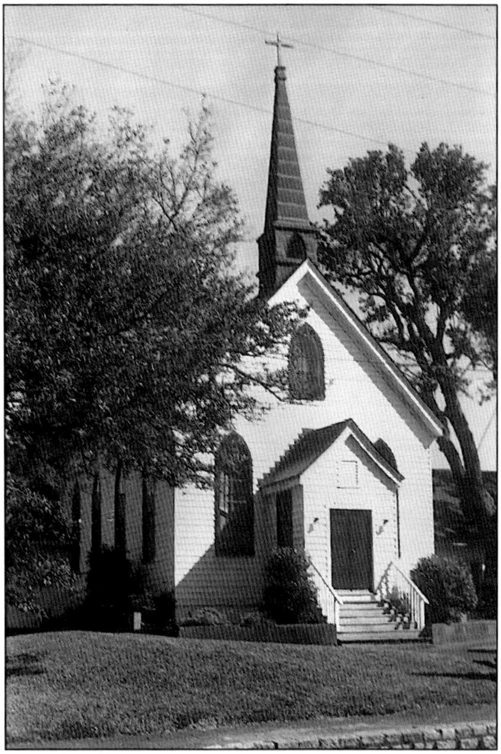

St. Paul's Lutheran Church was built in 1884 on the corner of Pitt and Queen Streets by the small group of Germans who had been worshipping together since around 1881. They were first called the Church Society of the Concordia Association. Then in 1884 the name became the German Evangelical Lutheran St. Paul's Parish of Mount Pleasant. The Germans were a dominant force in the town at that time, running stores and a bakery. From 1898 until 1911 the Lutheran Theological Seminary was located in Mount Pleasant in the former Berkeley County Courthouse; in 1911, it moved to Columbia where it is still located.

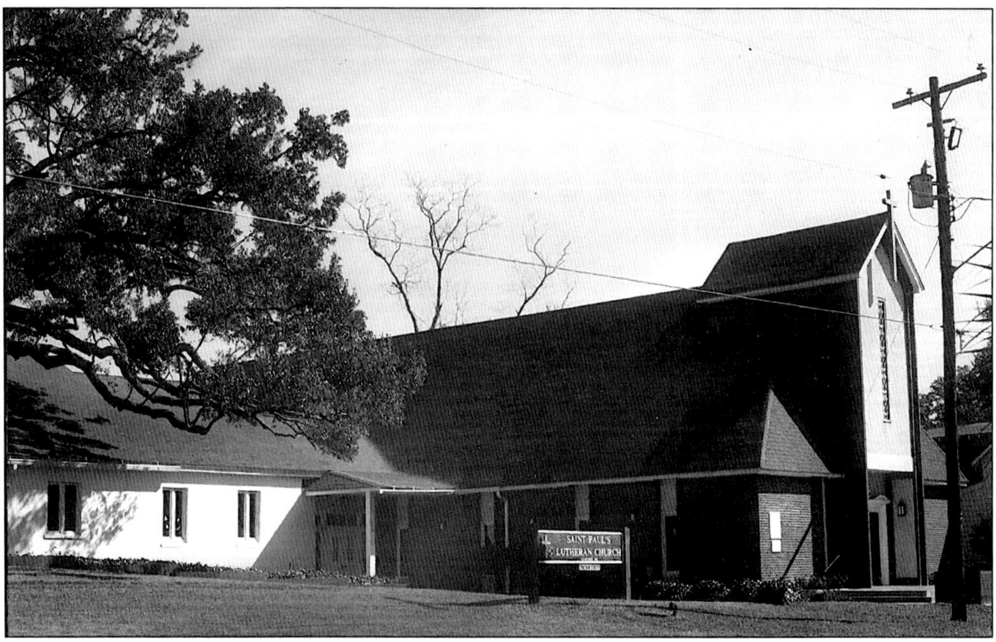

In 1972, St. Paul's congregation moved into their new sanctuary just a short distance from the first church building. Since 1889 they have owned the cemetery on McCants Drive that is known as the Lutheran Cemetery, even though people of many faiths are buried there. It was originally a part of the Ocean Grove Cemetery on Greenwich Commons owned by the town. The oldest stone is to the memory of Angeline Jervey, who died in 1893.

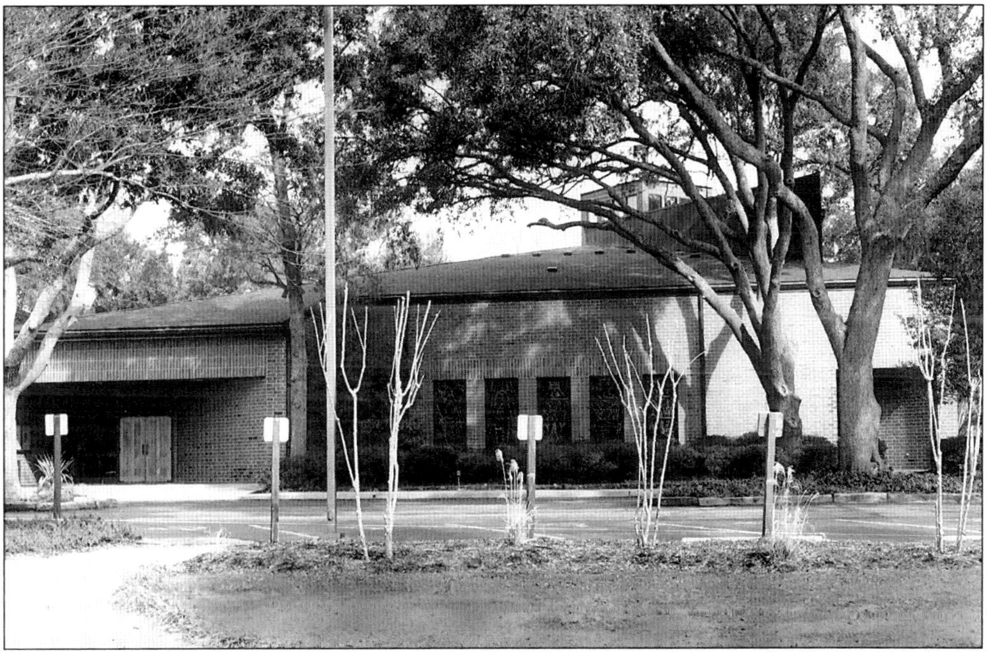

Christ Our King Catholic Church is a contemporary structure located north of the original little villages and geographically would be in the northwestern part of the 1784 plat of Haddrell's Point Plantation. This plantation of 471 acres included the land from Shem Creek up to Myrick Road over past McCants Drive and down to Simmons Street.

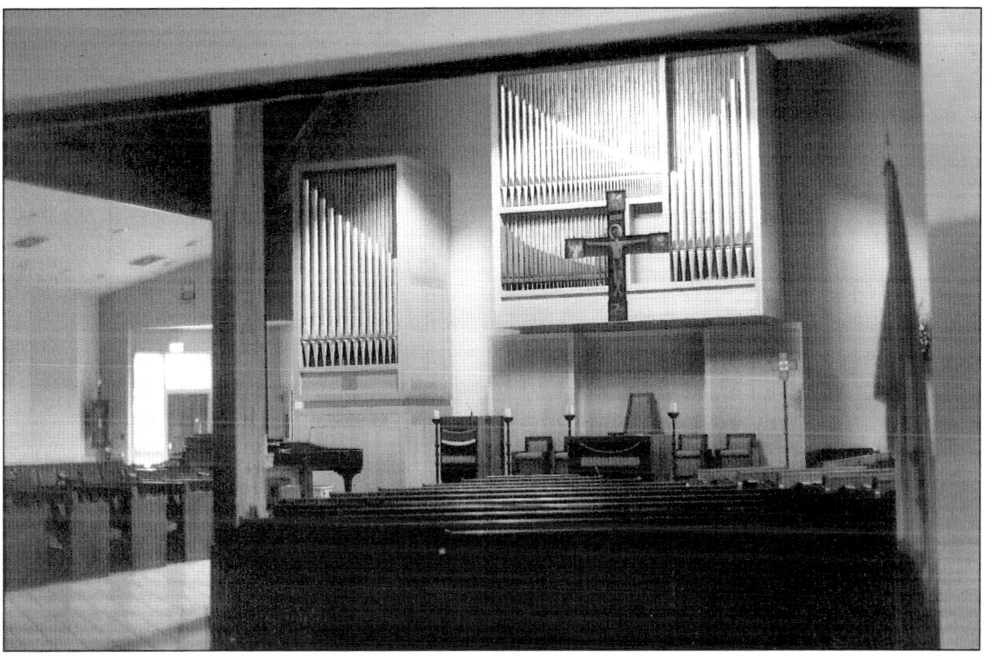

This view of the interior shows the recently installed Holtkamp pipe organ. Christ Our King church emphasizes a strong music program. Together with Stella Maris Church they have an elementary school on the Coleman Boulevard part of their property. High school students go to Bishop England School on Daniel Island.

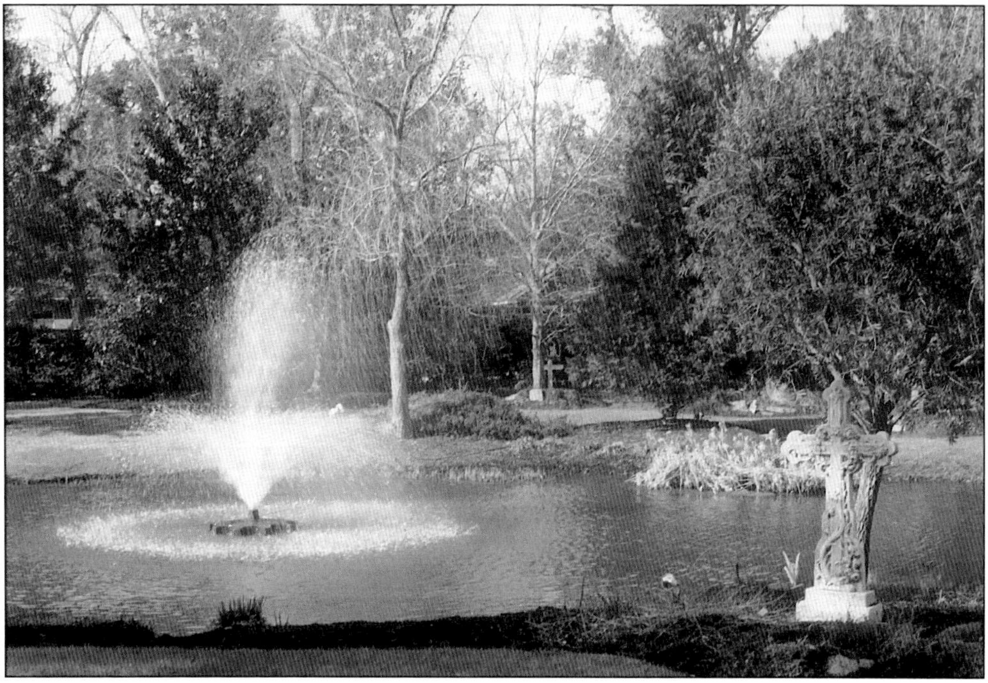

On the grounds of Christ Our King Church is a unique garden area developed after Hugo destroyed the woods. The visitor can walk the circumference and stop at various places which commemorate Jesus's last day on earth and meditate on this great mystery.

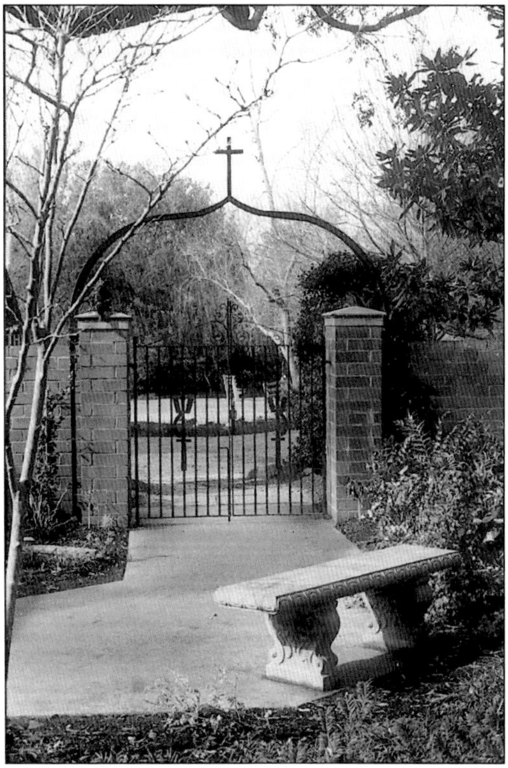

The Way of the Cross Park provides a peaceful setting for contemplation in the midst of a busy town. Flowering plants and trees add to the beauty of the place. Visitors are welcome.

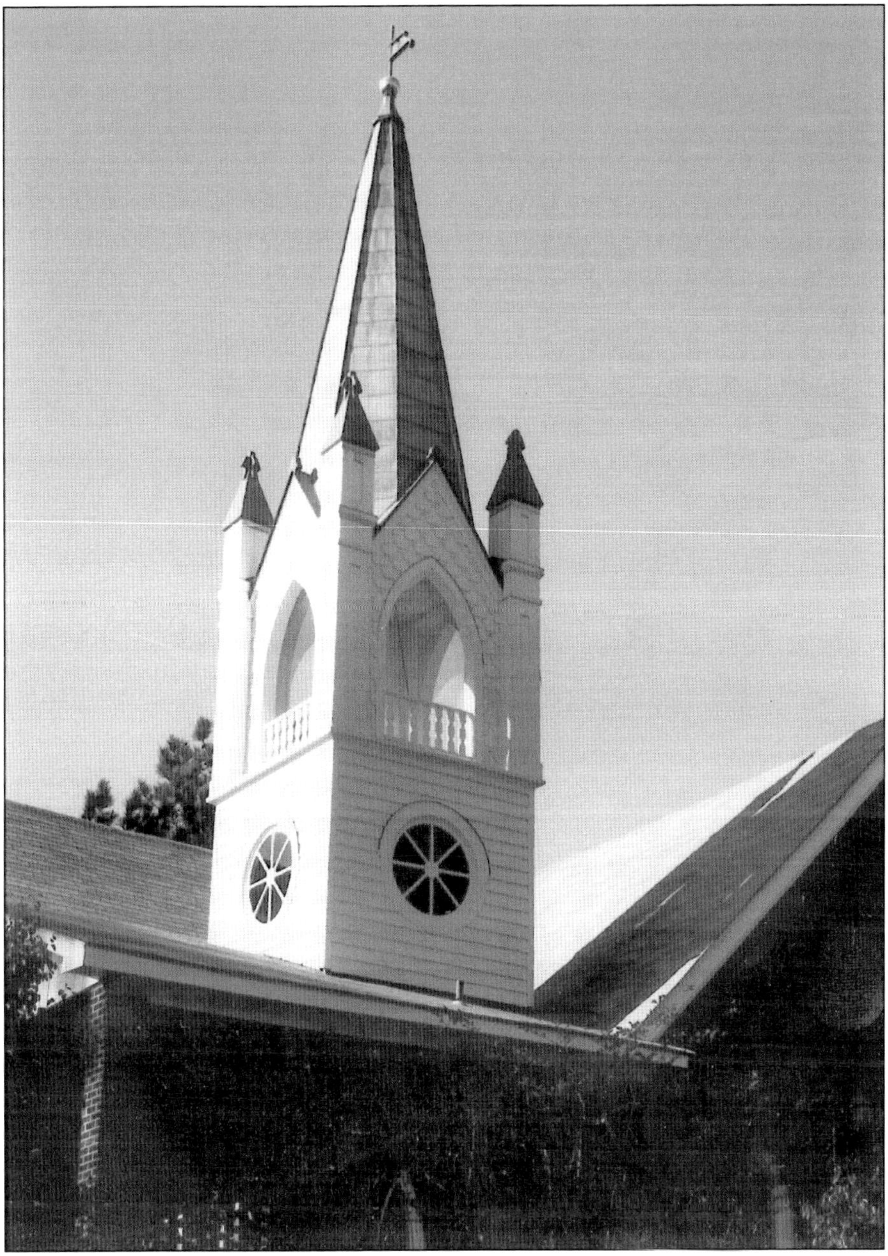

The African-American community is an integral part of Mount Pleasant. Within the Old Village area are Friendship A.M.E. and Ebenezer Baptist Churches. In the early days, whites and blacks worshipped together. During Reconstruction building lots were given to the Baptists, Methodists, and Presbyterians to build churches. Friendship Church features the lovely steeple pictured here. It has recently been restored so it is structurally sound. With pride in their heritage, the congregation is erecting a marker approved by the South Carolina Department of Archives and History documenting their history. Ebenezer Baptist Church a few blocks away has rebuilt their church after Hurricane Hugo demolished the previous one. Zion Presbyterian is no longer in existence. References in Presbyterian records indicate Vacation Bible Schools were held there in the 1950s.

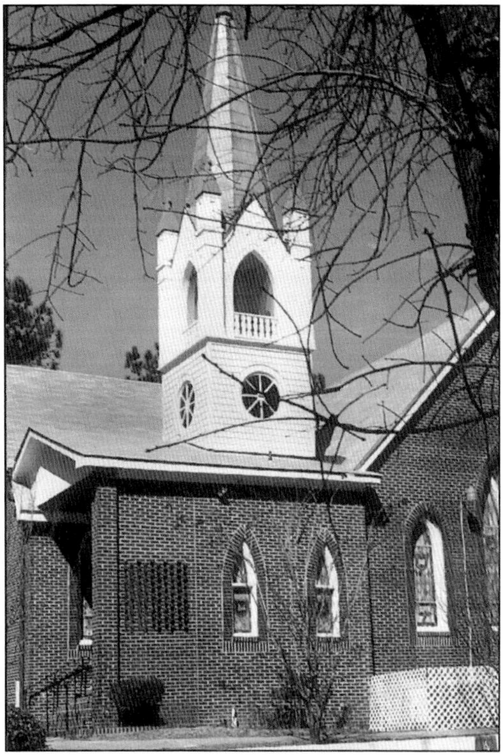

Friendship African Methodist Episcopal (A.M.E.) Church is located on Royall Avenue. It has a most decorative steeple, beautiful brickwork, and attractive windows. An educational building and offices are connected to the church, while a recently surfaced parking lot provides much needed parking places nearby.

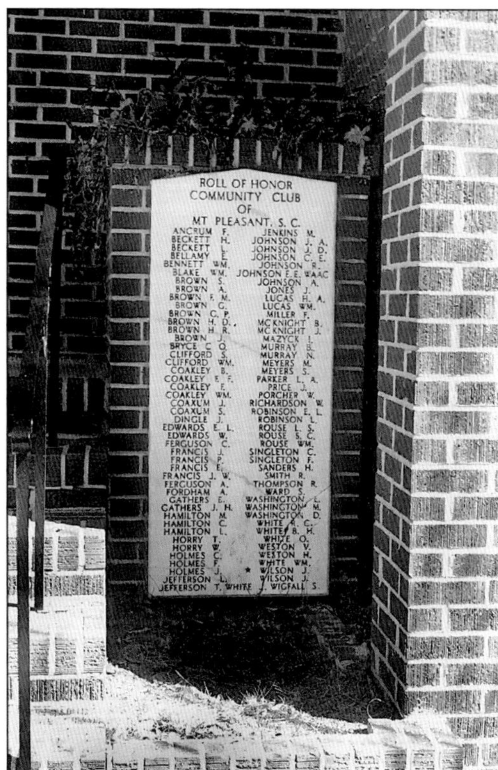

Two marble plaques are attached to the A.M.E. church building. One, a cornerstone dated July 25, 1961, contains names of the trustees, stewards, pastors, presiding elder, and bishop. The other is a "Roll of honor Community Club of Mt. Pleasant" that lists almost 100 names. Not many blocks away is a street which was recently named for Hamp Fludd for his contribution to the town. He was an excellent brick mason. He, his family, and many friends attended the ceremonies ending with a reception at Friendship Church.

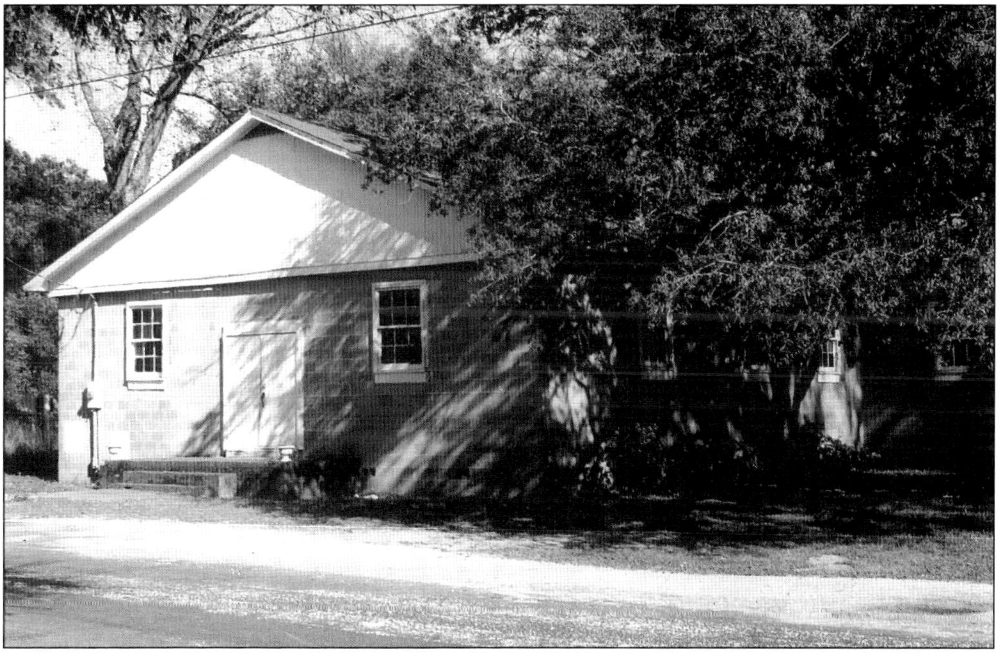

Ebenezer Baptist Church is a neat concrete block building located on Morrison Street near Whilden. The cornerstone on the church indicates it began in 1951 and was rebuilt in 1991, after the hurricane. It is on the original lot given for the Baptist church in the 1890s. The lot that was given to the Presbyterians was around the corner from this church. Their church was called Zion and no longer exists.

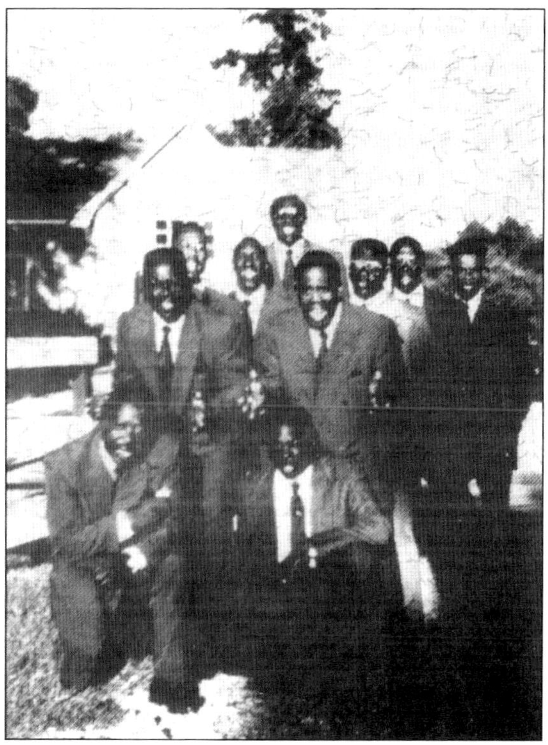

The Brotherhood Gospel Singers, a group of young men who have performed in many places in the U.S as well as Europe since 1977, were members of Long Point Missionary Baptist Church. Some have been ordained and pastor their own churches now. In 1994 they sang a series of concerts in Switzerland in the Cathedral of Lugano and in Italy. They are heard on television in "Gullah, Gullah Island." They present over 60 concerts yearly and have received recognition and honors for their music. This photo was taken by John Blais of Charleston.

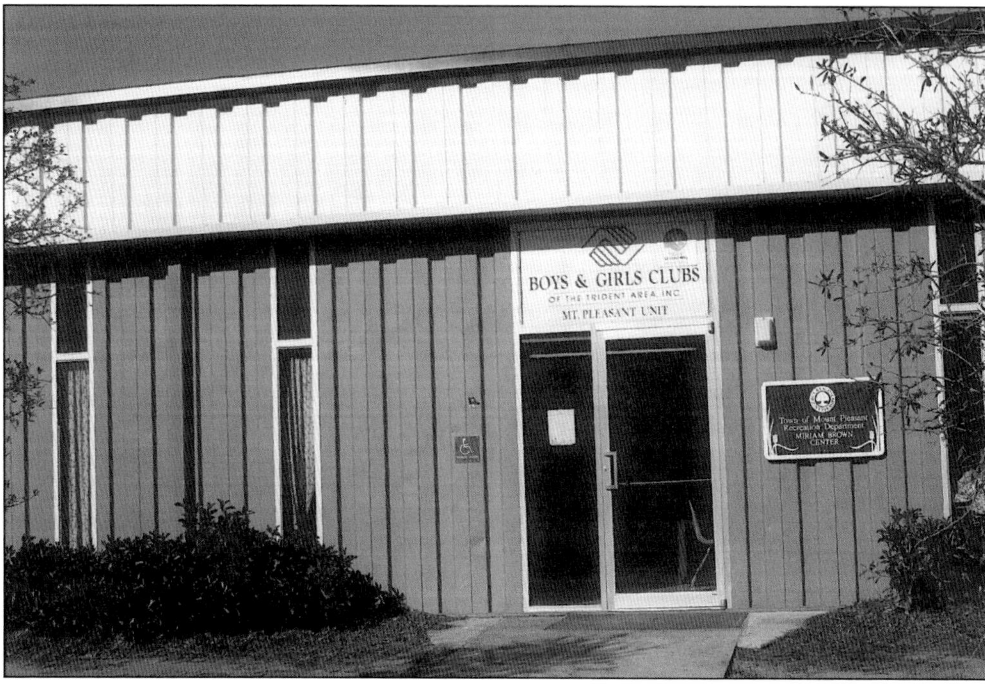

The Miriam Brown recreational facility honors the educator of that name. A longtime teacher and principal, Miriam Brown instilled moral values in her pupils as well as "book learning." The building and adjoining playground are located on the corner of King and Royall Streets where the Laing School was when it was operated by the Quakers.

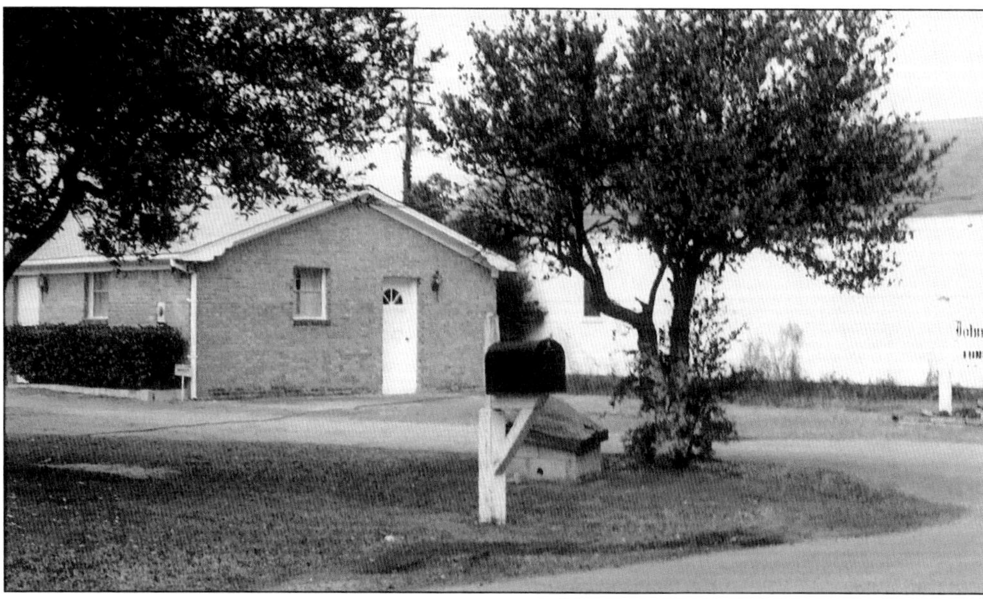

The Johnson-Halls Funeral Home has been operated for many years by an outstanding African-American family. Marguerite Johnson was particularly talented in helping the bereaved express their emotions in this difficult time in their lives. Ocean Grove Cemetery on McCants Drive has provided a resting place for many of the town's citizens since 1883. It is separated from the Lutheran Cemetery by Hallelujah Lane.

Six

EDUCATION

Mount Pleasant Academy was the first school organized after Mount Pleasant Plantation became the Village of Mount Pleasant in 1809. Today there are numerous elementary schools, middle schools, and a large high school in the East Cooper area.

The early history of the Mount Pleasant Academy is quite interesting. Mrs. Elizabeth Fleming's bequest resulted in a board of eight trustees being incorporated and a school built in Mount Pleasant in 1809. Two years later, to complete it, they were authorized to raise funds by means of a lottery. In 1908 the school was located on the corner of Pitt and Venning Streets where it remained until a larger building was constructed in 1938 on Boundary (now Simmons) Street and Highway 40 (now Coleman Boulevard). Both buildings have been demolished. In 1940 Moultrie High School was begun in the vacated academy building on Pitt Street. In four years it was relocated to a campus adjacent to the new academy building. Following desegregation and rapid growth of the area a new high school, Wando, was built at the intersection of Mathis Ferry and Whipple Roads.

A middle school was begun where the high school had been, continuing the name of the Revolutionary War general William Moultrie. Laing School as originally planned no longer exists. It was established after the War between the States by the Quakers. The name is retained in the middle school some six miles north on Highway 17. The Laing alumni association is still active and provides scholarships for worthy African-American students.

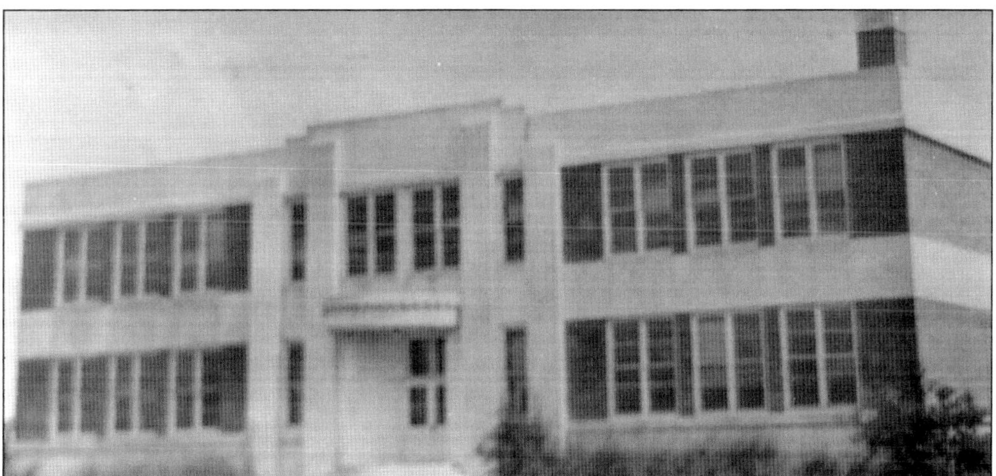

The new building of the Mount Pleasant Academy, shown above, was dedicated in 1938 in ceremonies under the direction of the Parent-Teacher Association (PTA).

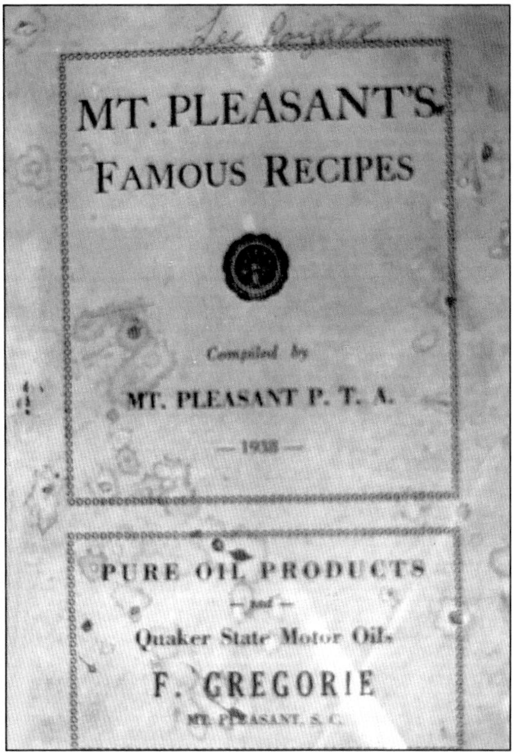

Not only did the PTA of the Mount Pleasant Academy plan the celebration when the school moved into its new facility in 1938, it published a 115-page cookbook, *Mount Pleasant's Famous Recipes*, which has become a local best seller. It has gone through several revisions, the latest in 1976. The recipes were contributed by many Mount Pleasant housewives and included such local favorites as shrimp pie and two-cent cake. The advertisements are also interesting and provide a retrospective of the businesses in the area in 1938.

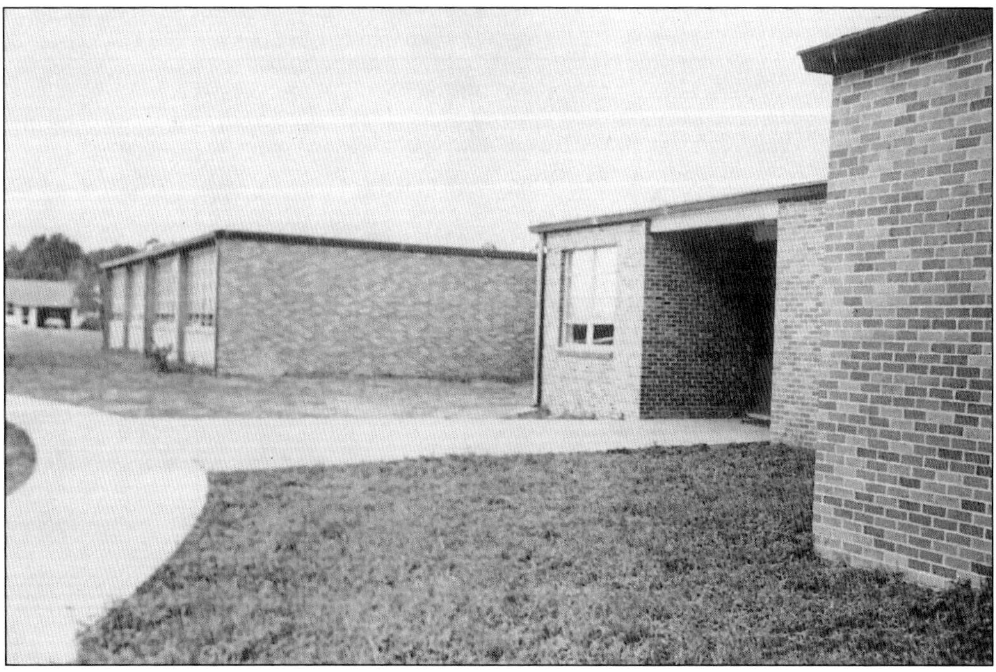

Mount Pleasant Academy had excellent teachers, including Mary P. ("Miss Mamie") Whitesides, who had a tenure of almost half a century. She was honored in 1953 by the Exchange Club as "Woman of the Year." After teaching for some 46 years, she became principal of the Academy. The elementary school (above) on Rifle Range Road is named for her.

The academy celebrated its sesquicentennial on Friday December 18, 1959 with a chapel program. Mrs. W.W. McIver, a pupil from the 1890s, gave an historical sketch in which she recalled old times with stories of various customs. Mayor Francis F. Coleman also spoke, offering many memories from when he had been a student there. A particular recollection concerned a Christmas when Santa Claus caught on fire from the candles on the tree at the Christmas party. Luckily no serious injuries occurred.

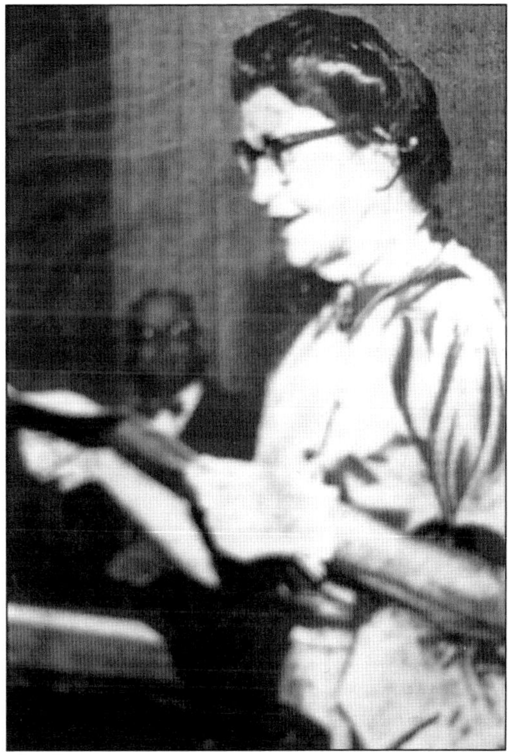

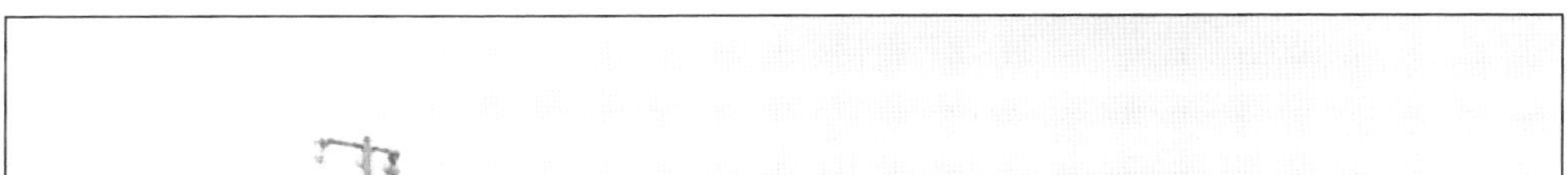

In 1999 the faculty, students, and friends celebrated the academy's 190th birthday with a party and historical skit. The play, which the students had compiled from anecdotes of former pupils, was enthusiastically received. The display on loan from the Museum on the Common about the Academy illustrated how things once were. The Academy is now located on Center Street. It remains an elementary school in the South Carolina School System.

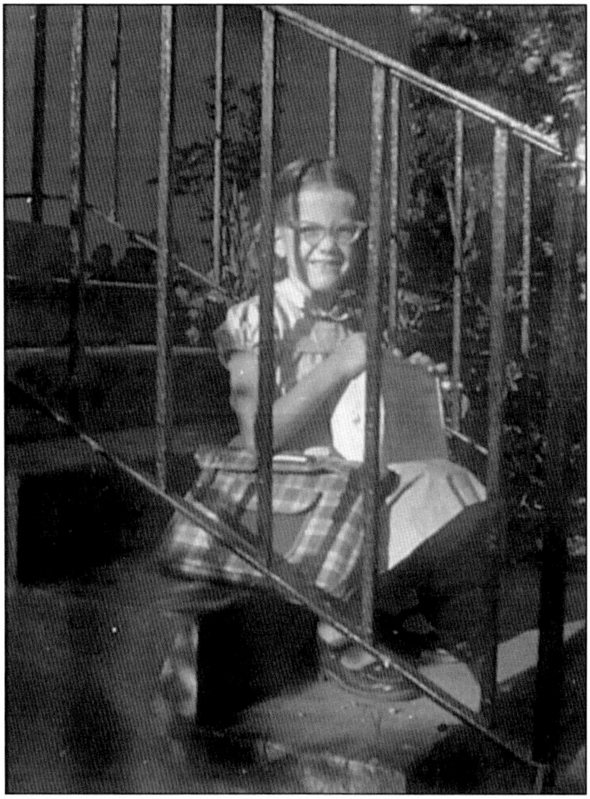

To be ready for the first day of school in the 1950s, girls felt it necessary to have a new dress, a bookbag, and lunch box with a thermos. This young miss is ready to meet the challenges of the school year. In those days, bookbags were either carried by a handle or a strap over the shoulder, as backpacks had not been thought of yet.

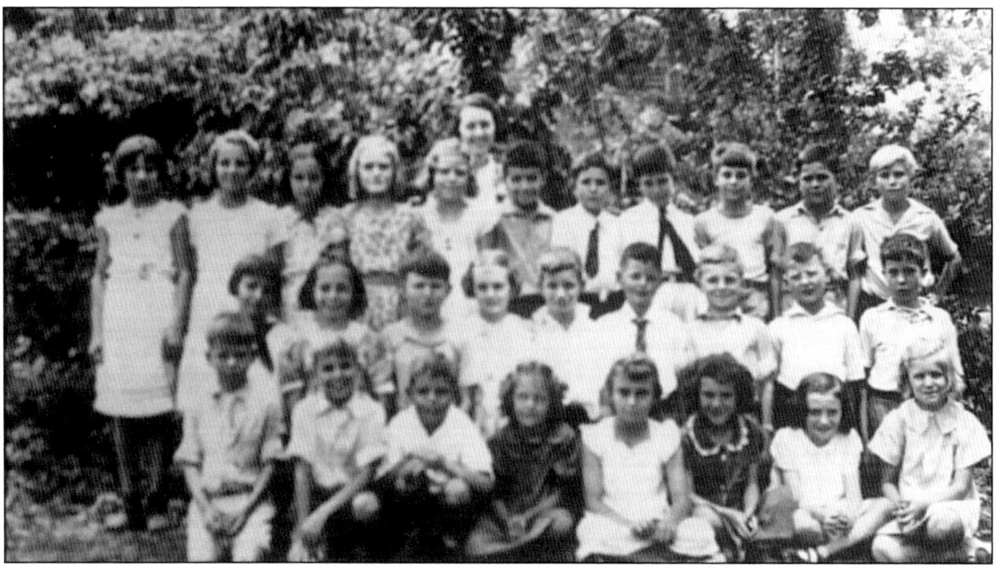

These 28 boys and girls pose with their teacher Miss McIver. They represent a class at the academy in the 1940s. The teacher had an excellent solution for quieting a noisy class. She would speak very softly. In order to not miss hearing what she said, they would become quiet.

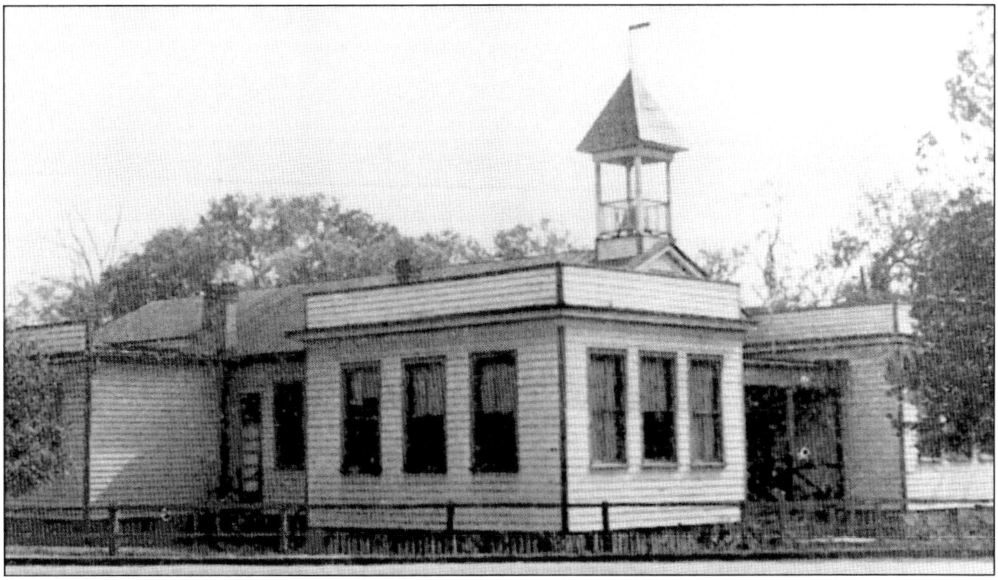

Although Mount Pleasant has had an elementary school since 1809, it was not until 1940 that the town had a high school. Before then students had to catch the ferry, or later the bus, to go to high school in Charleston. Boys went to Charleston High, girls to Memminger. A high school was begun in the vacant academy building shown here. Twenty-three seniors graduated in 1941 from the school named for the Revolutionary War hero, General William Moultrie. When the school moved to property near the new academy there were only eleven grades. The twelfth was added in 1946. A new gymnasium was built in 1964. It was said that in the old gym basketball games could be rained out because the roof was in such bad shape. In 1971 desegregation occurred; Laing High School north of Mount Pleasant was closed and the students went to Moultrie. Moultrie's last graduating class of 170 took place in 1973. Wando High School opened, and the old campus became Moultrie Middle School.

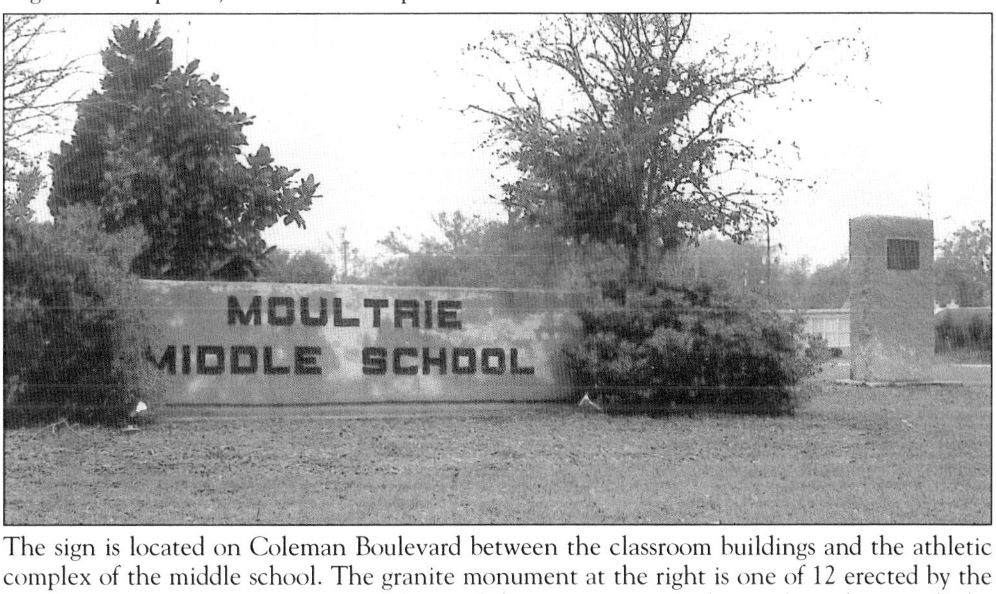

The sign is located on Coleman Boulevard between the classroom buildings and the athletic complex of the middle school. The granite monument at the right is one of 12 erected by the Rebecca Motte Chapter of the Daughters of the American Revolution (DAR) to mark the King's Highway which President George Washington traveled in 1791 on his southern tour.

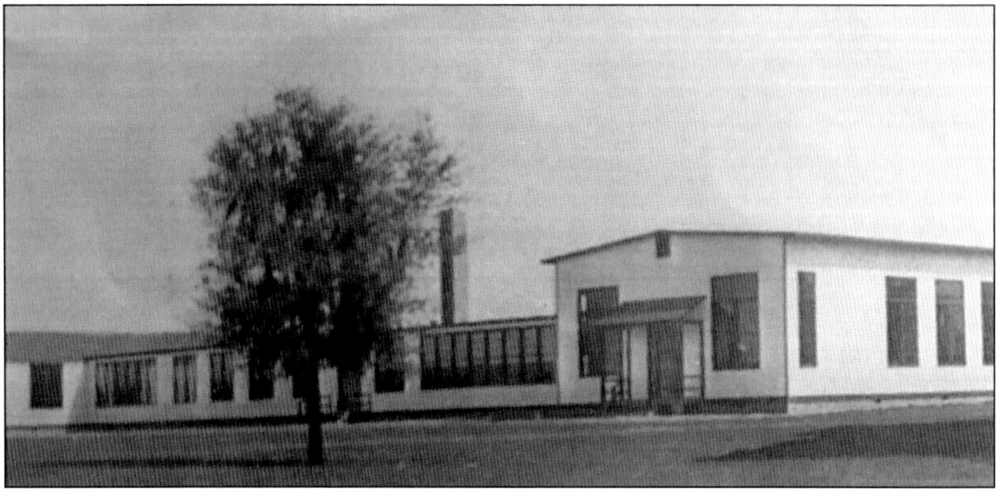

When World War II was over, parts of the military installation on Sullivan's Island were no longer needed and were sold to the general public. The high school was built of material from the old barracks. Though the facilities seem spartan, there were many excellent teachers on the faculty.

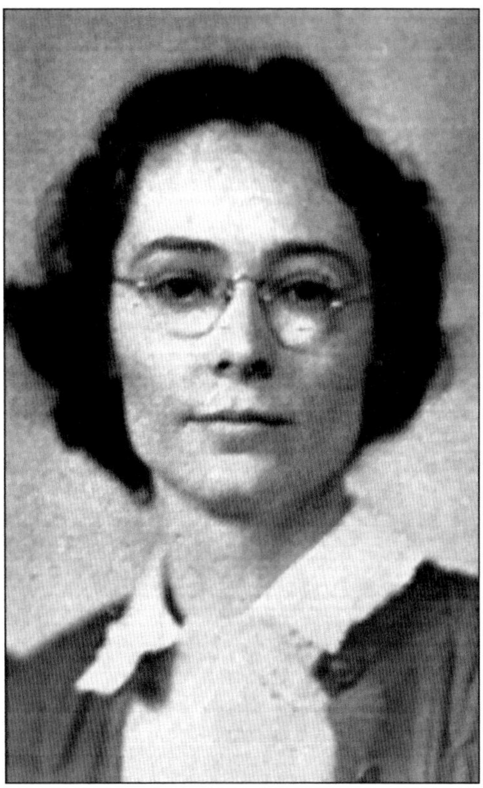

Eunice Caldwell taught English, French, and Latin. She was a member of the original staff when Moultrie High School opened in 1940 in the former academy building on Pitt Street. She moved with the school in 1944 to the new campus on Coleman and Boundary (now Simmons). She was a member of the faculty for 27 years.

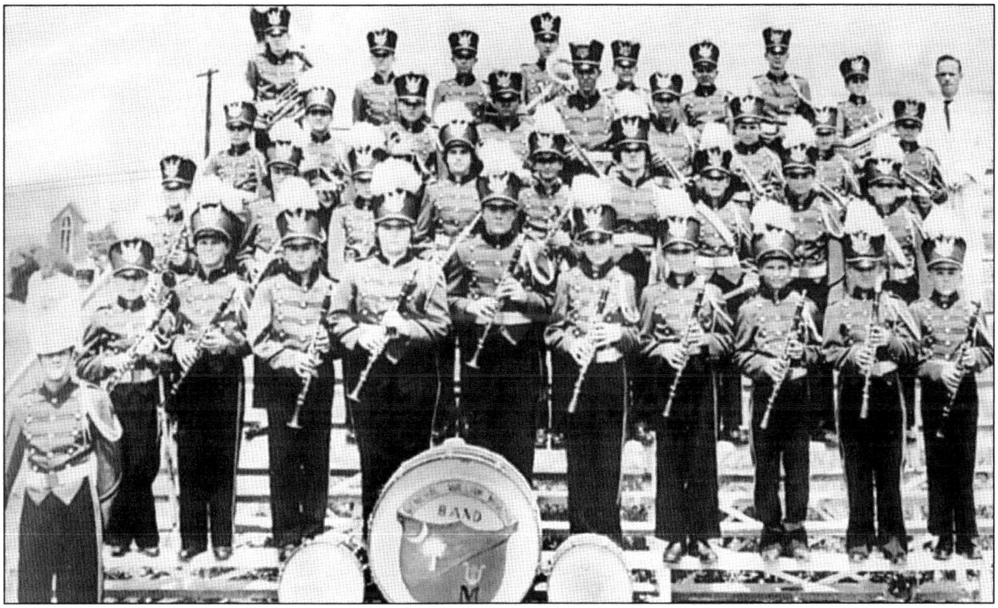

The Gen. William Moultrie High School Band of 1962 poses on the bleachers of the Sergeant Jasper field. The Revolutionary War theme was carried out in names and uniforms. To cheer them on, the teams had pompom girls and cheerleaders to inspire them to victory. Though not a large school, there was a great spirit for the team. Parents assisted in selling refreshments at games.

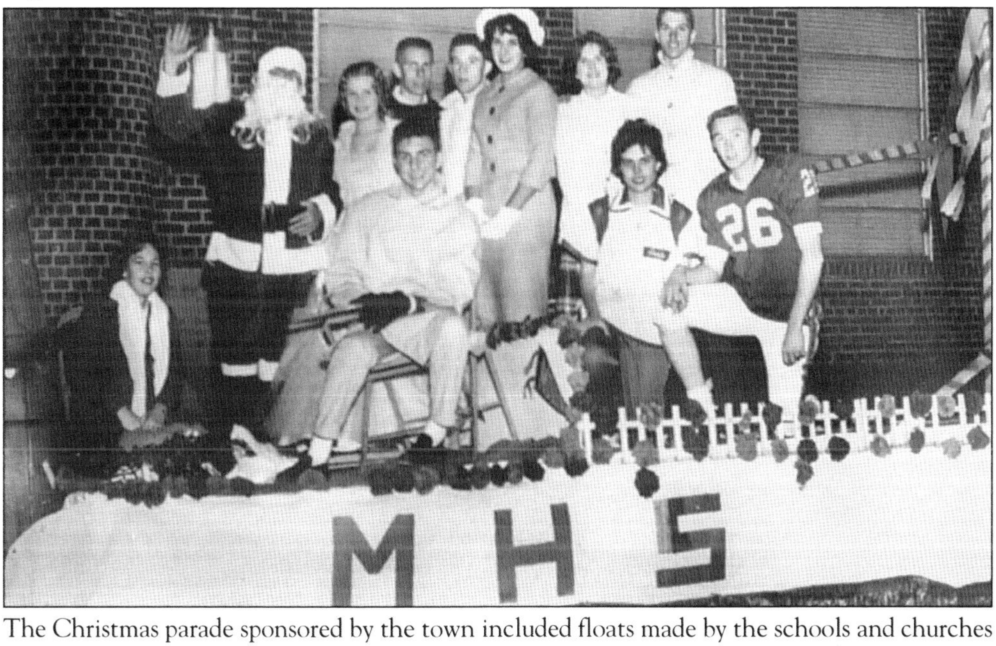

The Christmas parade sponsored by the town included floats made by the schools and churches as well as businesses. In 1963 the Moultrie float representing various school activities was constructed, but alas, it was not destined to be in the parade. One mishap after another befell it. However, the photographer certainly gave it his best shot. Every year, the big secret was kept over who had been selected as "Miss Merry Christmas." She got to ride in a convertible and wave to the crowd.

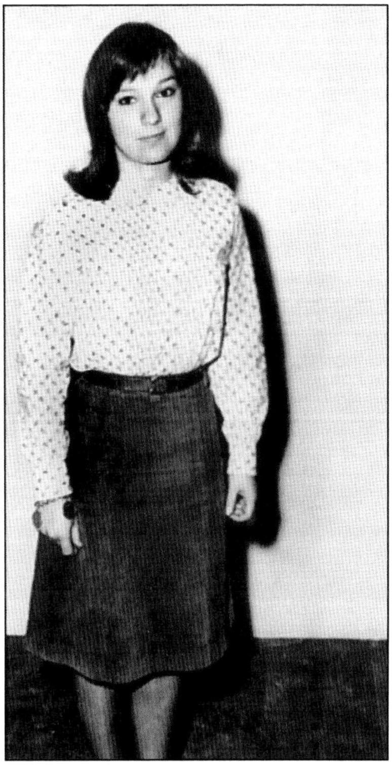

Moultrie High School participated in a program whereby students from foreign countries came to America and lived with local families. Karen Laursen from Denmark was an exchange student at Moultrie during the 1966 school year.

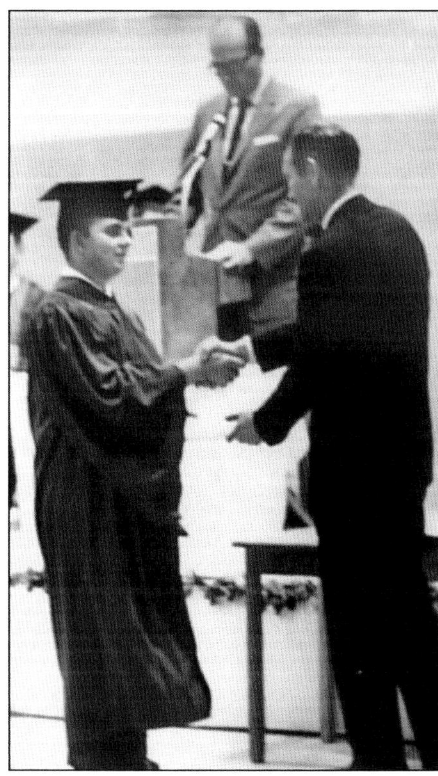

The long-awaited day had come for this young graduate in the Class of 1963. Moultrie High School graduations were held in the gymnasium. Rehearsals, directed by Mrs. Merle Catlin, a teacher, preceded the event with much ado about seating and the correct protocol of walking up and receiving one's diploma. Usually a trustee gave it to the graduate while the principal read the names. Relatives and friends filled the stands. The program included speeches by the honor graduates and music by the band and chorus.

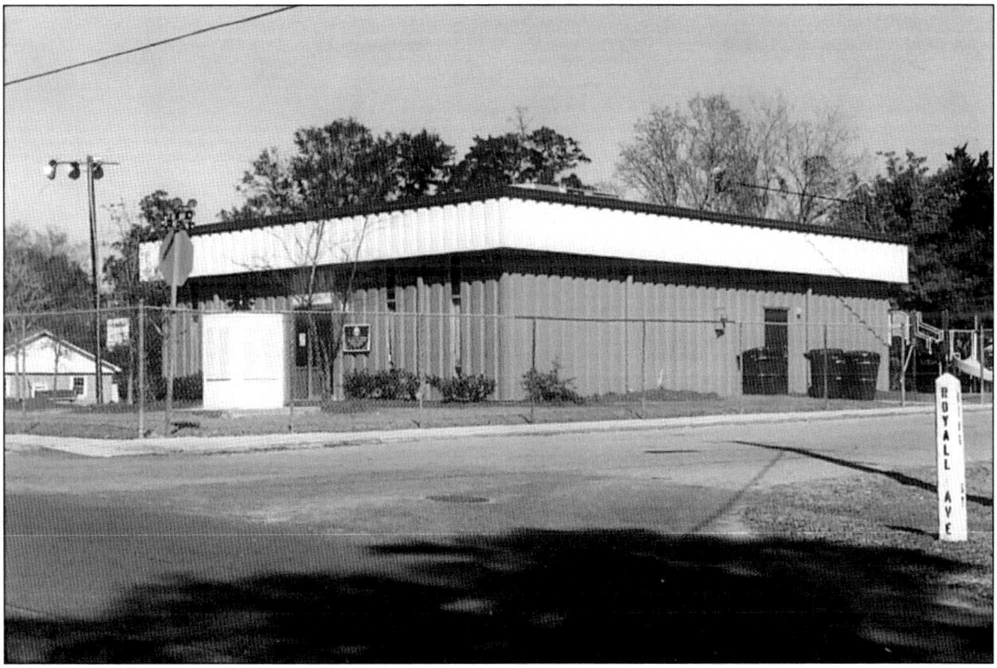

Laing School was begun just after the Civil War by the Quakers with Cornelia Hancock as the head of it. After a few months in the Presbyterian Church, they moved to Bennett Street, then to their new building on the corner of King and Whilden Streets. That building was ruined by the 1886 earthquake. A large frame structure was built on the same site that provided space for the classes. Many kinds of industrial classes taught trade skills to the boys and sewing to the girls. Many names are included on the marker on the school's site, which is in front of the present Miriam Brown Recreation Center.

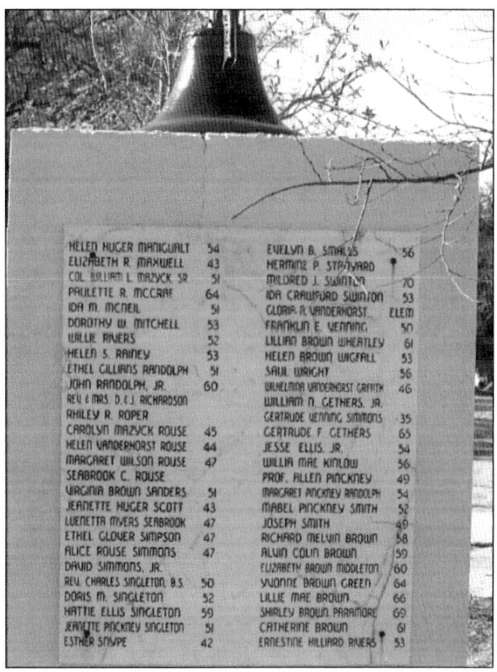

The school bell has been placed on the top of the marker which lists names of teachers and alumni of Laing.

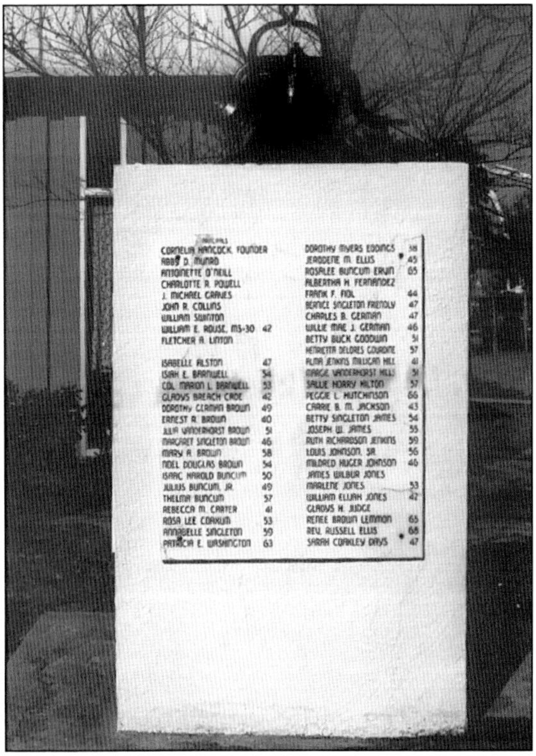

Names of many who attended Laing School are inscribed on the sides of this marker. The founder, Cornelia Hancock, and an early principal, Abby Munro, head the list.

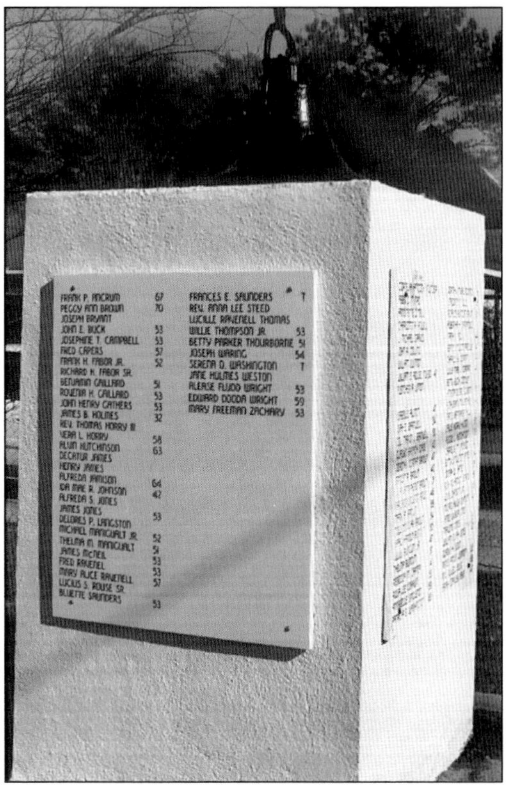

Many listed here have become outstanding in their particular profession. There is an active alumni group who keeps alive the impact Laing School had on their lives, although the school as originally designed is no more. The name continues as Laing Middle School on Highway 17 North.

Seven

CUSTOMS

In this chapter, various customs are remembered; many of these remain, while a few have vanished. Some include families eating Sunday dinner together, followed by a ride in the country; Easter egg hunts for the youngsters; Memorial Day at the Confederate Cemetery; taking walks in the good old summertime, and sitting on the porch afterwards; taking the grandchildren fishing or going for a picnic at the beach and feeding the gulls; mountain getaways to escape the heat; Halloween costumes; the occasional snowfall; and oyster roasts. The year ends with Christmas in the little town.

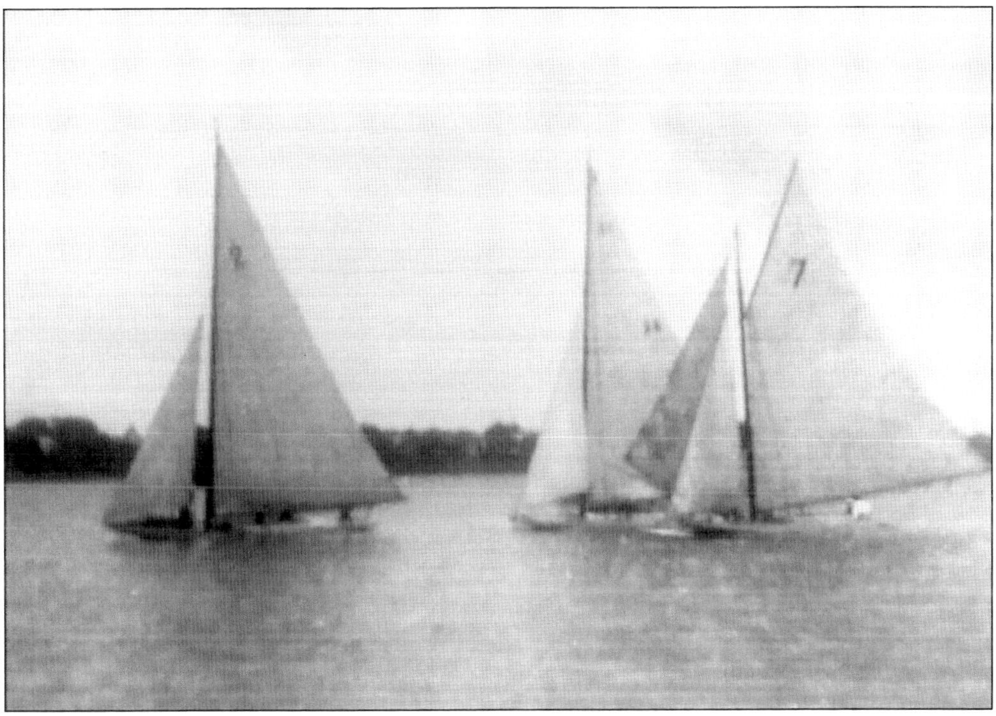

One of the most enjoyed customs was that of sailing. It was a part of summertime, both for individuals as well as teams in organized regattas. Competition was keen among the enthusiasts. Races were held in various locales, from Rockville up the coast to Mount Pleasant. The headquarters for the sailing group here was at Alhambra Hall.

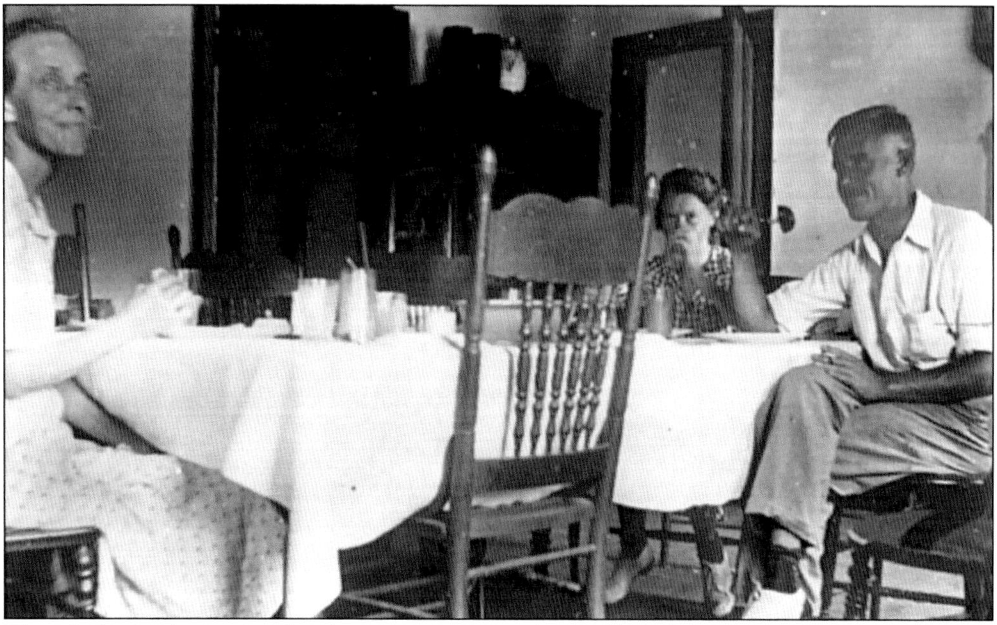

The whole family ate Sunday dinner together in the middle of the day before World War II. Conversation followed the meal, accompanied with an after-dinner cup of coffee served in thin china cups.

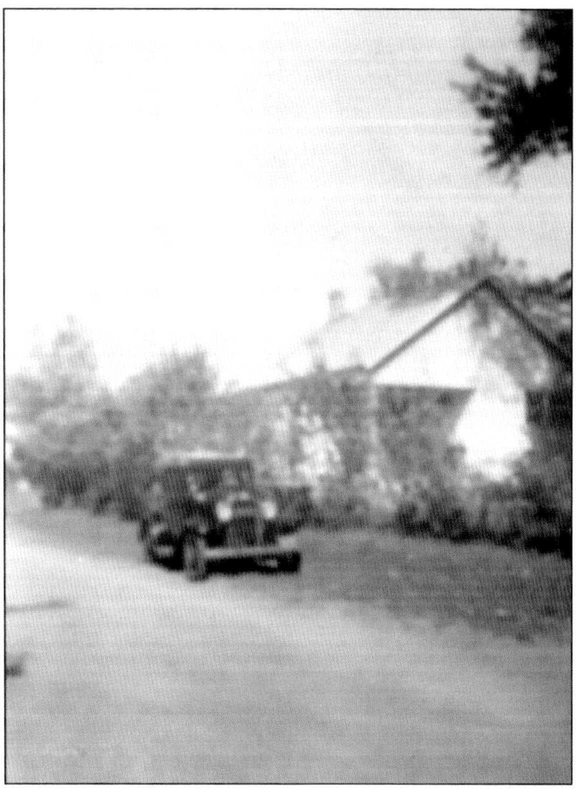

A Sunday afternoon drive out in the country after dinner was a happy experience. Nearby fields and forests provided diversity from the town. This 1935 car is gassed and ready to go.

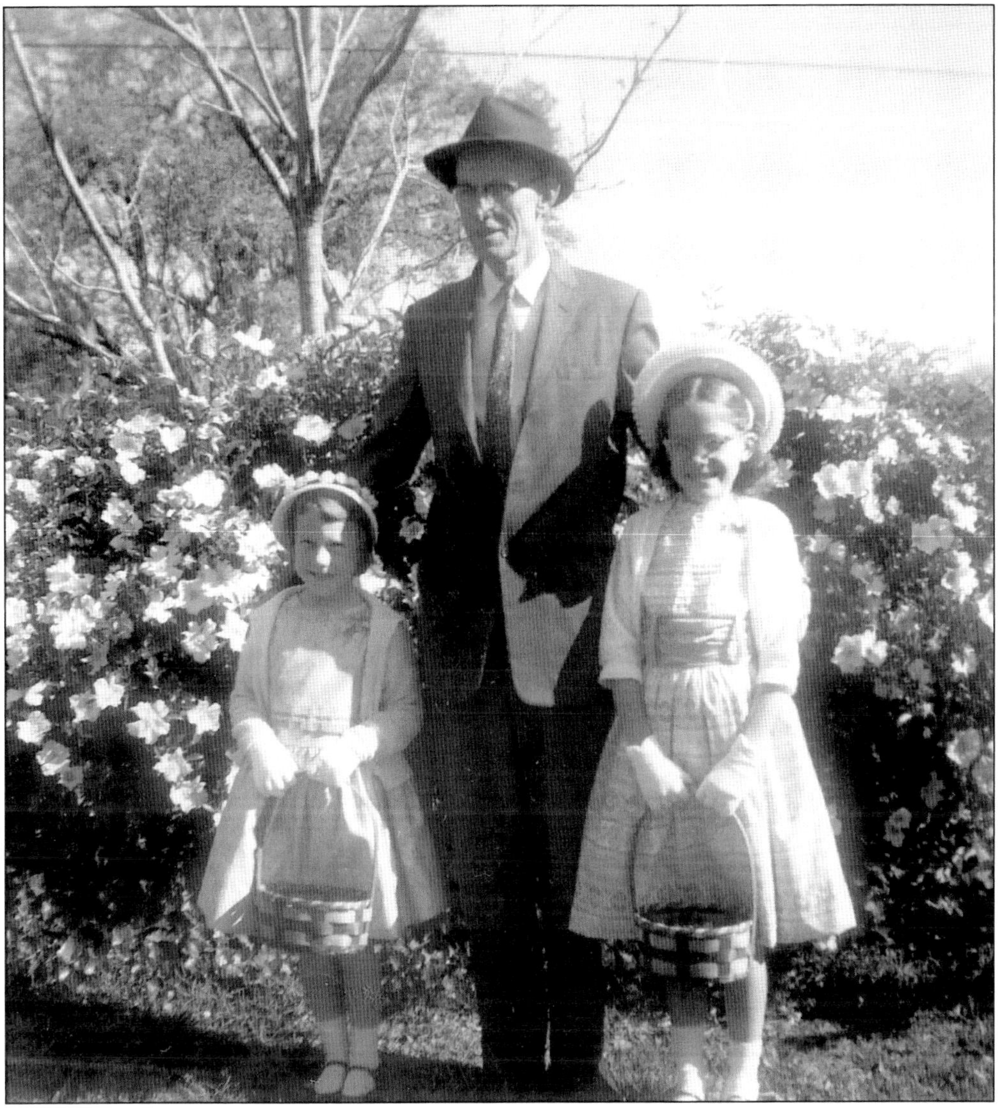

Easter in 1961 for these children meant a visit from beloved grandparents. Here they pose with their grandfather in front of a flowering Cherokee rose, with their Easter baskets in hand.

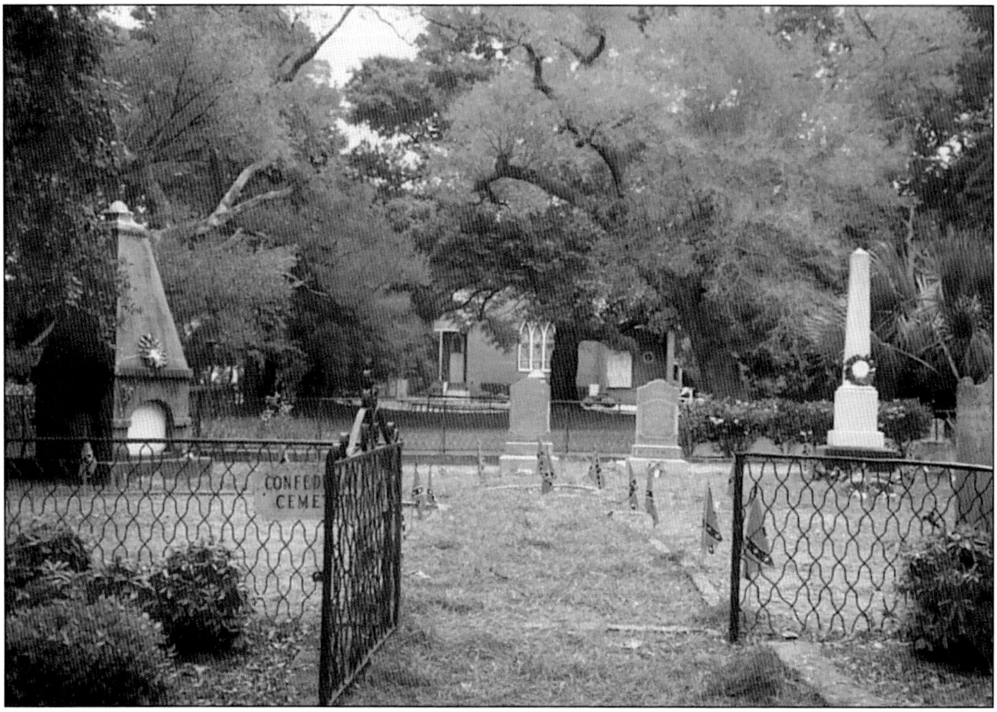

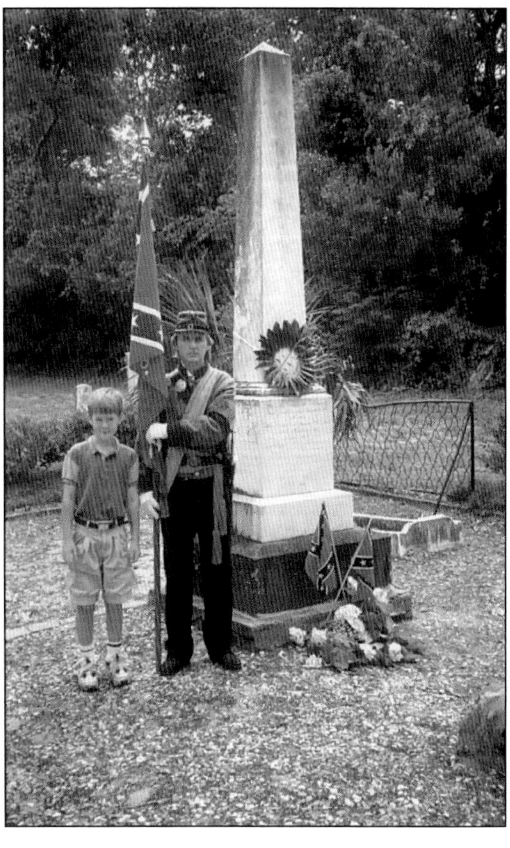

Each May 10, Southern Memorial Day, the Confederate Memorial Association of Mount Pleasant meets at the cemetery on Carr Street. Their short ceremony consists of members reading a prayer by Bishop Capers; a poem, "Ode to the Confederate Dead" by Archibald Rutledge, first poet laureate of South Carolina; and "Ode" by Henry Timrod, the Laureate of the Confederacy. The names of those who served from Christ Church Parish are read. After a brief dedication, flowers are placed on the graves. The Confederate monument is on the right; the monument for those who died in the War of 1812 is on the left.

The fenced area of an old cemetery on the corner of the Common is referred to as the Confederate Cemetery, although some of the stones predate the war. Confederate soldiers' remains were re-interred near the tall marker, marked by a small concrete monument. They are said to have died in a hospital here. Re-enactors frequently join the association's observance. In days gone by, school children came as a group, and after the ceremony, they had the rest of the day off from school.

These ladies out for a walk pose in the Rue de Muckle near home. This short street behind Moultrie Plaza acquired its name, when Primus, a World War I veteran, told his friends that he lived "in the muckle" (meaning myrtles, a native aromatic shrub). The property owner suggested that with his war service in France, Primus should say he lived on the "Rue de Muckle." It has been called this ever since.

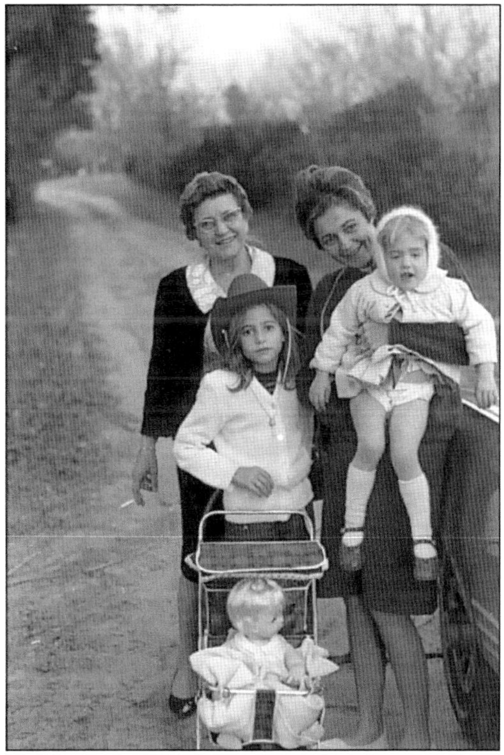

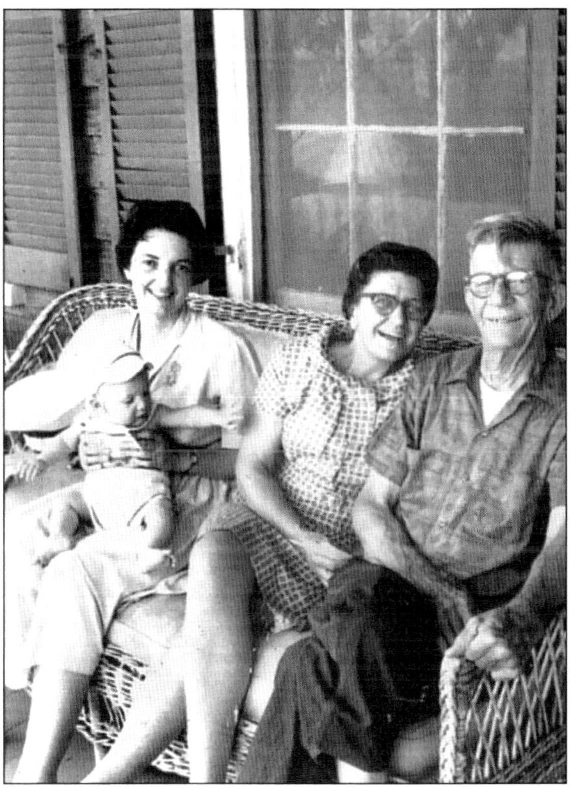

Four generations are relaxing on a porch that faces south where summer breezes blow. Window blinds, such as these, when closed, kept the interior of the house much cooler, as well as shielding it from showers. Sitting and talking is delightful, but wait, a song or story just may be forthcoming to the delight of the ladies. After all, Ned and Burl Ives had swapped songs when Ives' boat was down on Shem Creek.

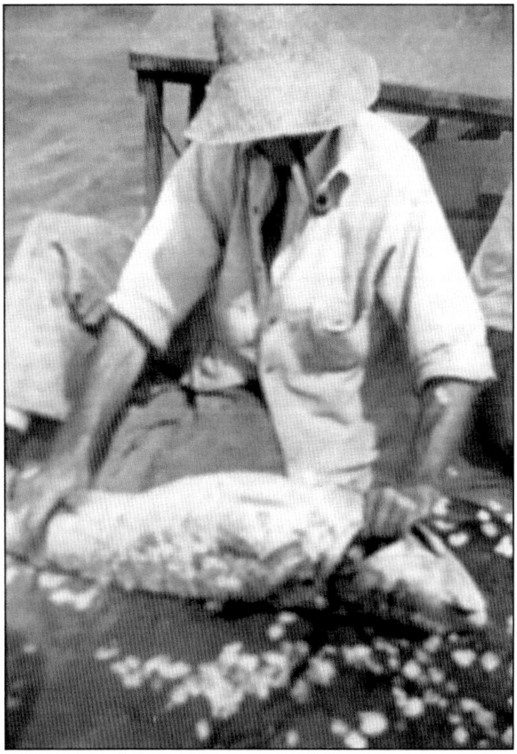

This big one obviously did not get away. Shrimping, crabbing, bogging, and gigging were all water-related activities. Not only did they provide food, they were also recreation. No expensive equipment was necessary and the source was right at hand. Should more than was needed be caught, it could be divided with neighbors. Youngsters made spending money by selling a "plate" of shrimp for 25¢; a quart of oysters brought 15¢. The creek was also a wonderful place to swim, as was the front beach. Pollution had not been heard of in the 1930s.

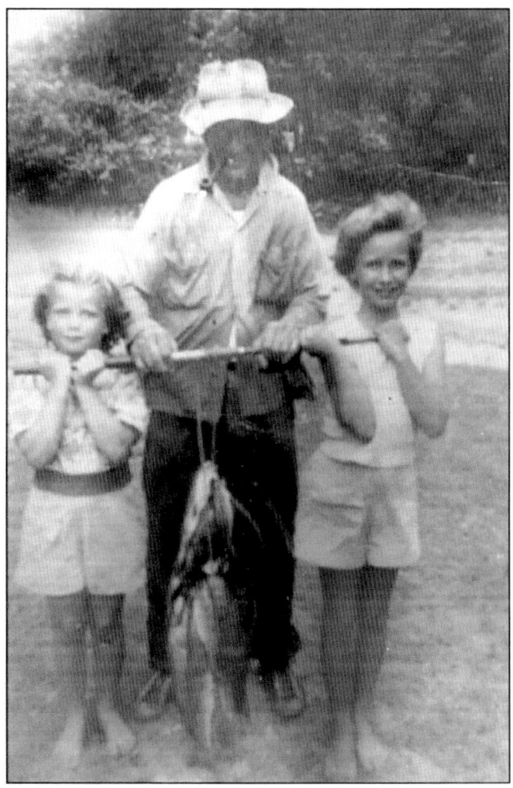

What could be better than spending a morning down on Shem Creek with the granddaughters going fishing? The string of fish and the happy faces express the 1950s as a happy era.

Three generations are enjoying the beach in 1946, probably after having a picnic. The tide is out, leaving an expanse of sand on which to find shells before going home. Spring high tides have left sedge (dead marsh grass) washed up on the sand. Of the string of barrier islands along the coast, Sullivan's Island is the nearest to Mount Pleasant, and trolleys used to take residents there. Numbers still designate the streets, harkening back to the trolley stops or stations.

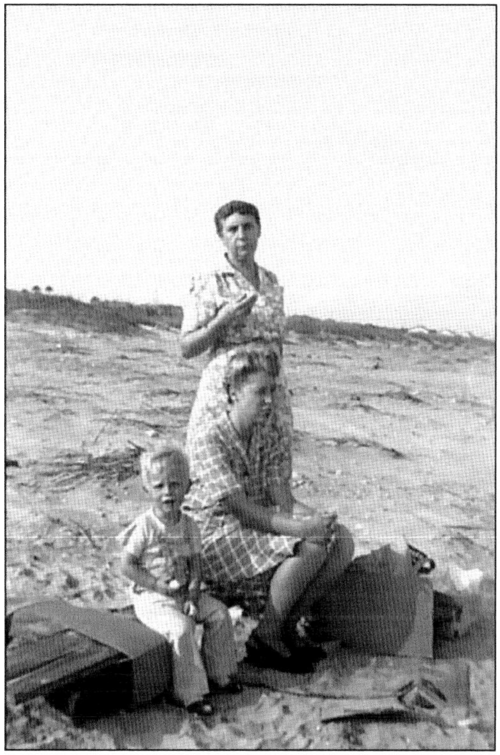

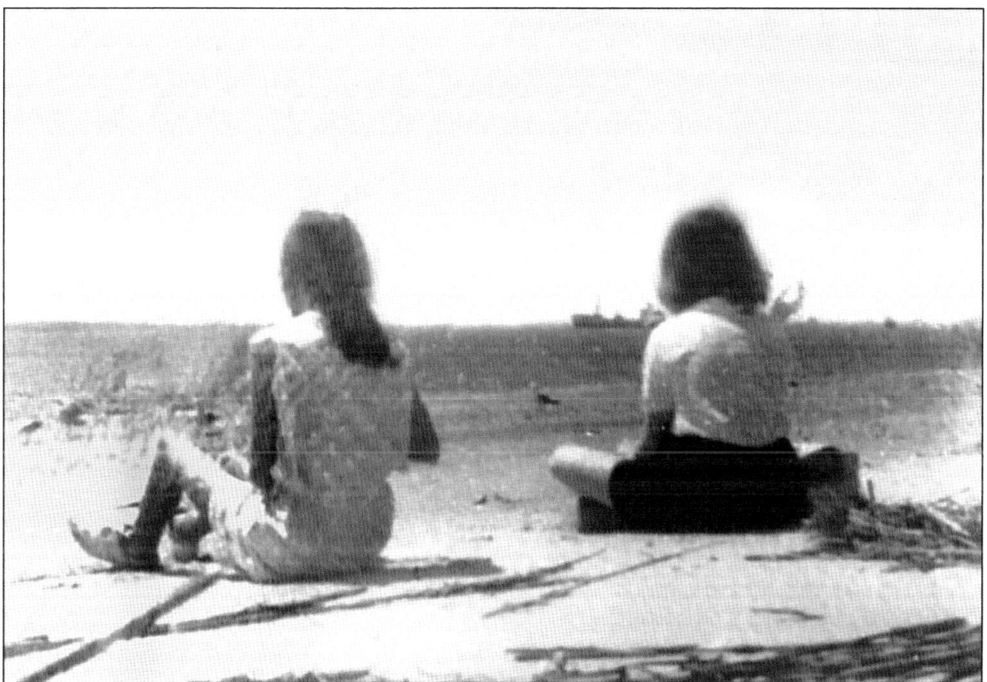

These young ladies have brought bags of bread to feed the sea gulls. Swooping down, the birds catch the morsel before it hits the ground. Probably 20 years have passed between these pictures, but the beach remains virtually the same.

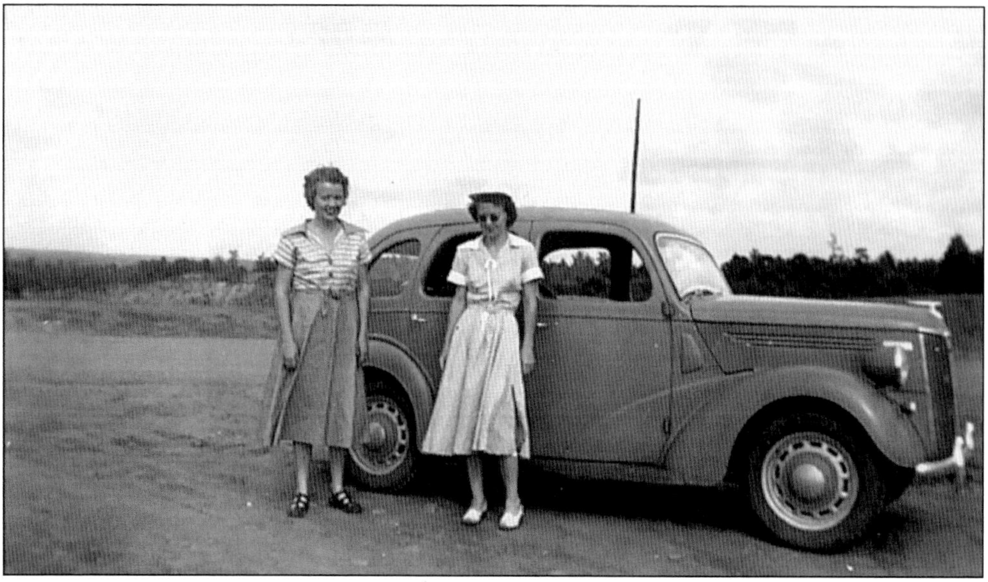

A trip to the mountains from Mount Pleasant provided a cool respite from the oppressive summer heat of the coast. A drive of about 300 miles brought these travelers to the Blue Ridge mountains. After World War II cars were in short supply, and the little English Ford import proved it could compare with the bigger American cars of the 1950s, even when climbing the hairpin curves of the two-lane roads on the Saluda grade.

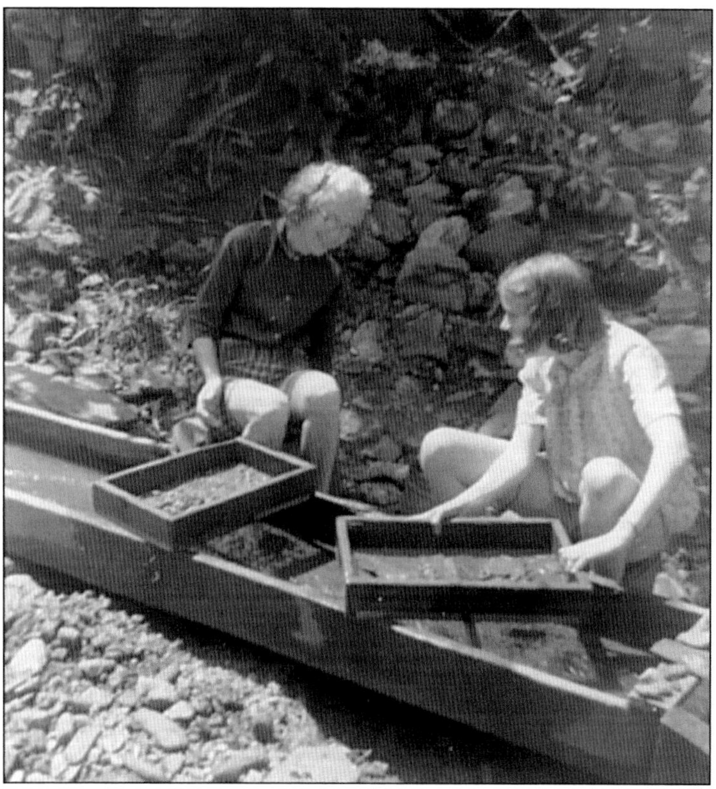

One activity in the mountains was panning for gemstones, or perhaps even gold! The treasures that they found were brought home and put in a rock polisher, even if they were nothing more than pretty rocks.

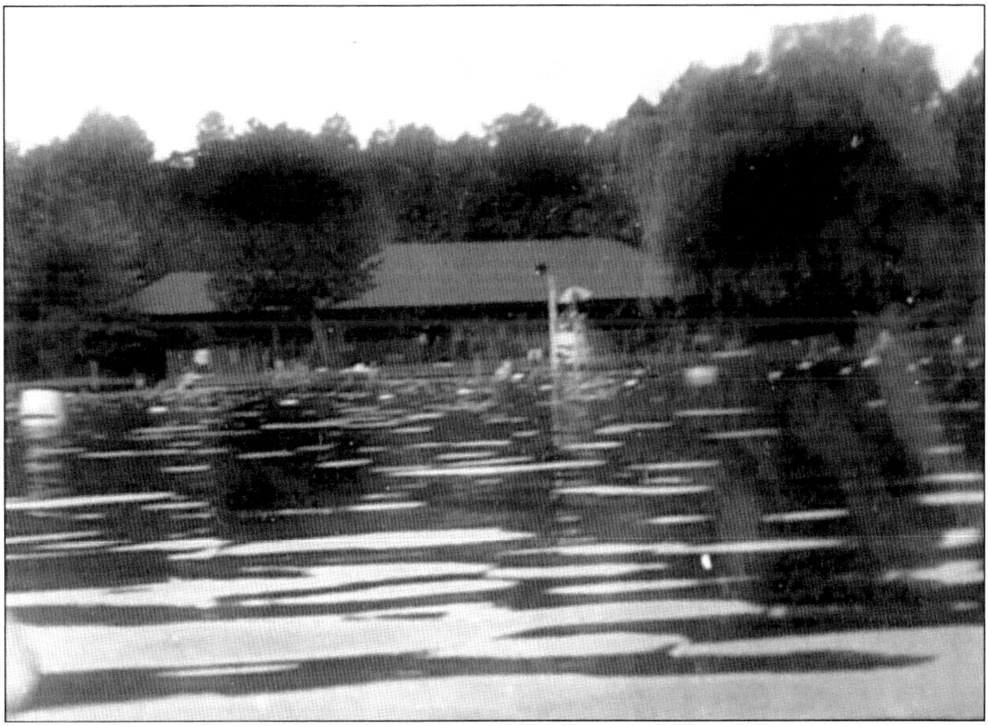

A trip to a state park in the upstate was a welcome change from the Lowcountry heat. Oconee State Park near Walhalla was operated under the watchful eye of the director, Mr. Ray, during the 1960s. The South Carolina state parks are a heritage from the Civilian Conservation Corps (the CCC) of the Great Depression era. Originally the cabins were quite primitive, but as time went on, they became more like the facilities campers would have at home. They were popular; by 1938, almost half a million people had visited the ones in South Carolina.

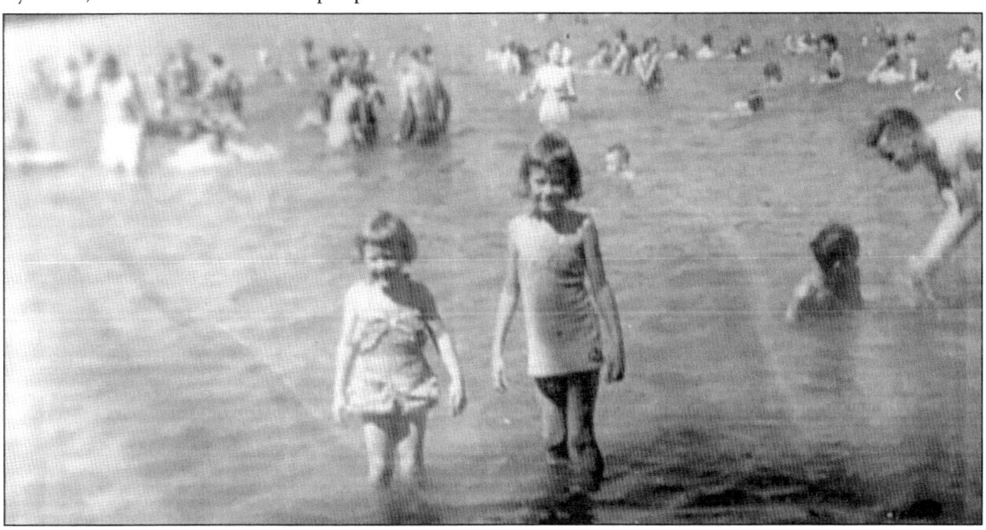

The lake was delightfully cool and gradually deepened. Life guards kept close watch on the swimmers. Application for a week at one of the parks had to be made early in the year, because they were popular vacation places for the whole family at a reasonable price. They also served as a home base for trips into the more distant Great Smoky Mountains.

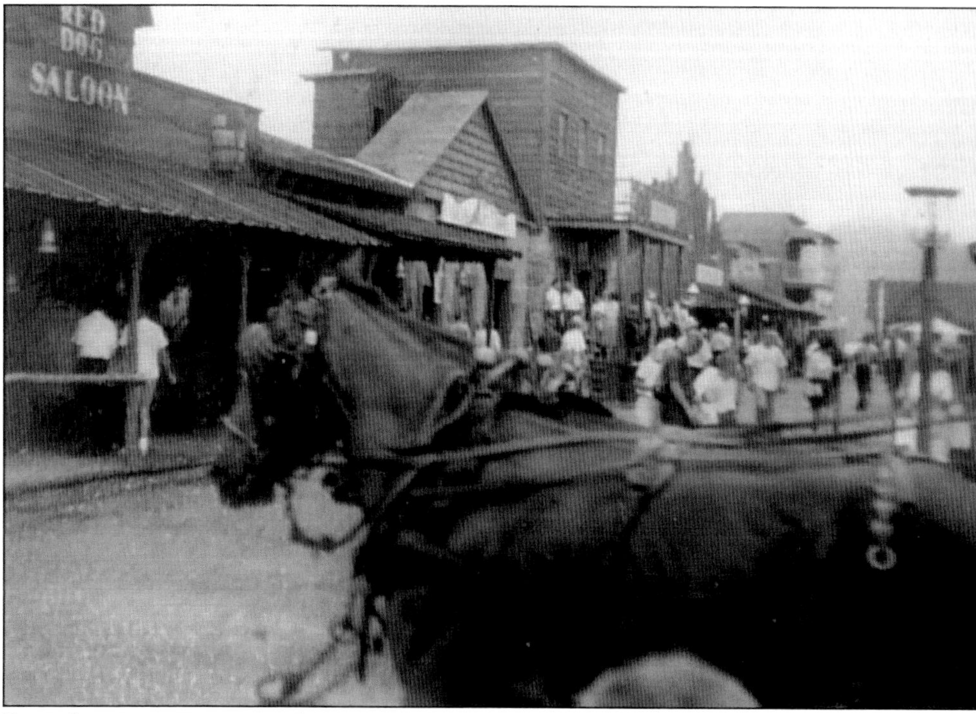

By mid-century, visitors to the mountains wanted action. Maggie Valley in the western North Carolina mountains featured a make-believe town of the old West. At stated intervals gunfire erupted and one of the actors convincingly "dropped dead" to the delight of the tourists.

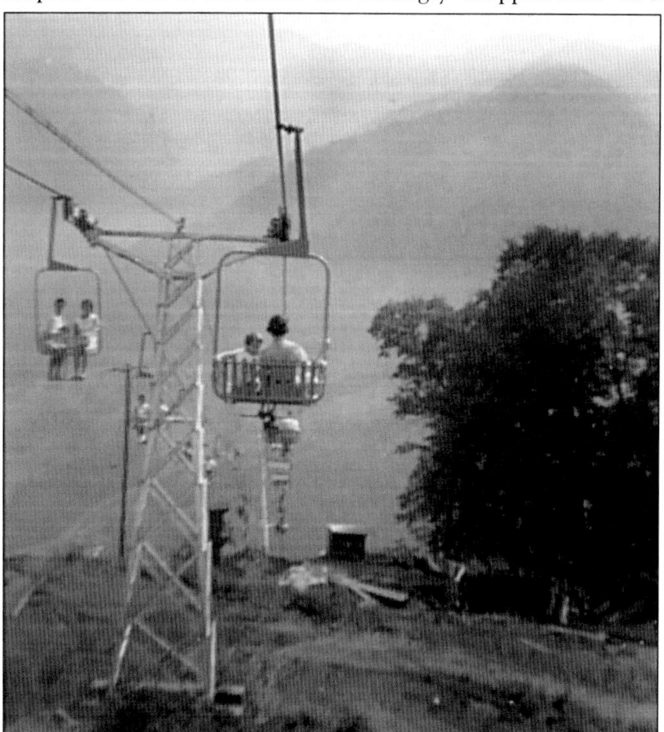

The summer attractions kept the ski lift operating all year round, not just in winter. Occasionally as the cable cars passed each other, tourists recognized friends from their home town! It was the era of outdoor dramas such as *Horn in the West* and *The Lost Colony*.

Hula Hoops were popular nationally in the 1960s, and Mount Pleasant was not to be left behind. The little girl pictured here was taking hers to school.

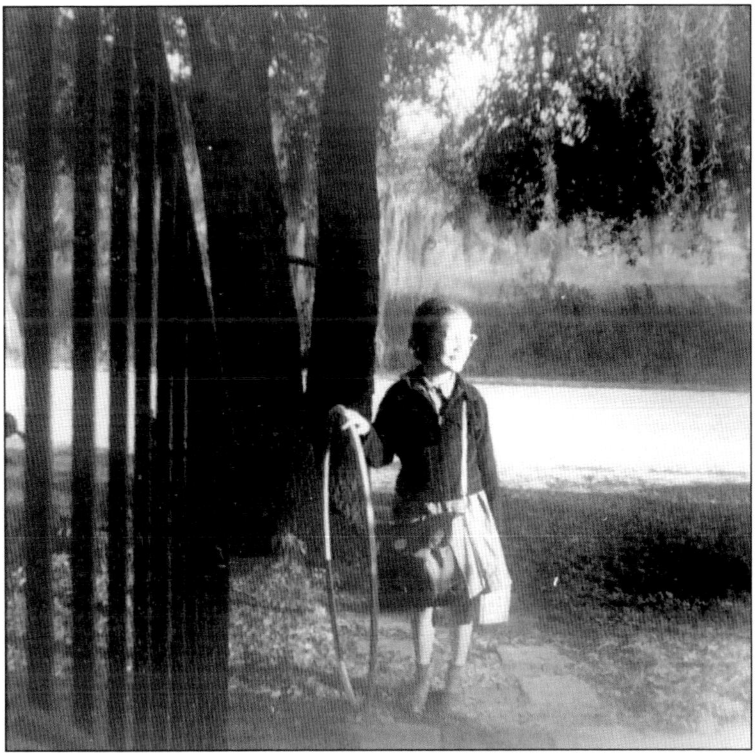

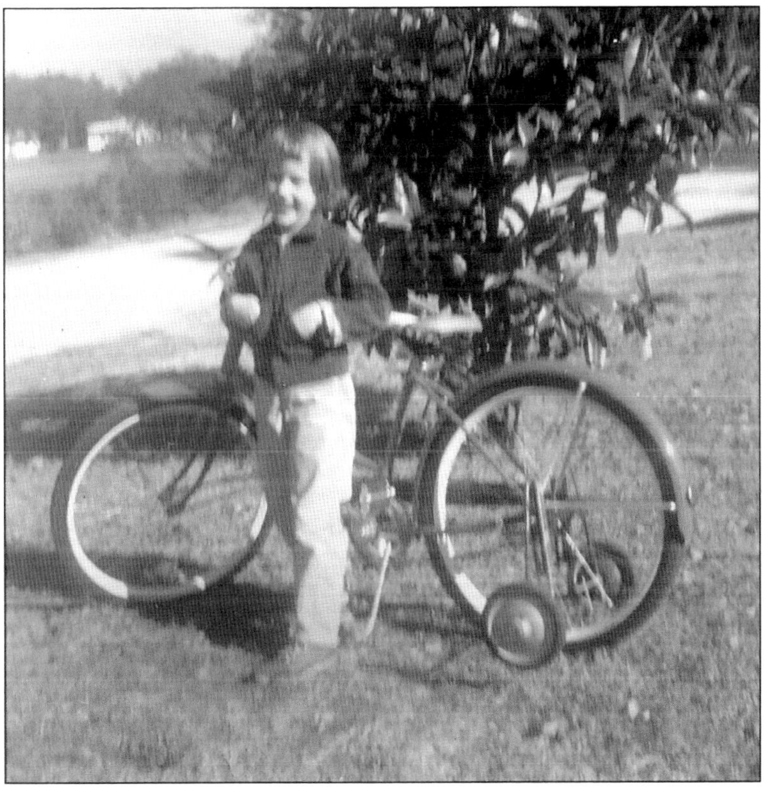

After-school activities included playing jump rope accompanied by merry little rhymes and bike riding. Since the streets were not busy with cars, it was relatively safe. The little girl pictured here practices with training wheels, so that when the time arrived, she could ride away without them.

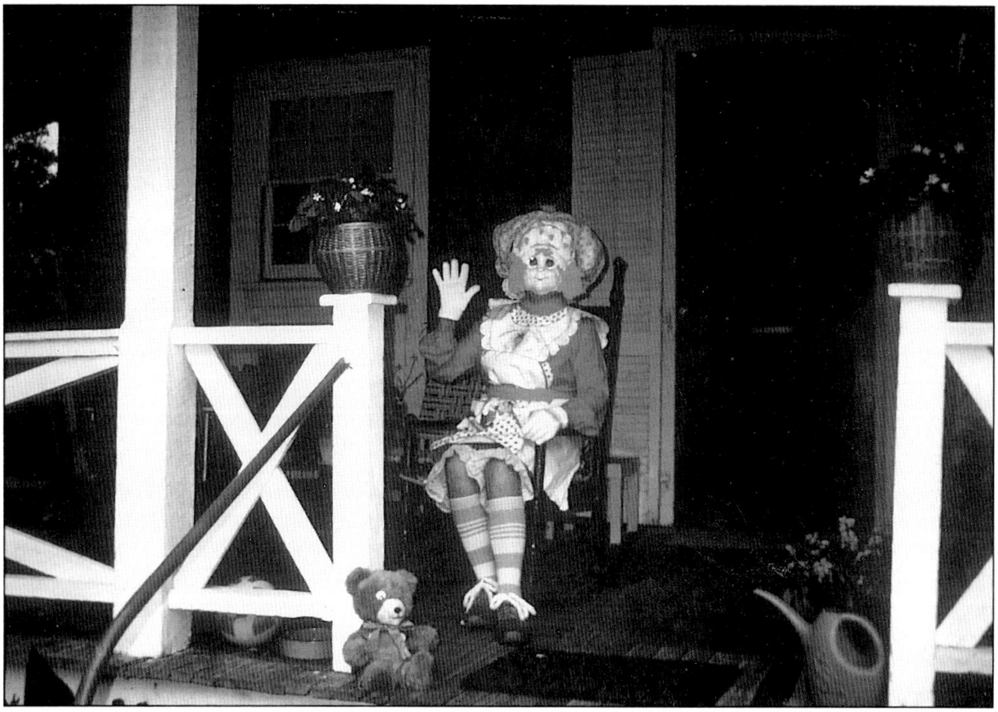

A surprise greeted the Halloween trick-or-treaters when they visited this house on Hibben Street and found someone in costume on the porch.

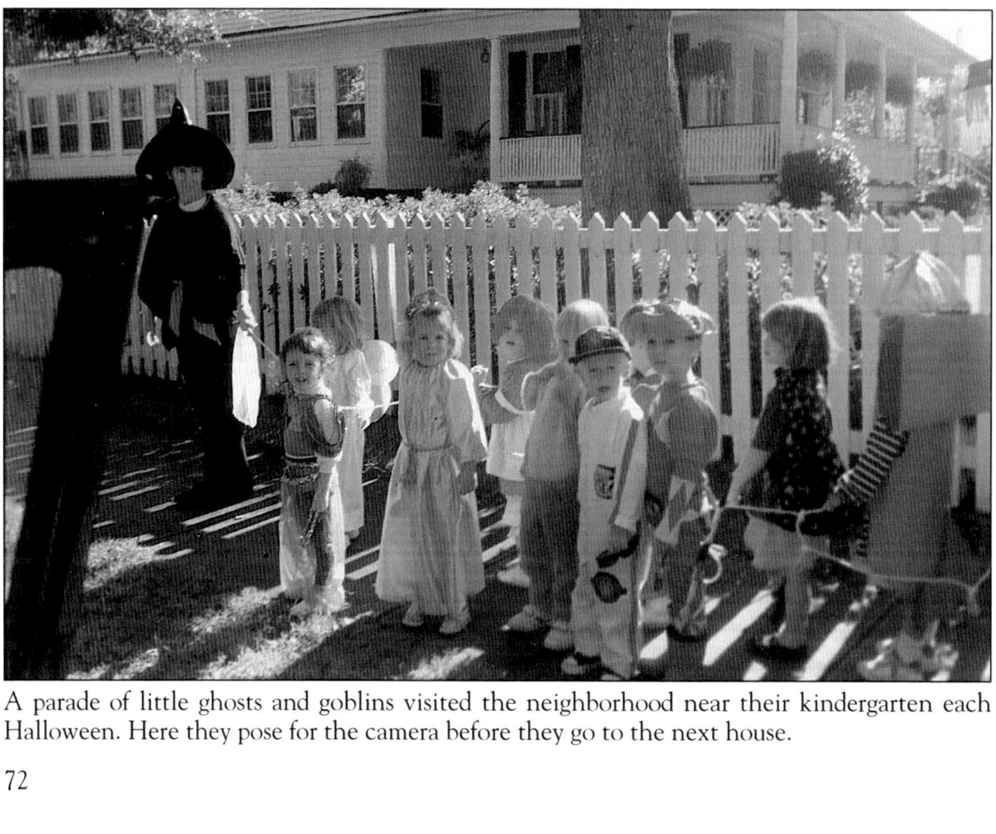

A parade of little ghosts and goblins visited the neighborhood near their kindergarten each Halloween. Here they pose for the camera before they go to the next house.

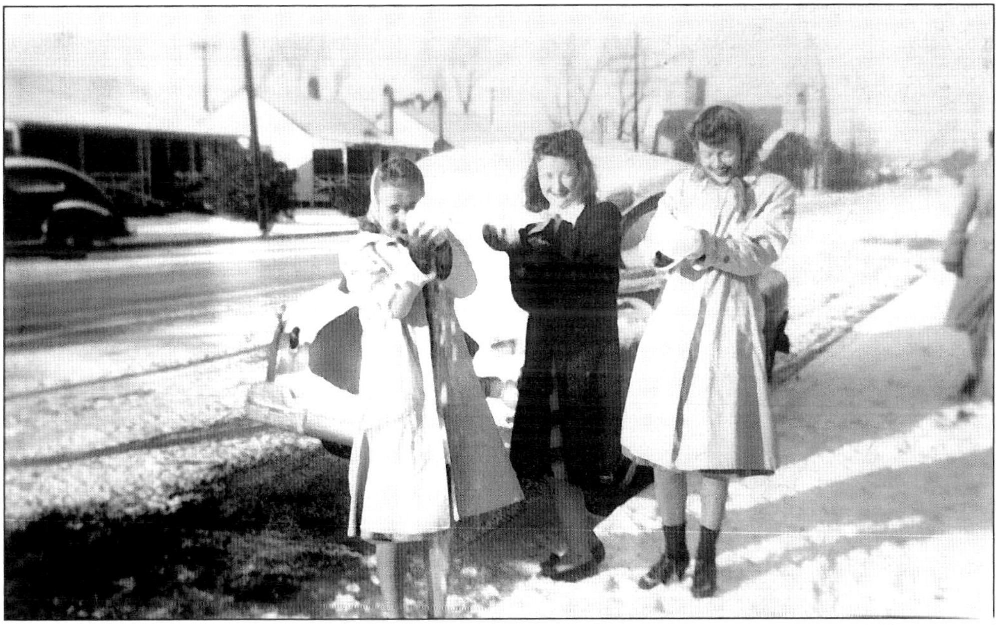

Probably not the white Christmas that Bing Crosby sang about, but these young ladies intend to make the most of it. Snow was a rare treat to be enjoyed while it lasted. The car in the background indicates the time to be the late 1930s.

Oyster roasts are a southern tradition; they can be elaborate or very simple. All that is necessary is a way to steam the bivalves until they begin to open, a heavy cotton glove or rag to hold them, and an oyster knife to finish opening the shells. Because of the many creeks around from which to retrieve oysters, Mount Pleasant has enjoyed these parties for years.

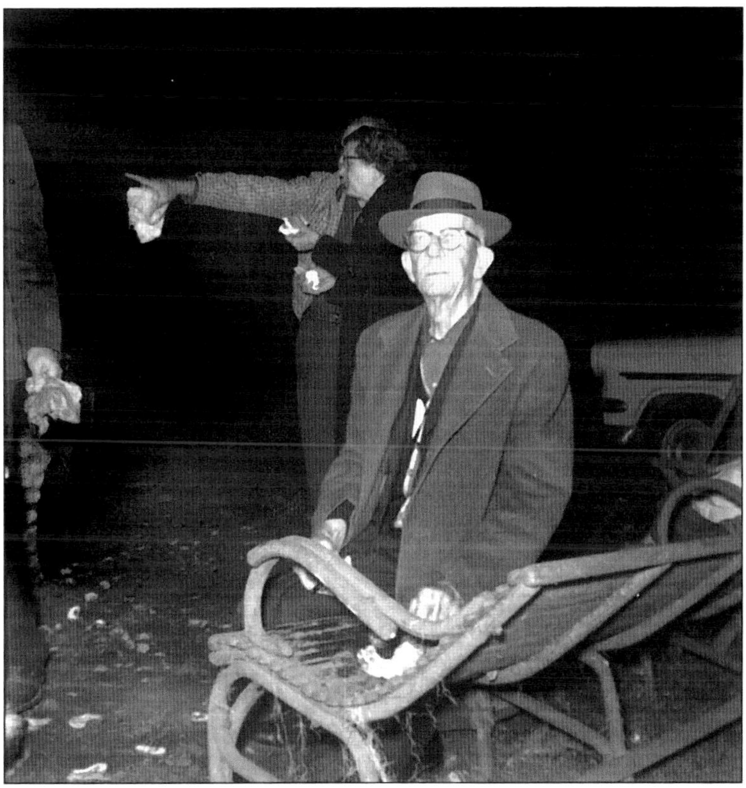

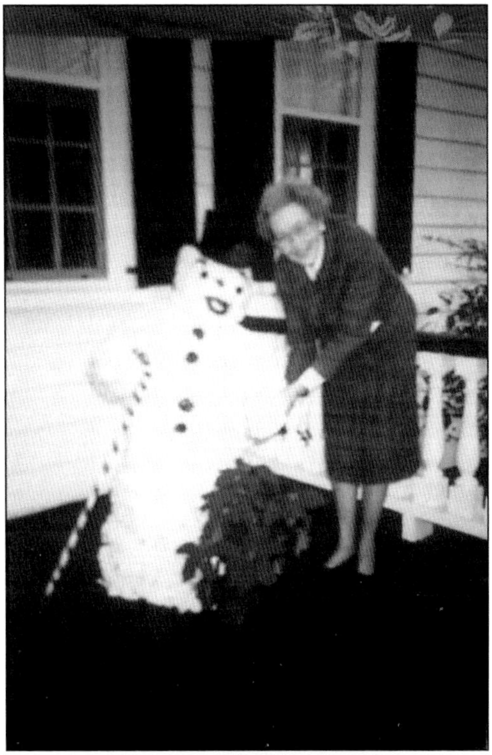

For many Christmases, the jolly snowman "Mr. White," attired in a different costume each year, greeted the passersby from the Hibben Street porch. Christmas parades were not the professional kind we see today. They were a lot of fun for the youngsters decorating the floats. School bands, dancing schools, scout troops, and horses all made up the parade.

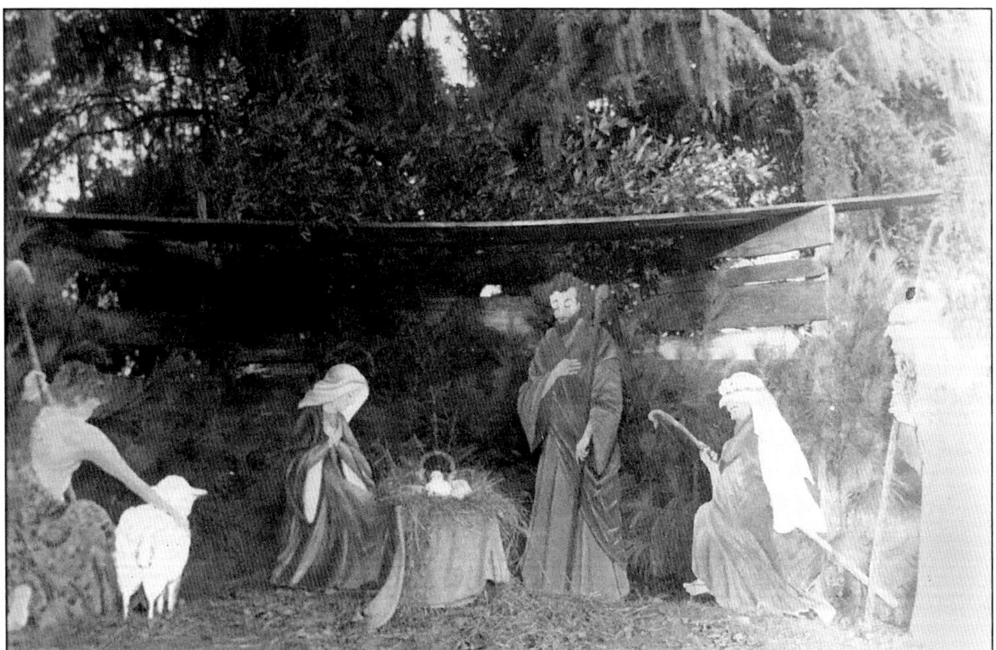

A nativity scene, made by the same lady who crafted "Mr. White," graced the yard of the Lutheran Church. In the 1950s giant nativity figures were placed on the porch of the Presbyterian Church to mark the Christmas season. It was also an era of Christmas pageants in churches. Choirs took part while the reenactment of the Bible story was presented.

Christmas dinner was a special occasion when family could come together. Many times, ambrosia made of oranges and fresh grated coconut served as a dessert, or possibly wine jelly or fruit cake.

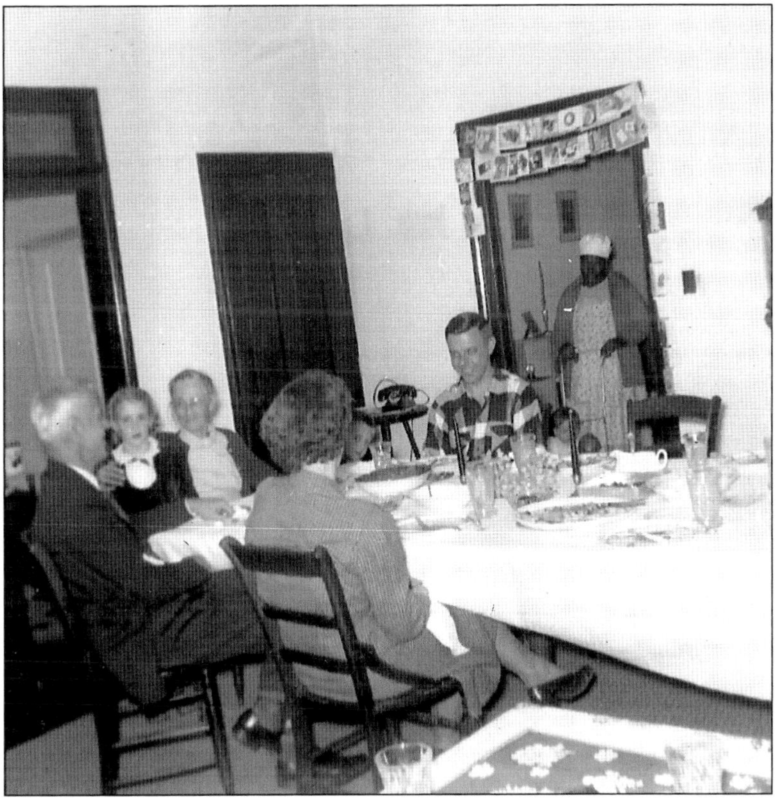

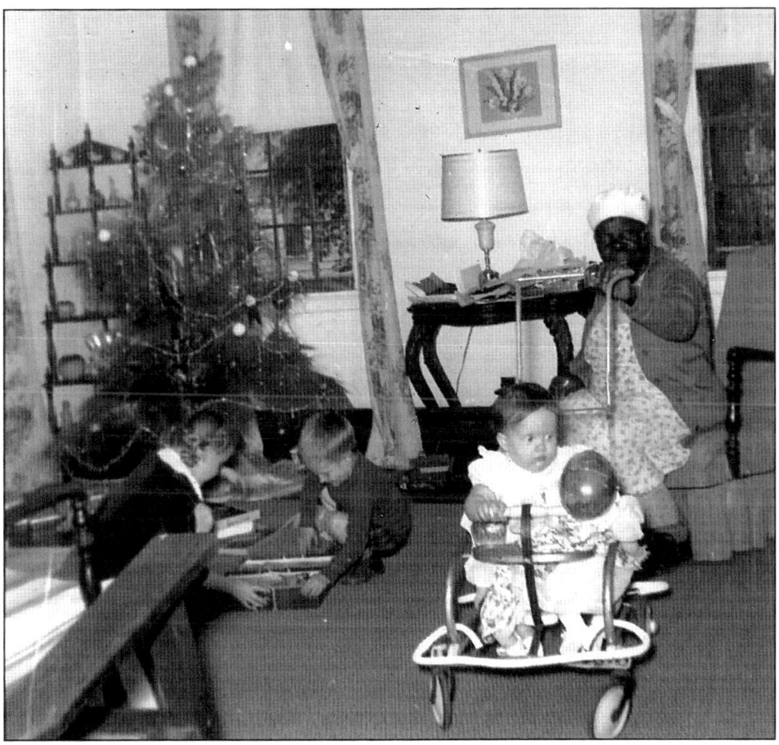

Christmas at a grandmother's house in 1951 brings wonder to the toddler's eyes. Belle proudly guards the stroller, while cousins play a new game in front of the Christmas tree. A trip to the woods to choose a tree was part of the of the season, as commercially grown trees had not yet appeared.

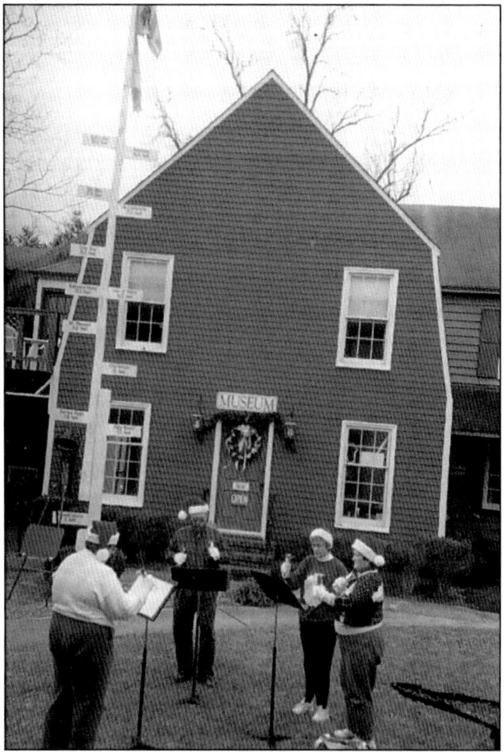

The bell ringers from a local church fill the air with tintinnabulation and signify that Christmas is coming. It is after 1989, indicated by the pole which marks the tide level's height in the various places when Hurricane Hugo passed through the area.

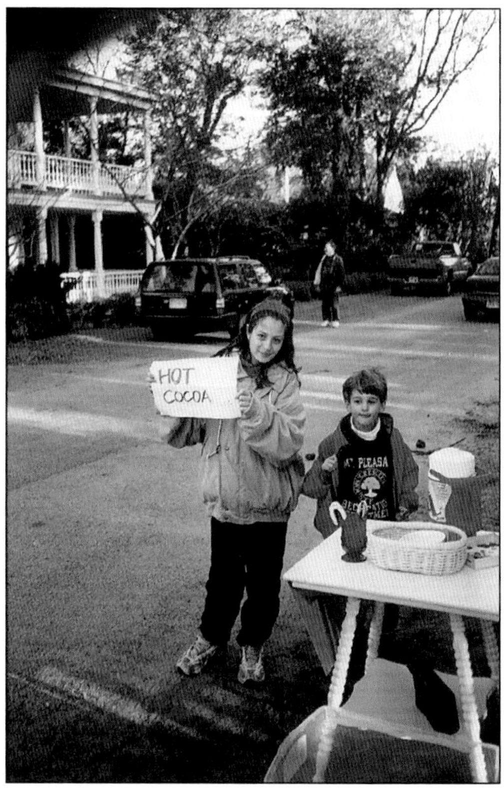

The chapter on customs through the year ends with this image of young entrepreneurs selling hot cocoa on a cold winter's day on Bennett Street

Eight

ARTS, CRAFTS, AND ENTERTAINMENT

Despite its relative isolation, Mount Pleasant supported arts, crafts, and entertainment. An Arts and Crafts Association has existed for many years. Art shows brought young artists to people's attention. Among the artists of the mid-century, Edward von Siebold Dingle is outstanding. Entertainment has ranged from traveling shows, plays, and television, to movie-making.

Authors have chronicled the area's history for many years. Oral history was being preserved long before it was the popular thing to do. Two local newspapers served Mount Pleasant in this era. The East Cooper Pilot *ceased publication in 1979; however, Betty Lee Johnson collected into two books interviews she had done of the older citizens.* As I Remember It *was probably the first printed oral history of the area. The* Moultrie News, *first published May 28, 1964 as a biweekly, later became a weekly. For several years local history articles have been written by Suzannah Smith Miles, who also has a number of books to her credit dealing with the Lowcountry.*

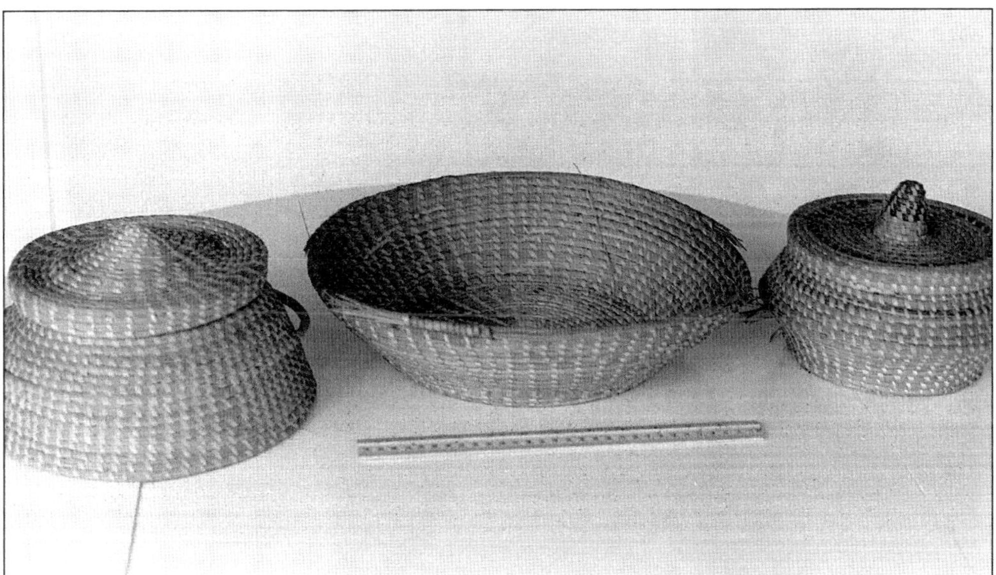

The sweetgrass basket craft, brought from Africa, is unique to the area. These baskets have been sold along the roadside in Mount Pleasant since the 1930s.

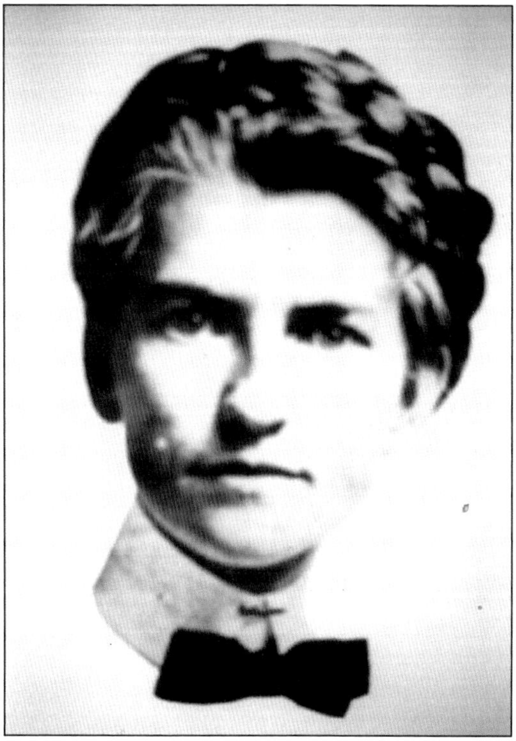

It was natural that Petrona Royall McIver (1883–1973) became the historian of Mount Pleasant. She wass a member of the Parish History Club (1926– c.1933); the group visited places all over the area and documented their findings in articles. Brochures containing her information included the opening of the Cooper River Bridge in 1929, articles in the waterworks dedication booklet in 1935, and the overview in the 1939 directory. In addition, she published articles about the area in various historical and genealogical magazines. Her book, entitled *History of Mount Pleasant*, has gone through several printings since 1960.

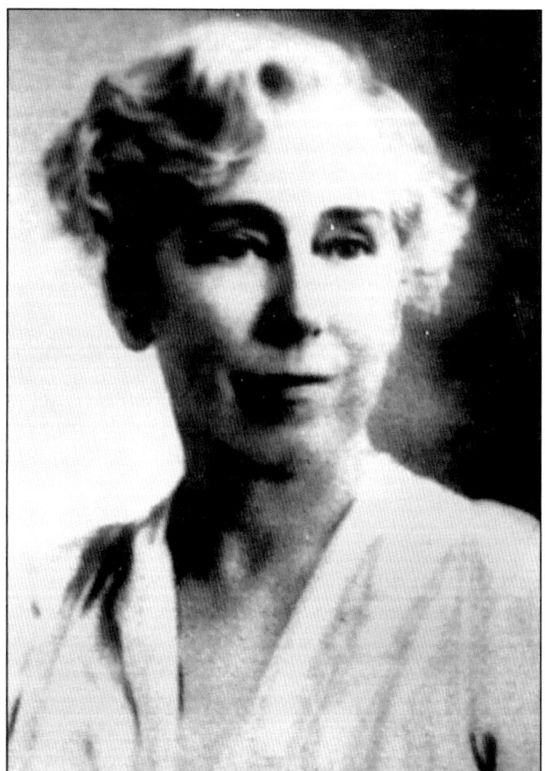

Another outstanding author was Anne King Gregorie (1887–1960). Although her home was outside the little town at Oakland on the Marsh, Porcher's Bluff, she documented the history of the area in *Christ Church, 1706–1959, a Plantation Parish*, of which the town is a part. Her other literary credits include a biography of Thomas Sumter and many articles, and she was the editor of the South Carolina Historical Society Quarterly. Among her many interests was archaeology, and her collection of Native American artifacts from this area is extensive. Both McIver's and Gregorie's histories have been reprinted by the Christ Church Parish Preservation Society, Inc.

The East Cooper area can lay claim to a number of outstanding artists, and among them is Edward von Siebold Dingle, a noted ornithologist whose paintings are prized by museums. His summer home in Mount Pleasant was on Middle Street on the harbor near Alhambra. The bird prints shown here were made in Switzerland in the 1940s before this type of reproduction became popular in the United States. Many of his bird paintings were done at his Middleburg home on the east branch of the Cooper River.

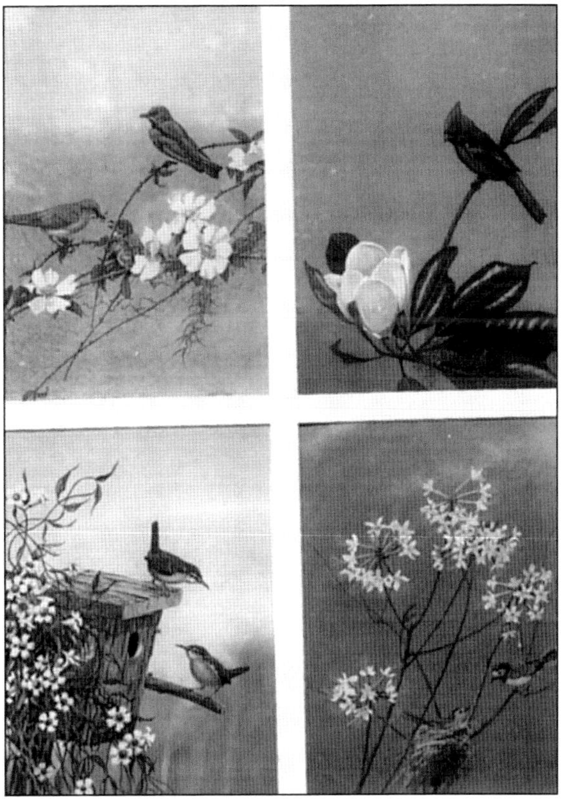

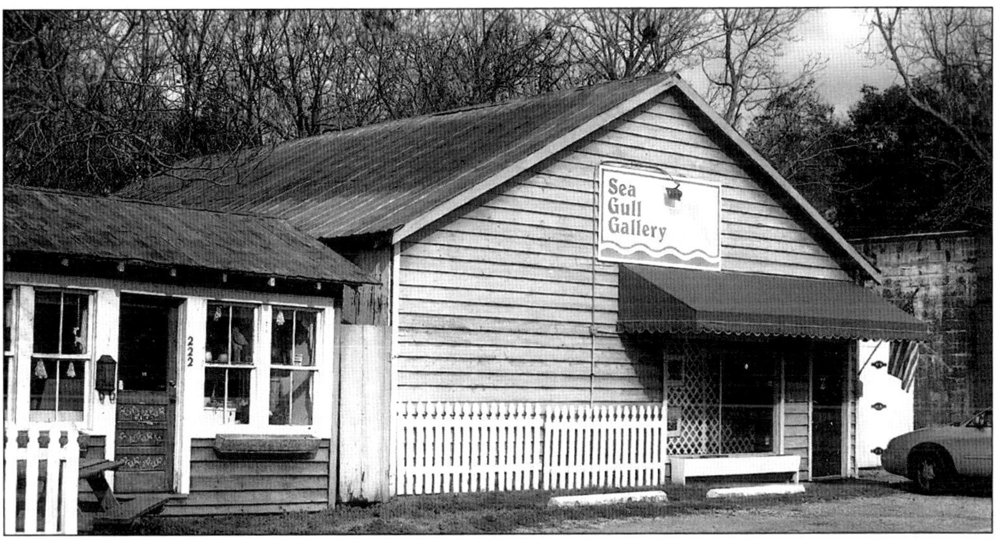

The East Cooper Arts and Crafts Association was formed in 1974 by Mary Milligan. The Sea Gull Gallery was its showroom and meeting place. The organization included painters, photographers, crafters, sculptors, and potters. They had workshops and promoted beginners. When Virginia Fouche Bolton taught art at Moultrie High School, the students exhibited their work on the fence in front of the school. Some of her pupils have become fine artists. Art shows have been held on the grounds of Channel 2 WCBD for a number of years. Tents of the individual artists create a colorful display in their own right.

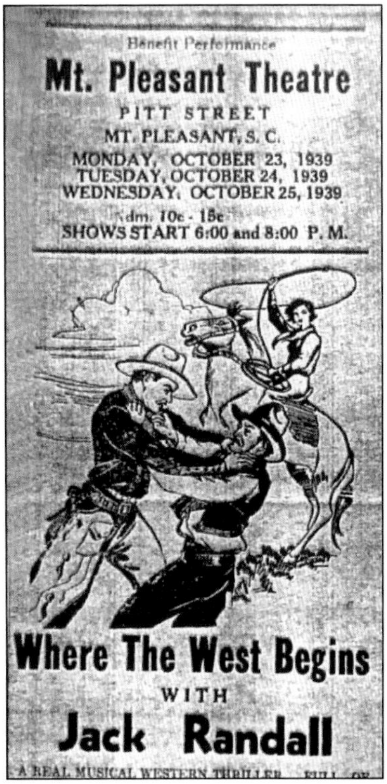

Traveling shows had stopped in Mount Pleasant for many years. "Medicine" shows promoted the sale of patent medicines guaranteed to cure all ailments. This advertising flyer for *Where the West Begins* dates back to 1939.

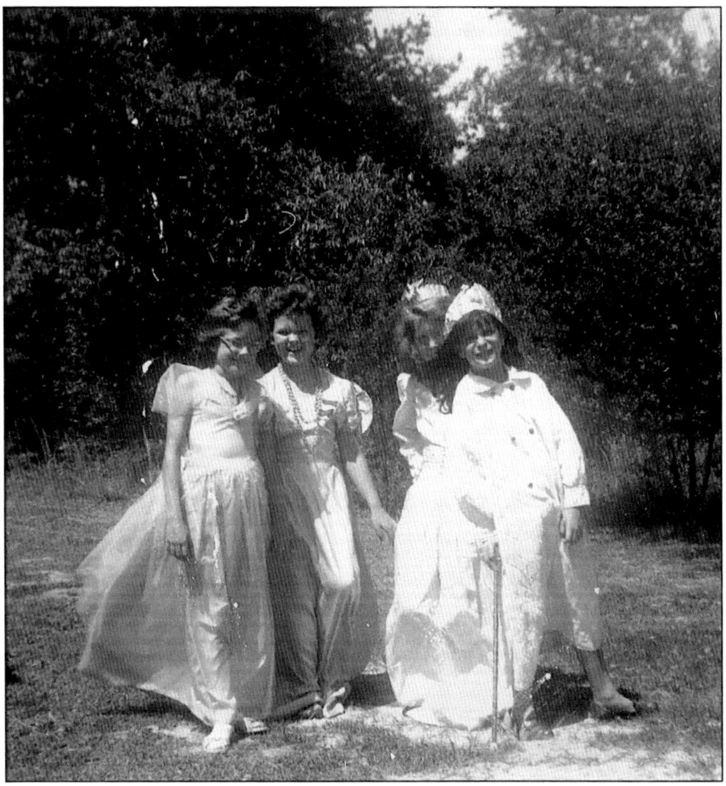

Impromptu play acting was a favorite summer pastime for the younger generation. Familiar stories could be acted out or a young magician would perform his sleight-of-hand tricks with a family audience clapping their approval. All that was needed was someone's screened porch and a curtain made from sheets to define a stage. Here we have the stars of one of these dramatizations.

In 1946 the Exchange Club sponsored the Mount Pleasant Little Theatre Group in a performance of *The Mikado*, a Gilbert and Sullivan Opera at Alhambra Hall. J. Wyman Frampton provided the musical direction, and it was staged by Mrs. E.M. Royall Jr. The program included the cast of characters and eight advertisements of local businesses. The dedication explained the manner it was presented with dialogue omitted. Mrs. Ferdinand Gregorie was the narrator.

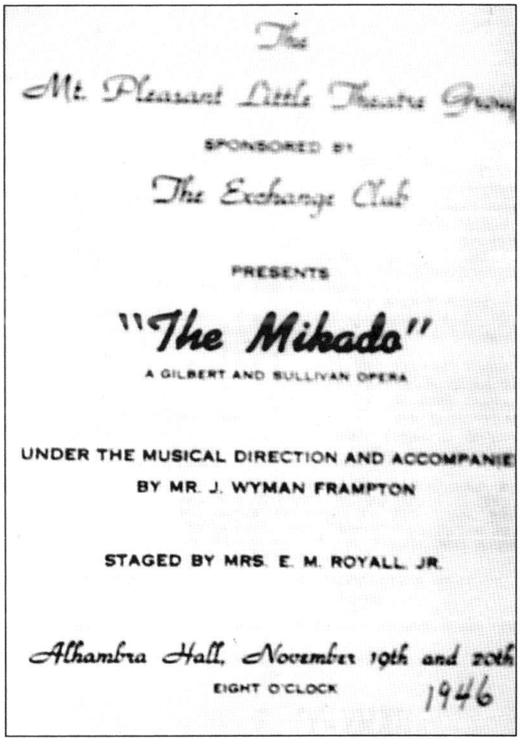

The
Mt. Pleasant Little Theatre Grou
SPONSORED BY
The Exchange Club
PRESENTS
"The Mikado"
A GILBERT AND SULLIVAN OPERA

UNDER THE MUSICAL DIRECTION AND ACCOMPANIE
BY MR. J. WYMAN FRAMPTON

STAGED BY MRS. E. M. ROYALL, JR.

Alhambra Hall, November 19th and 20th
EIGHT O'CLOCK
1946

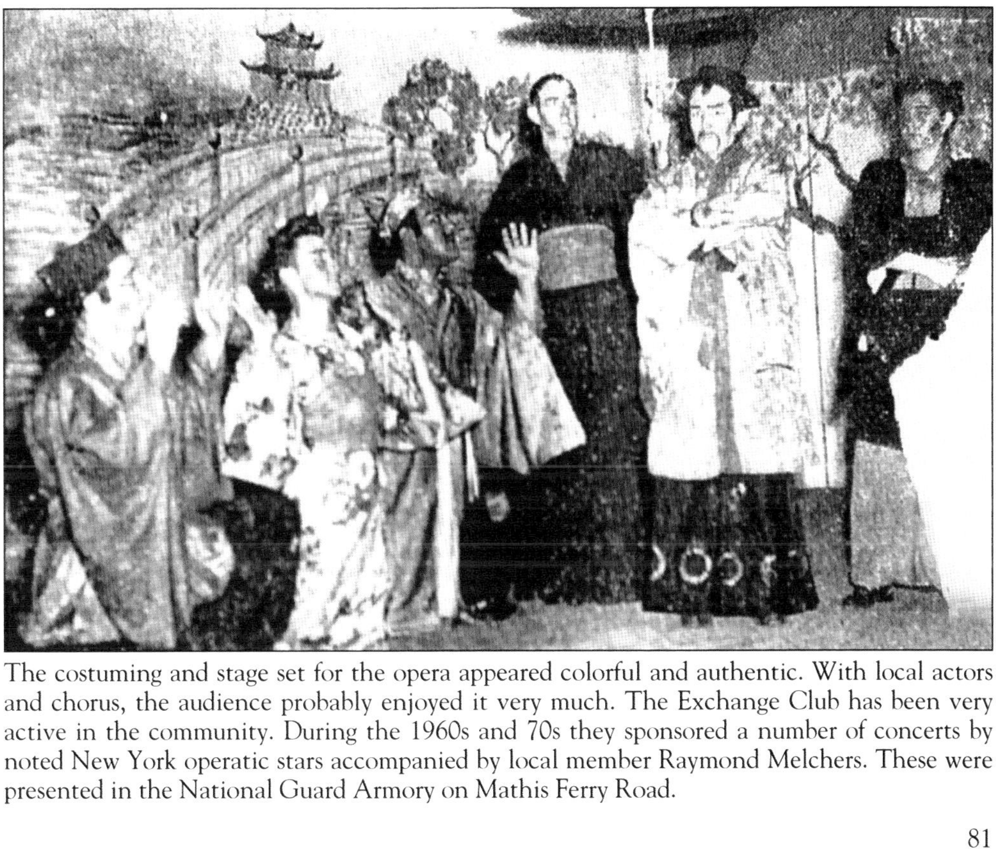

The costuming and stage set for the opera appeared colorful and authentic. With local actors and chorus, the audience probably enjoyed it very much. The Exchange Club has been very active in the community. During the 1960s and 70s they sponsored a number of concerts by noted New York operatic stars accompanied by local member Raymond Melchers. These were presented in the National Guard Armory on Mathis Ferry Road.

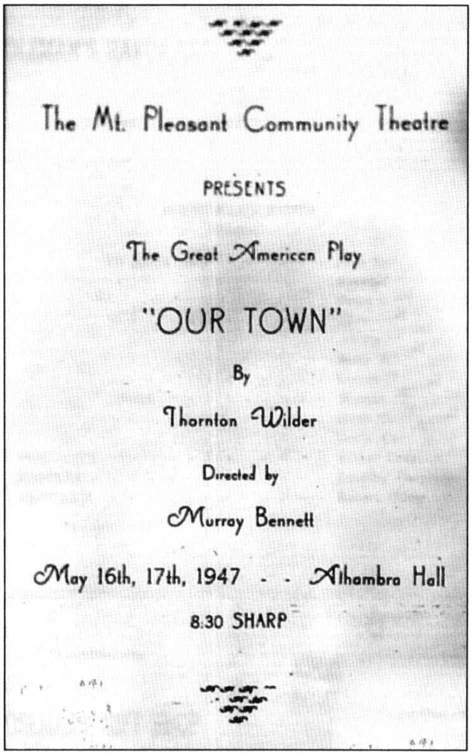

The Mt. Pleasant Community Theatre

PRESENTS

The Great American Play

"OUR TOWN"

By

Thornton Wilder

Directed by

Murray Bennett

May 16th, 17th, 1947 - - Alhambra Hall

8:30 SHARP

The next year, 1947, the Mount Pleasant Community Theatre presented *Our Town* by Thornton Wilder. No mention of a sponsor, but the number of advertisers had doubled. The director was Murray Bennett and the actors were all local people.

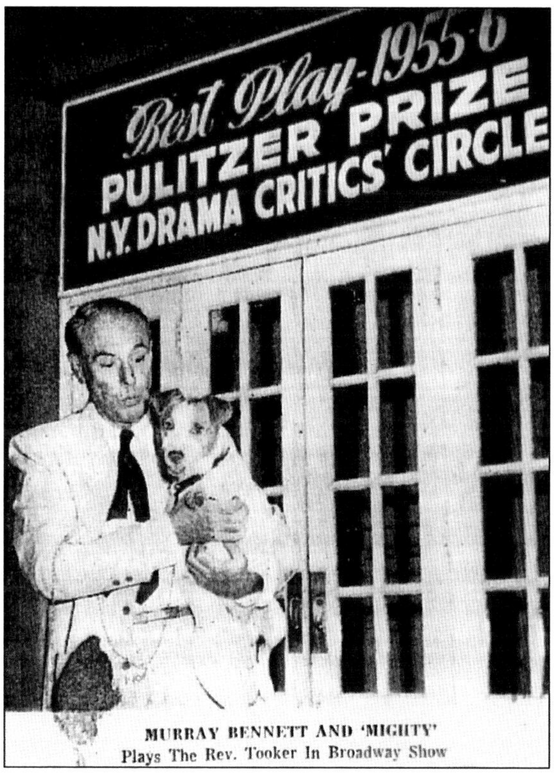

MURRAY BENNETT AND 'MIGHTY'
Plays The Rev. Tooker In Broadway Show

Murray Bennett, a well-known actor, author, and poet, resided in Mount Pleasant on upper Pitt Street (near Alhambra Park) for a number of years. He shared his talents with the local theatrical efforts before returning to New York City as Reverend Tooker in the Broadway show *Cat on a Hot Tin Roof*. Originally from Charleston, he first appeared on Broadway in 1921.

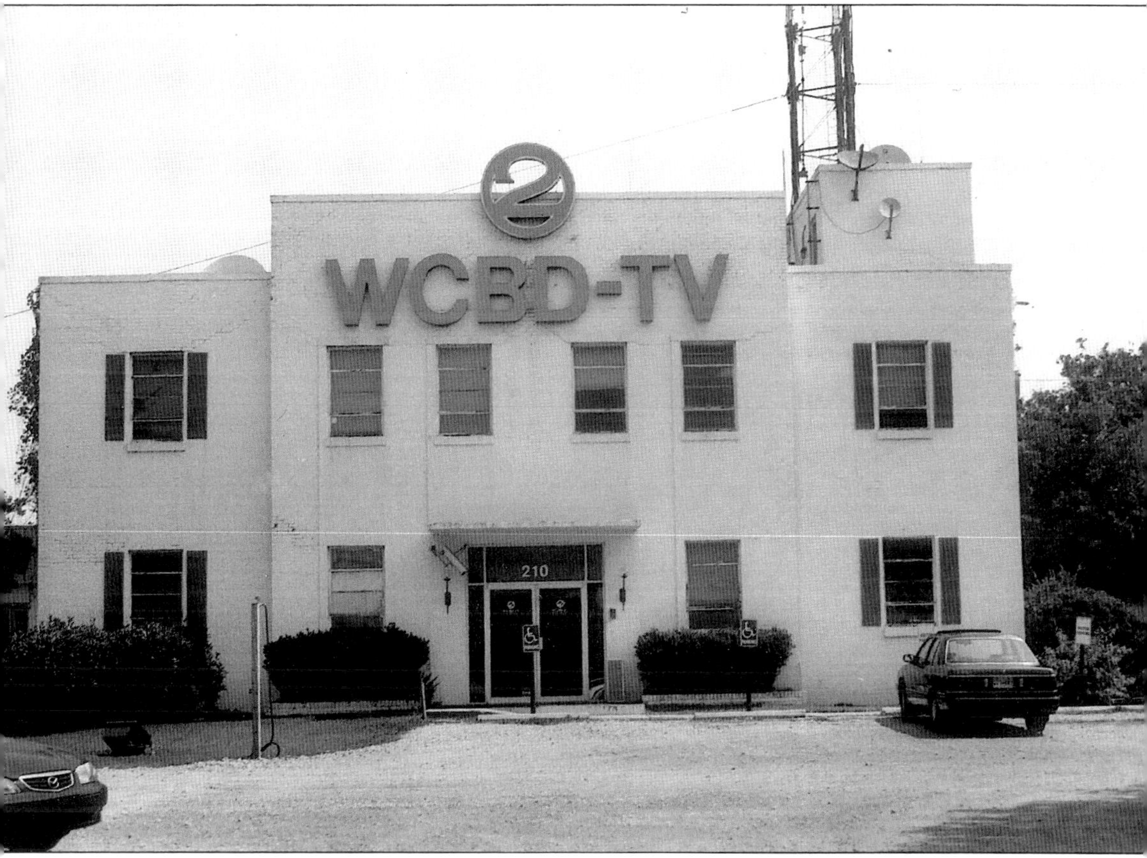

Two of Charleston's original three television stations were located East of the Cooper. WCBD, Channel 2, was established in 1954 on 27 acres at the foot of the Cooper River bridge, outside the town limits at the time, by C. Drayton Hastie. WCIV, Channel 4, was begun by a group of local businessmen in 1962 on Ben Sawyer Boulevard near the bridge to Sullivan's Island. Possibly the most unique "personality" was Suzy Q of Channel 2, an elephant. Occasionally she would escape and come trumpeting across the highway into Bay View Acres. Once when a sudden thunderstorm frightened her, she pulled up the oak tree she was tied to, and headed for her quarters. Oliver was her keeper and when the time came for her to go to a new home, he went on the trip with her. Annually at Thanksgiving a Christmas tree made of lights on Channel 2's antennae is turned on. The lights brighten the landscape until the New Year.

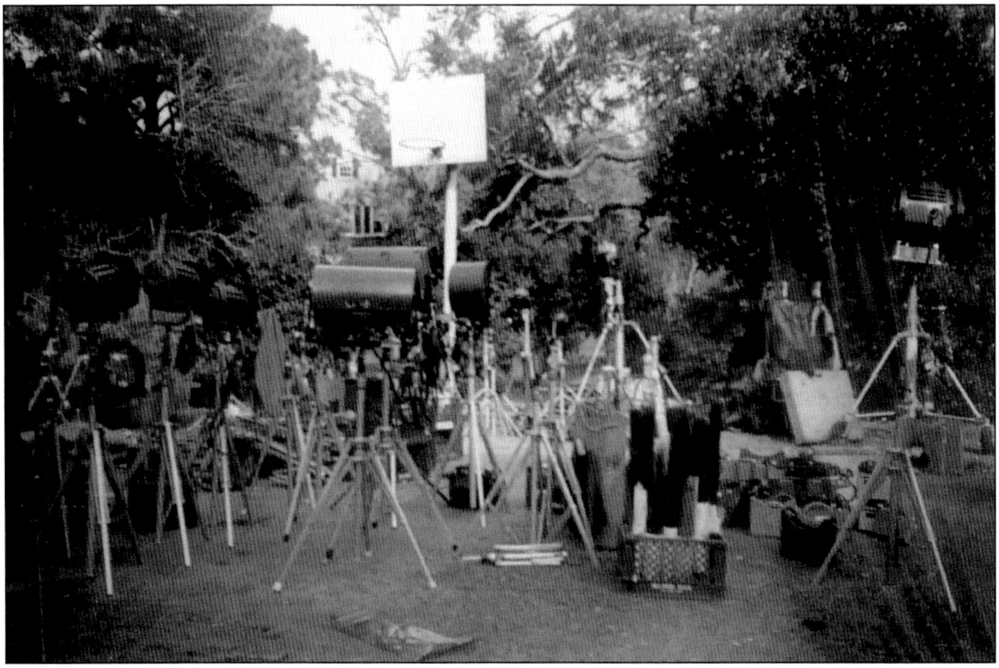

Mount Pleasant became a movie set for several movies. Pitt Street Pharmacy was featured in the Kate Jackson movie *Thin Ice*. *Rich in Love*, written by local author Josephine Humphreys, was turned into a movie and utilized almost the whole town during its filming. Cameras, lights, and other necessary equipment fill the yard of the house on Bennett Street.

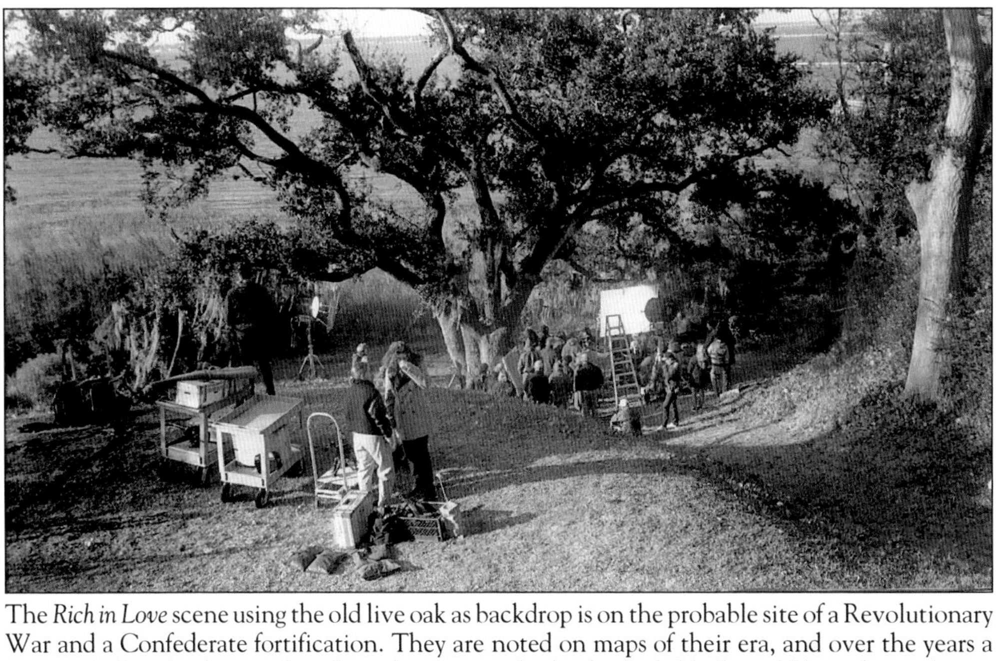

The *Rich in Love* scene using the old live oak as backdrop is on the probable site of a Revolutionary War and a Confederate fortification. They are noted on maps of their era, and over the years a cannon ball and other artifacts have been unearthed. The high bluff would have been chosen for protection against the enemy coming by water.

Nine

MEMORIES

The Friendly Town was a state of mind as well as a geographical place called Mount Pleasant. It is important to remember things of the past; such events will remind the reader of special occasions in his or her own life.

Many of these images may return to consciousness things experienced long, long ago. The image chosen to represent this chapter incorporates a number of things that might be remembered. Within the chapter are scenes of childhood beginning in the 1940s. Photographs of siblings, pets, activities, chores, and parties are some of the images you may associate with your own lives.

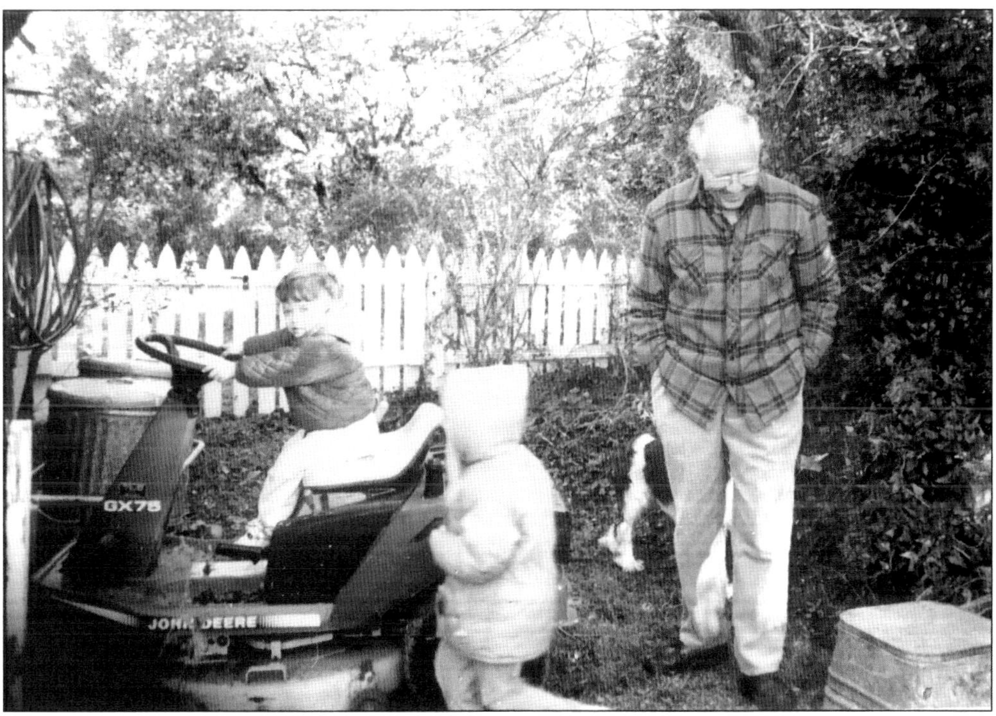

This child enjoys a visit to a grandparent's home, where he sits on the riding mower.

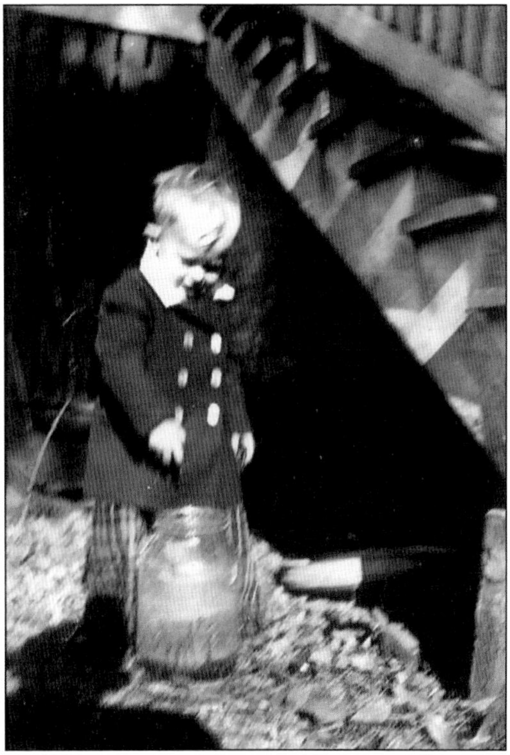

Watching his goldfish swim intrigues this two-year-old, pictured in the 1940s. Although it is cold enough for his overcoat, he is warm in the sun by the steps of his grandmother's house. World War II is of no concern to him.

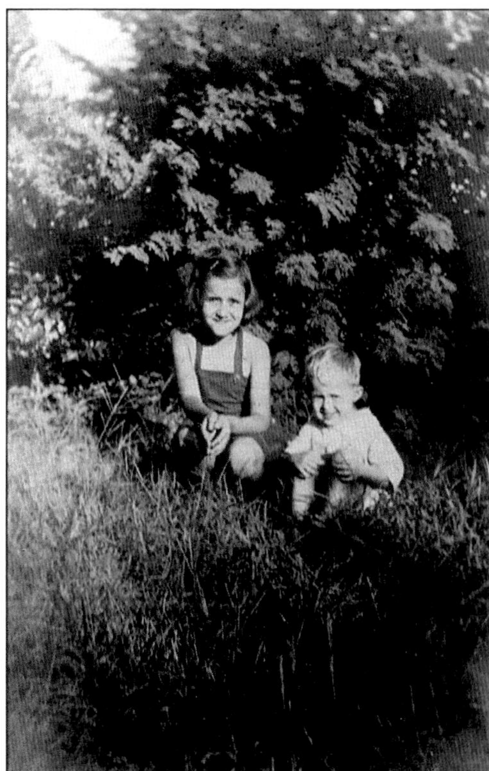

Childhood pleasures in the 1940s included playing in the yard. Before the days of plastic toys or computer games, youngsters relied on their imaginations.

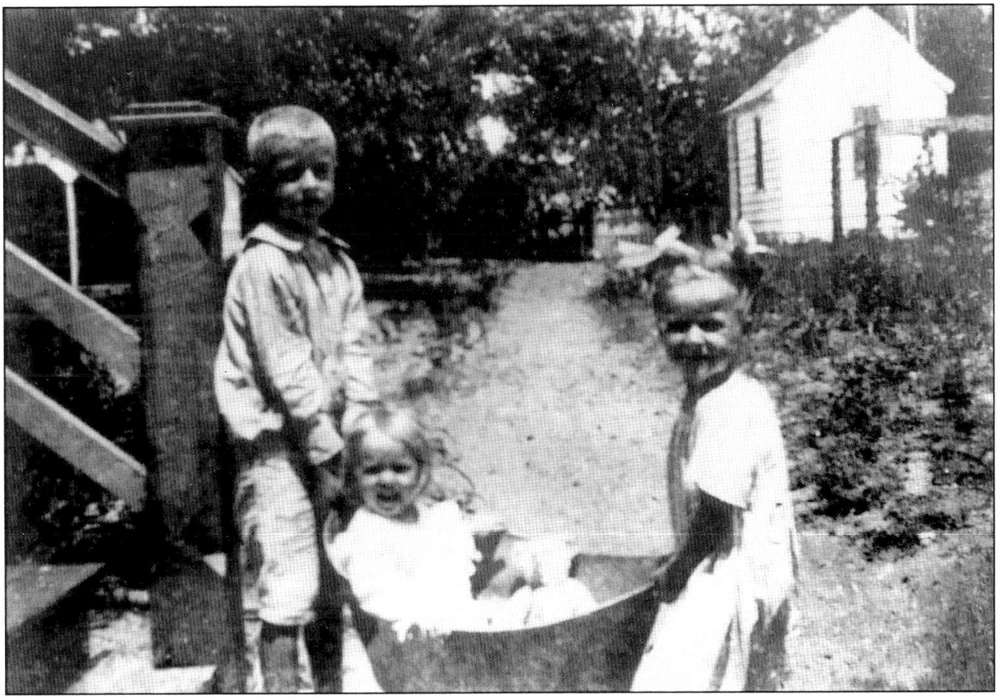

Older children are often fascinated with the younger siblings. Here the older brother and sister give their baby sister a ride in an old fashioned tub, which they found under the house. The little white house was Dr. J.Y. DuPre's office years before. Similar small buildings were found throughout the town. They served as offices, a library, and even an apothecary shop.

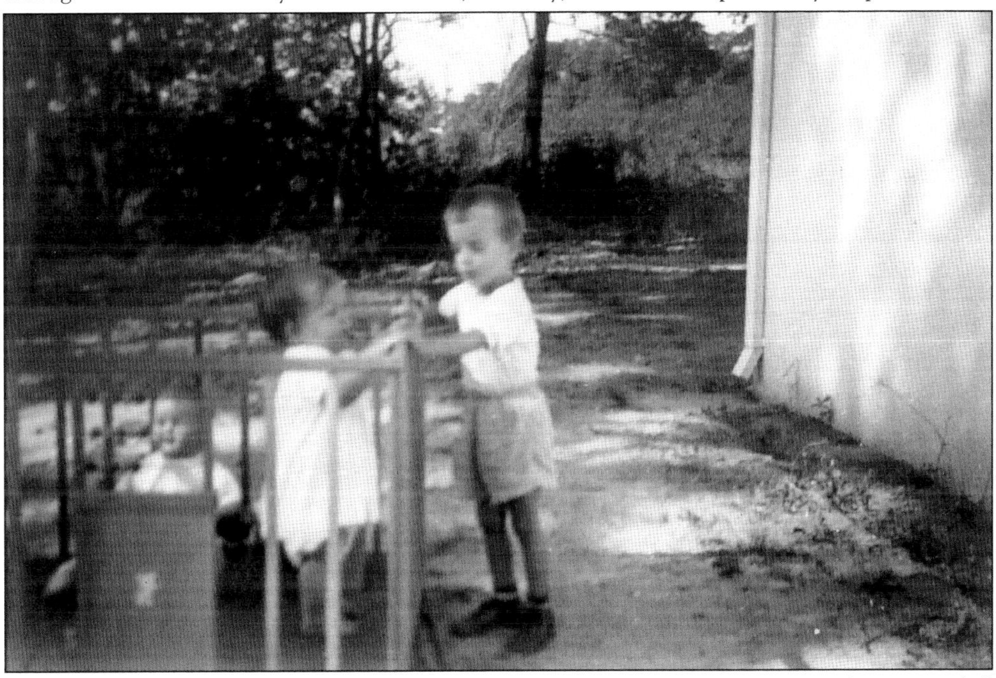

Here the older neighbor gives some pointers to the little one in the playpen outdoors. Her doll is almost large as she is.

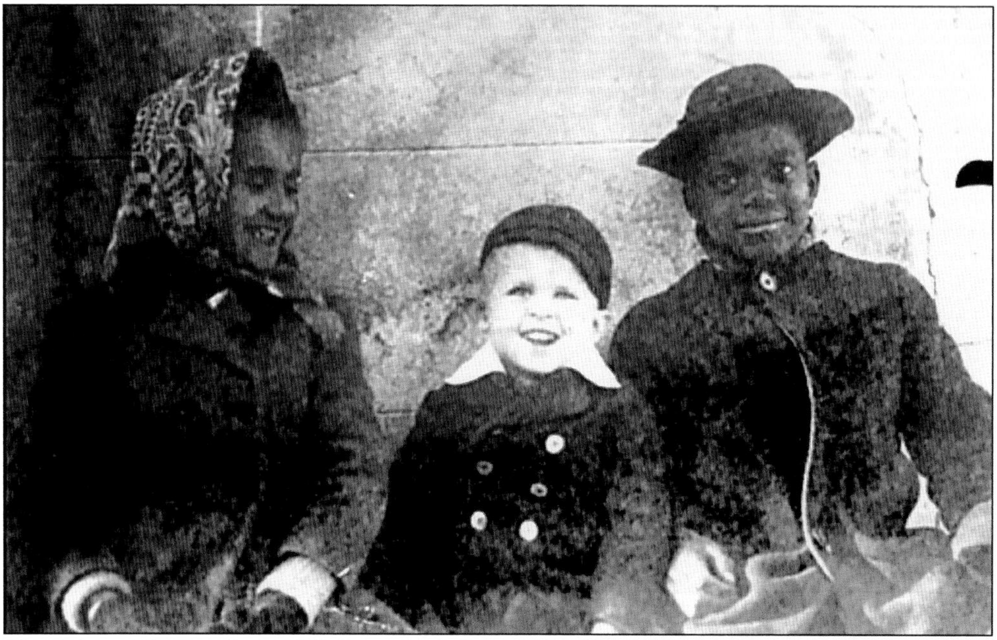

The color of skin made no difference in the 1940s for these children. They are all friends and are playing in the little boy's yard on Bennett Street.

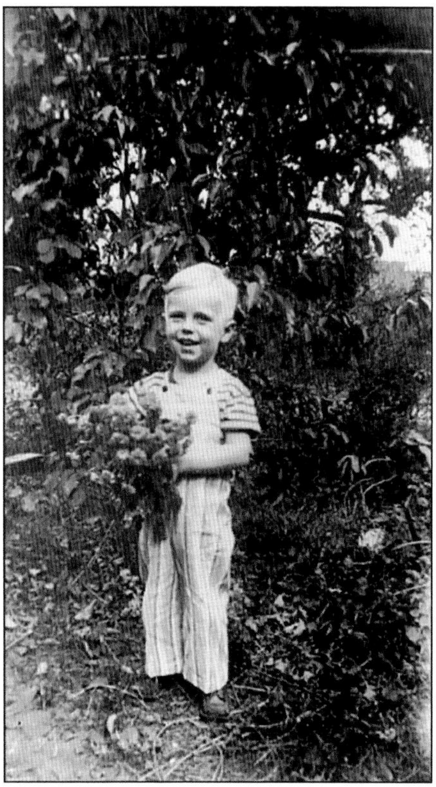

Summer has come and a child has gathered a large bouquet of flowers to take to someone, possibly his mother. He is pictured in his grandmother's yard on Live Oak Drive.

The little girl in this image cuddles with her kitten beside the telephone. In the 1950s, the rotary telephone was the latest way of dialing, and Charleston was no longer long distance. Not all houses had central heat, much less air conditioning. An oil-burning stove, like the one to the left, provided heat in many homes. There were also floor furnaces which fit into the floor in a central place in the house.

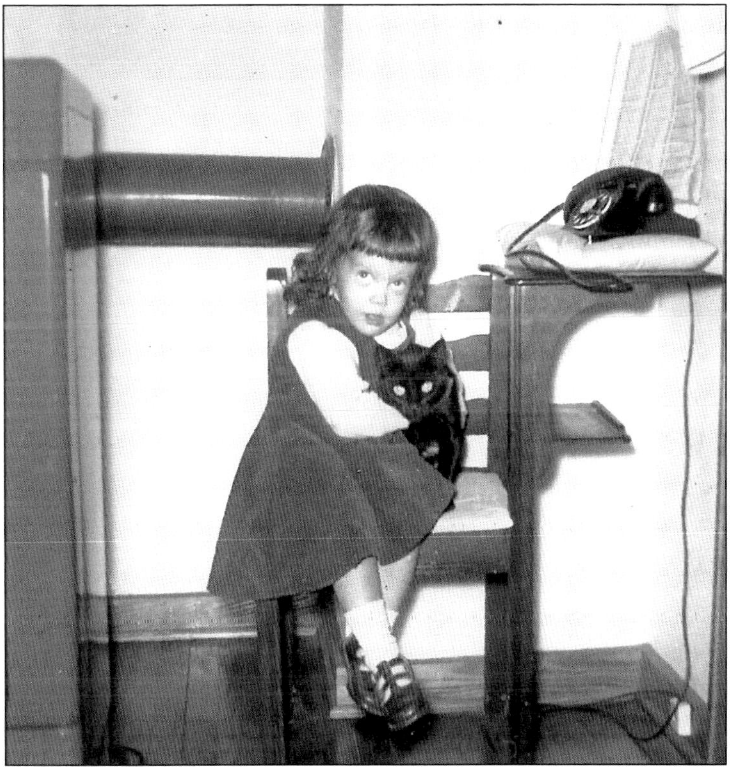

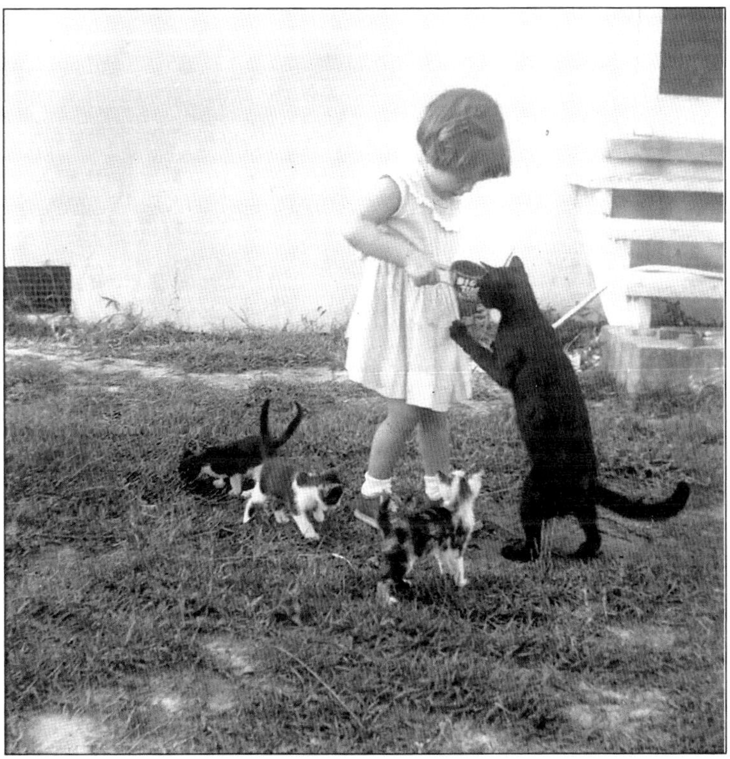

This cat knows her dinner is forthcoming, but she can hardly wait for it to leave the spoon!

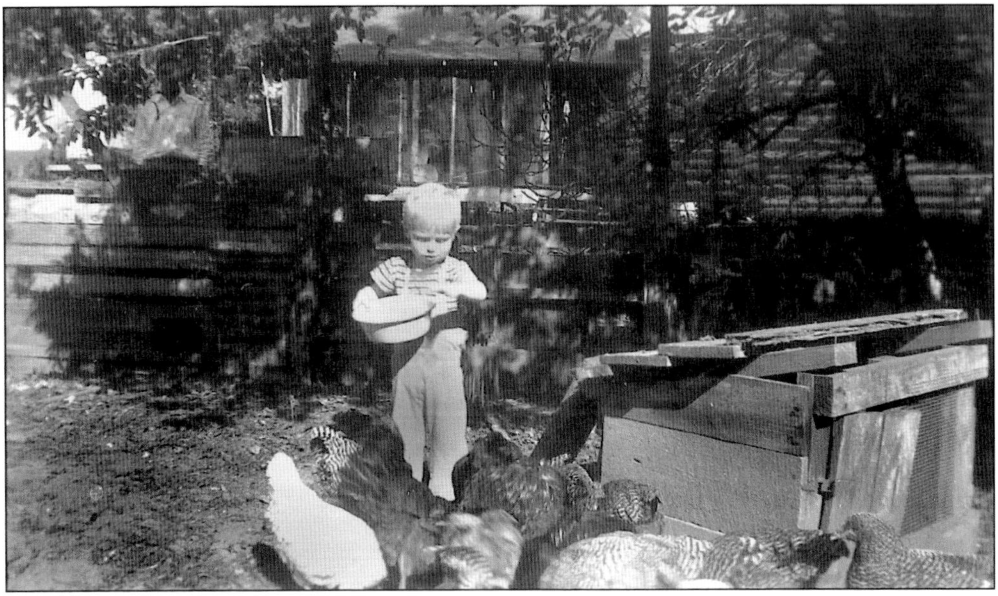

Feeding the chickens is a serious chore for the two-year-old in the backyard. His hens are barred rock, Rhode Island red, and a white one. Gathering the eggs was probably next on his list of chores.

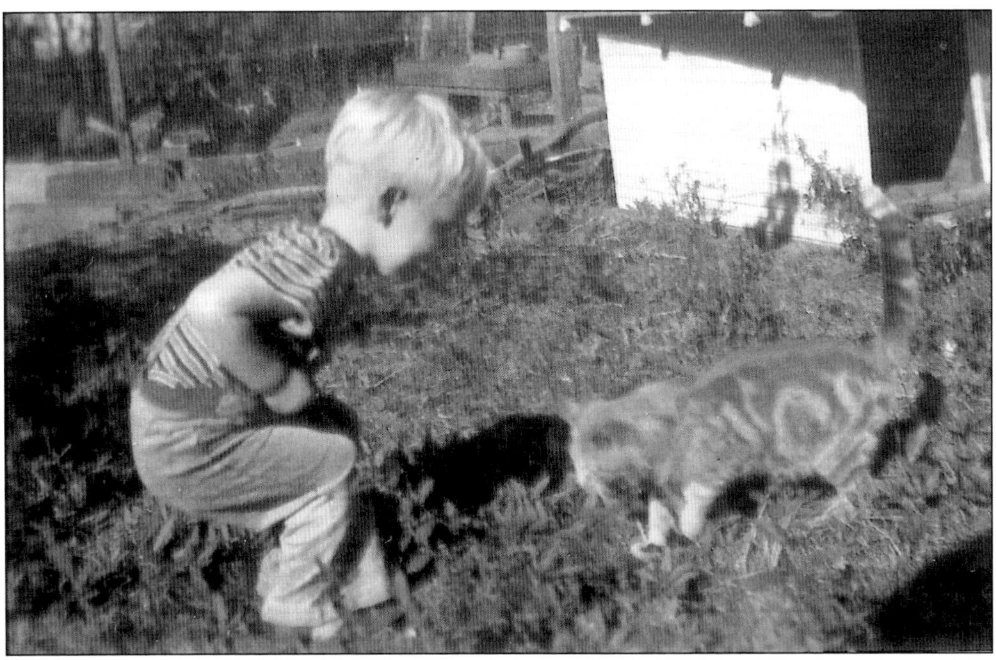

After his chores are finished, he spends time with his cat. In 1946, he has no cares in the world.

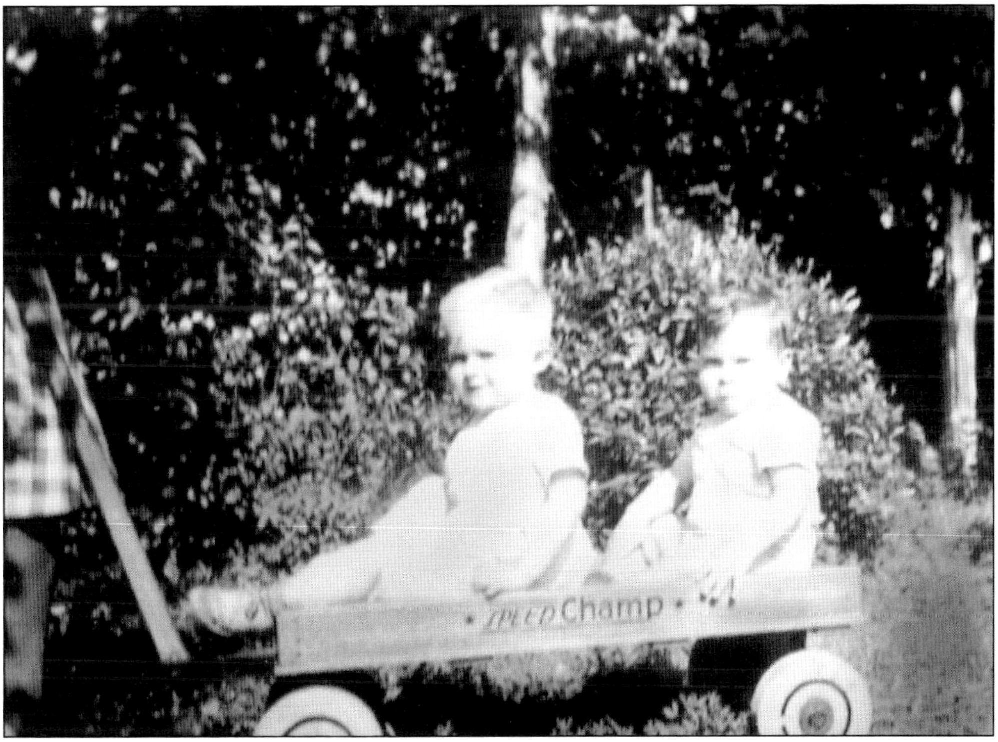

Two cousins both named John enjoy a ride on a "Speed Champ" wagon, which was probably painted red. Wagons haven't changed much since the 1930s. Medicine, however, has made great strides in the prevention of many diseases, such as polio, which one of these youngsters suffered. Happily he recovered and has lived a productive life.

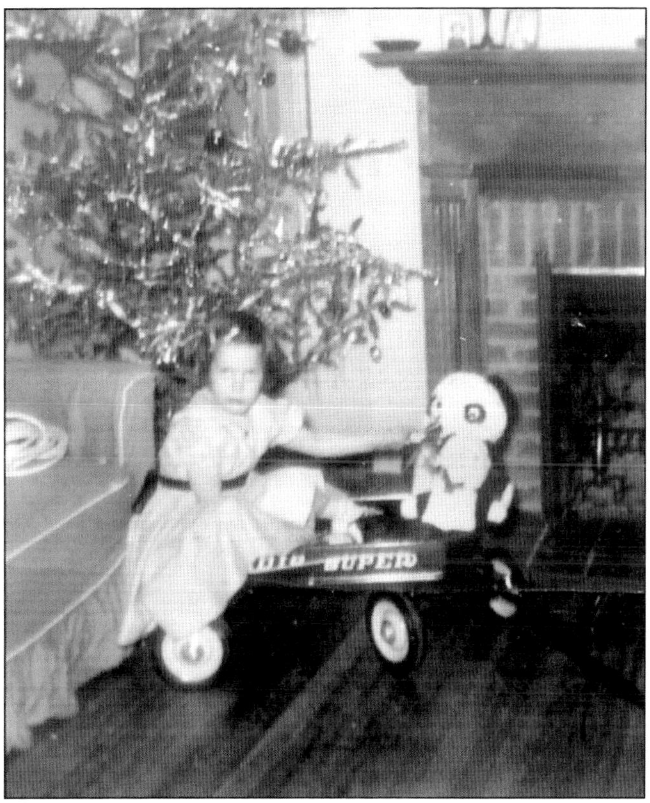

Girls liked wagons, too, and Panda almost fills this one. Bears have always been popular toys. In the mid-1950s, the Panda joined the ranks of favorite stuffed animals. Grocery stores began offering stamps for purchases, which were pasted in books and redeemed for many things including toys.

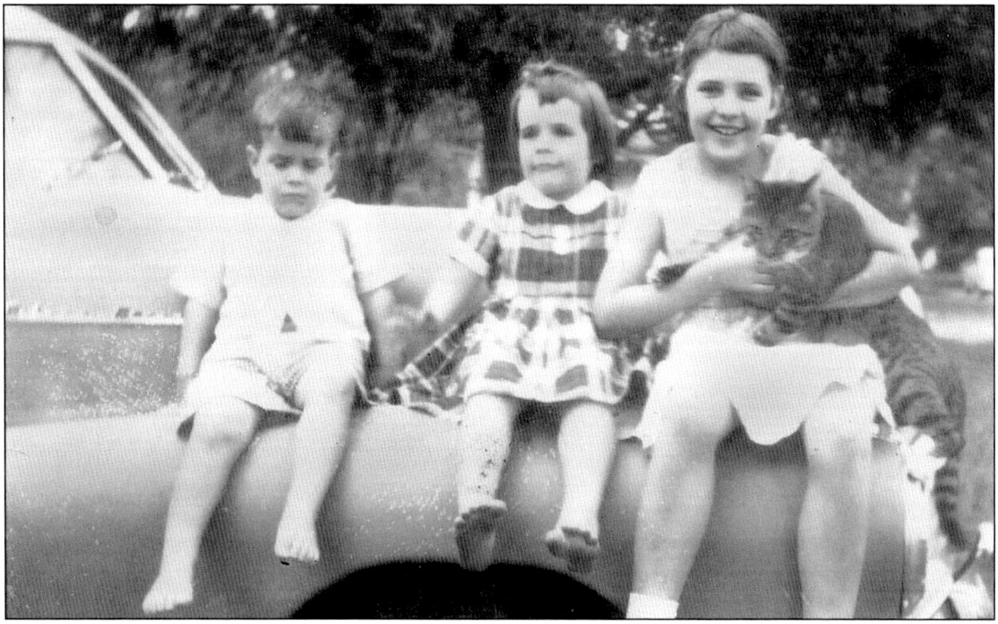

These youngsters are all dressed up and ready to go somewhere. Going barefoot was much fun in the summertime as the two younger children will agree.

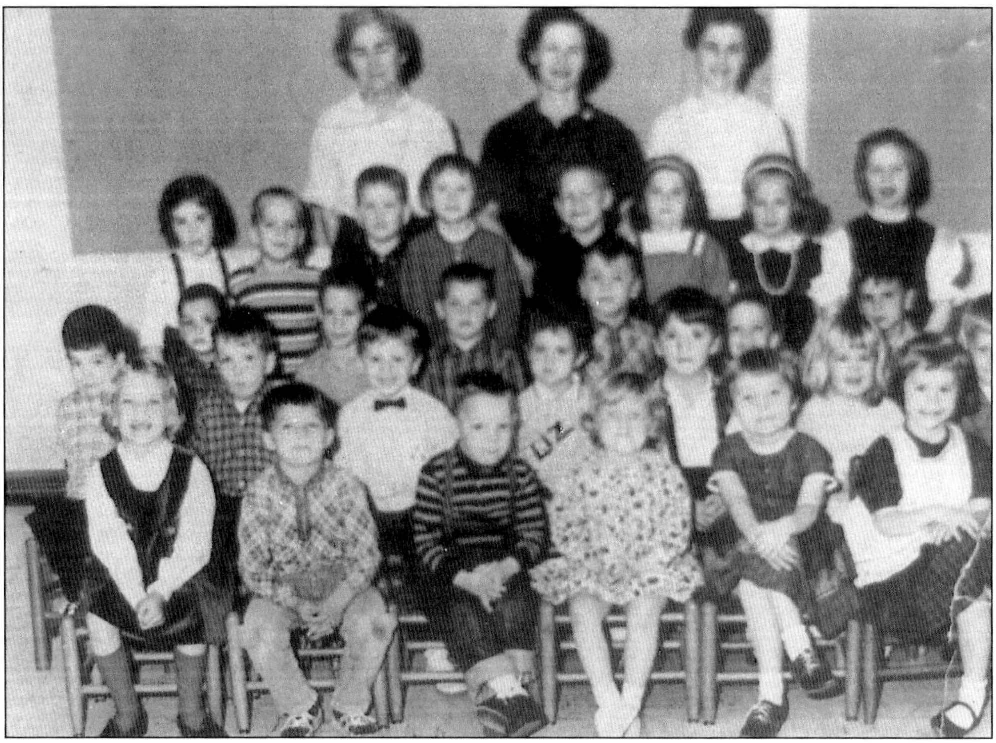

These 27 children pose for their class picture with their three teachers at the Mount Pleasant Presbyterian Church Kindergarten. Churches sponsored kindergartens with classes for three-, four-, and five-year-olds at a reasonable cost for parents. Public schools started with first graders at age six.

Some 50 years ago, radio and record players provided entertainment for children. Programs on radio included "Big John and Sparky" while 78 rpm recordings were geared toward songs that children could sing along with or march to. A glimpse into the round glass-front china cabinet reveals the popular Audubon birds plates.

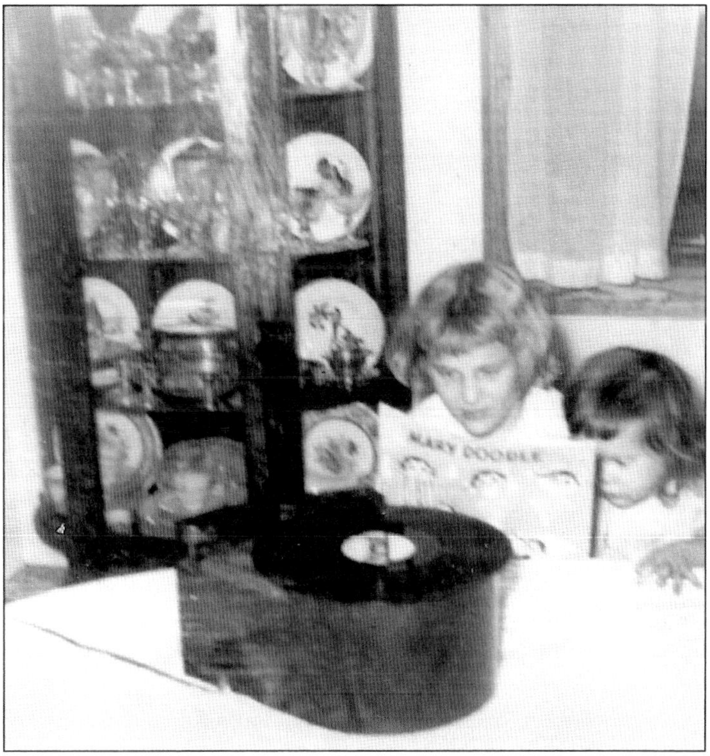

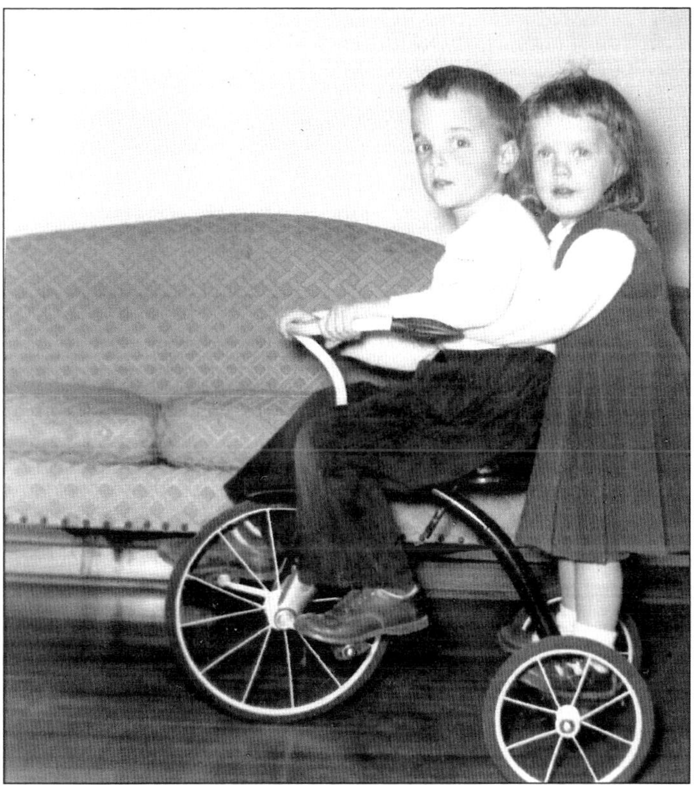

Tricycles were made of durable metal, not plastic. It was fun when a young neighbor came over, and the little girl could ride piggy back around the house. Her buckle-strap shoes were probably Jumping Jacks, a popular brand of this time period.

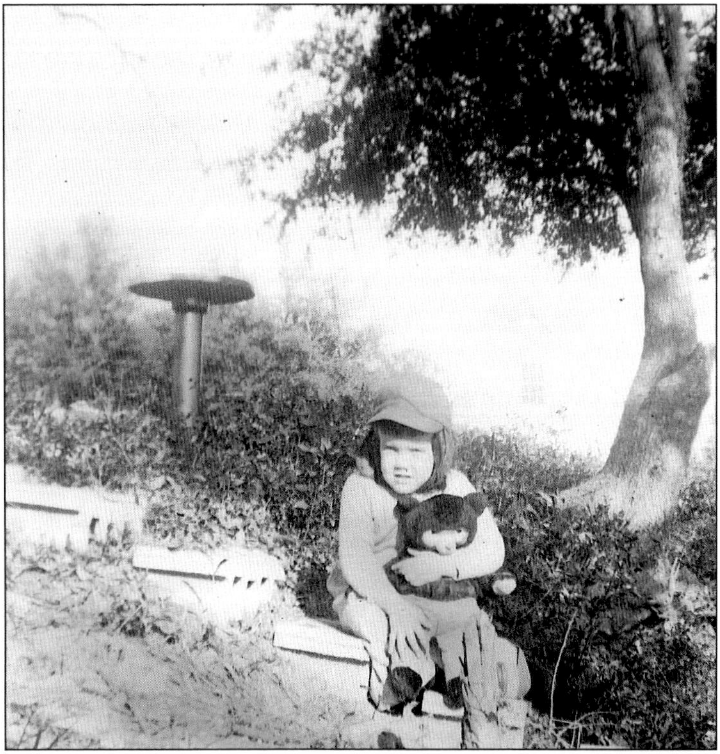

On cold days it was fun to play down the bluff near edge of the marsh, out of the wind. Smokey the Bear was a good toy to carry on such an expedition. Smokey was developed by the forestry department to help stop forest fires and used extensively in their advertising. His popularity spread to toys in the early 1950s.

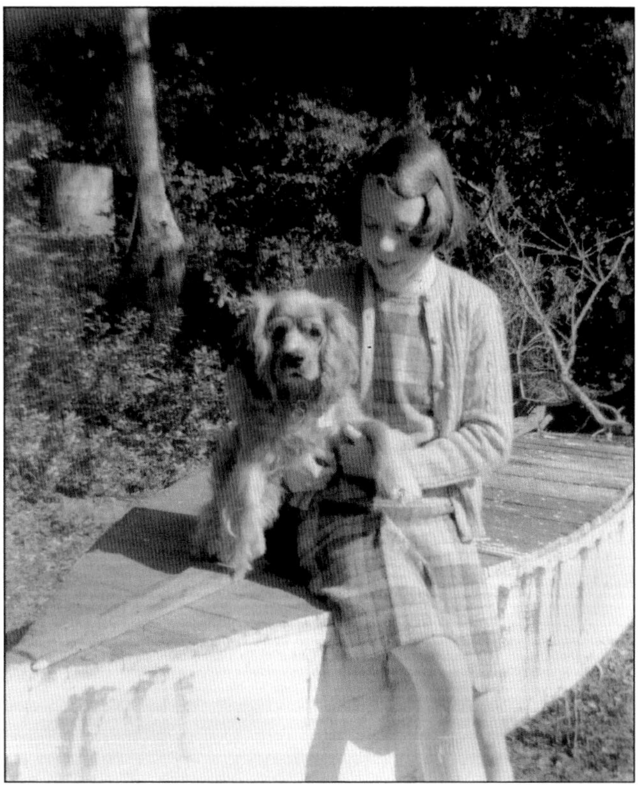

Anne and her dog, Happy, sit together on a boat in the late 1960s. Warm weather is here, so it won't be long before the bateau is put into the water. Cocker spaniels were a popular breed of dog in the 1950s and 1960s. They were small in size and loyal in disposition.

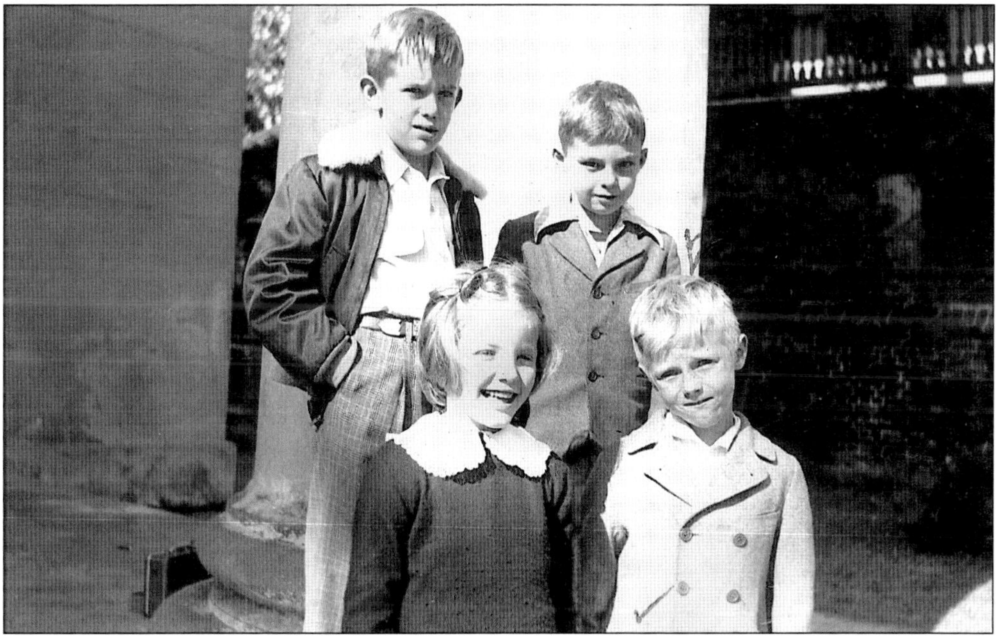

It's a birthday party for the young boy on the right front. His cousins and a friend help him celebrate turning four. He was born on D-Day in 1944.

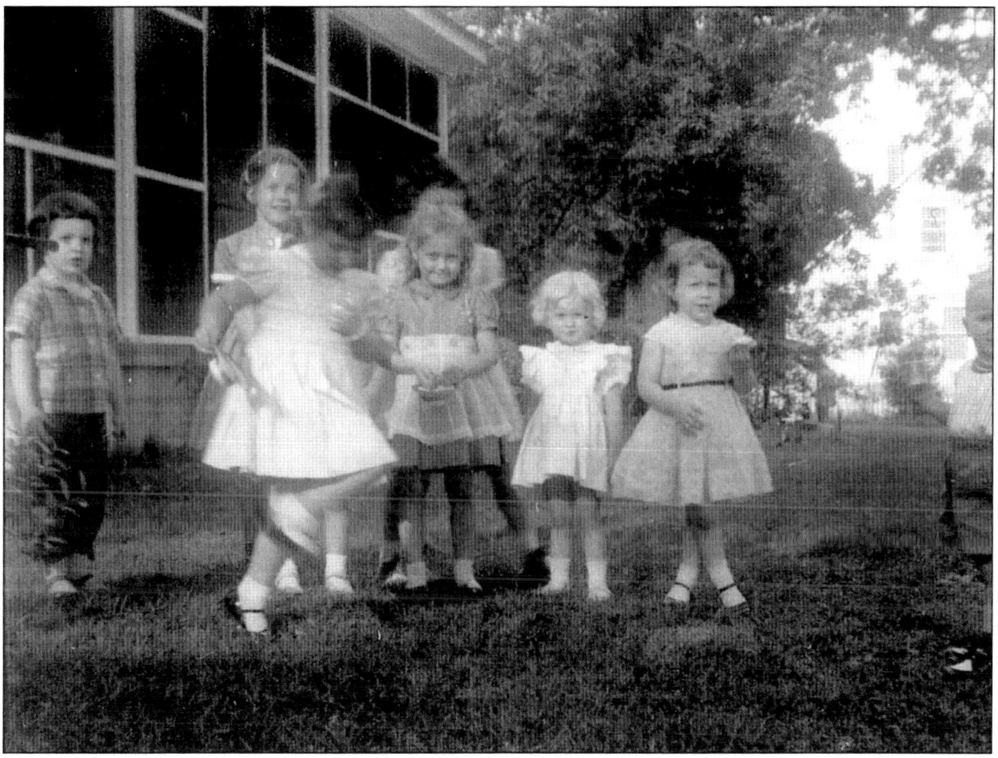

In 1958 friends help celebrate the fourth birthday of the young lady on the right. Their individuality is already apparent . It is the era of crinoline underskirts for party wear along with Mary Jane–style black patent leather slippers.

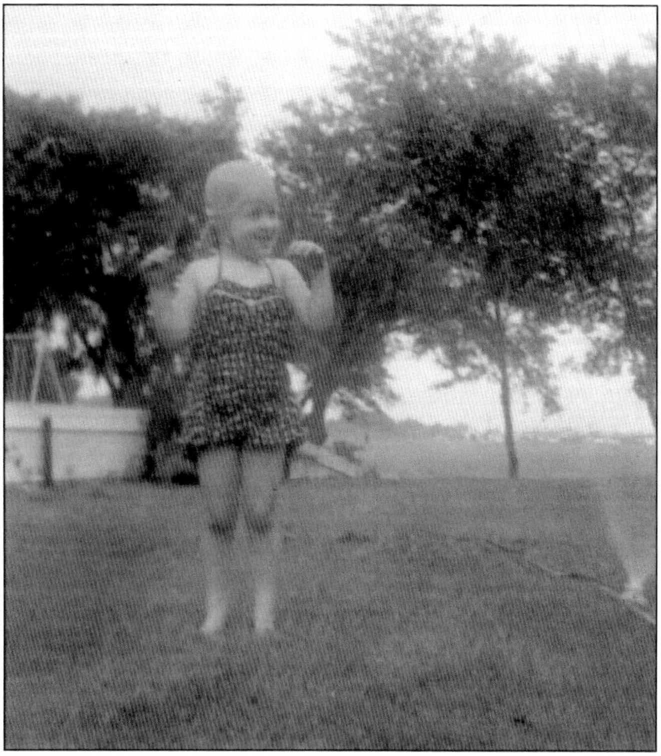

Outdoor fun in the summertime couldn't be any better. Complete with swim cap, this young miss enjoys the sprinkler in her own yard. This kind of entertainment at home was fun and useful—after all, it watered the grass.

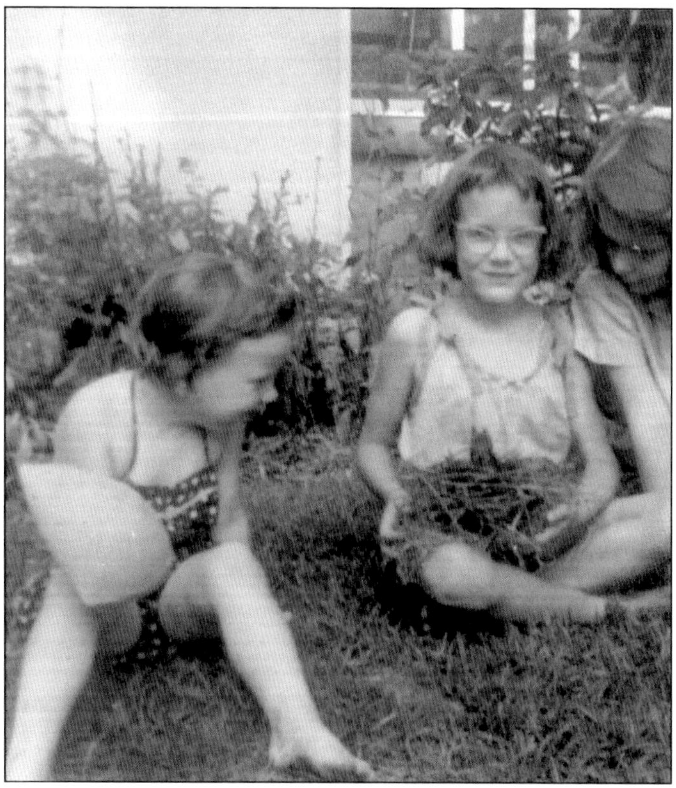

The two older girls appear to have found a bird nest, while the youngest one looks on.

It looks like this little guy is not too happy; he appears to have a bruise on his knee. Children haven't changed much since 1947—a little love will heal a lot of things.

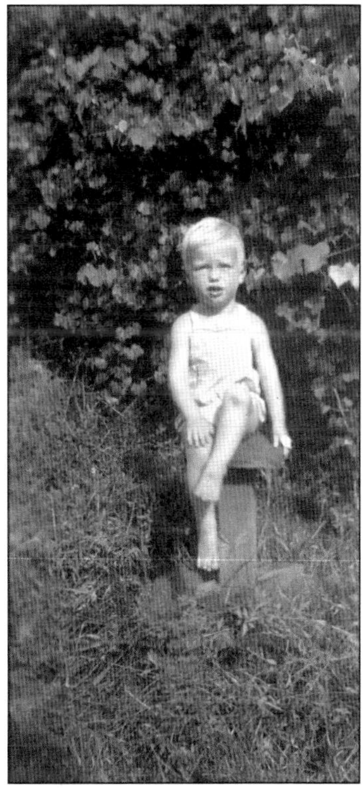

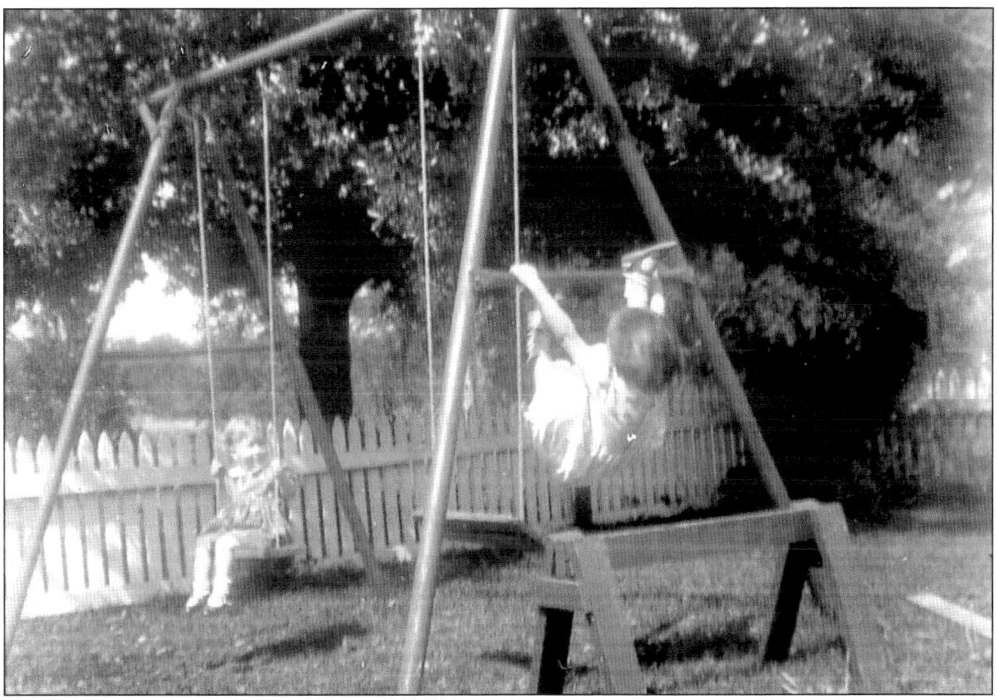

Swing sets provide hours of fun and exercise. Sparse by today's standards, those in the 1950s had everything necessary for swinging and "skinning the cat." A sawhorse was added here so the girls could grab the bar.

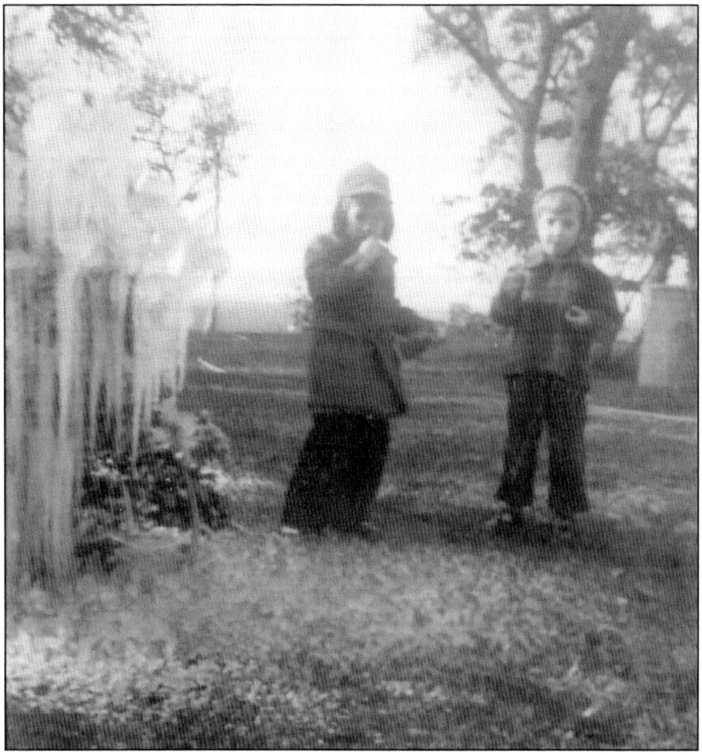

In the 1950s children still enjoyed the simpler things of life. These two little neighbors are eating icicles from an icicle tree, which was made by letting a hose run slowly over a bush on a night when the temperature was freezing.

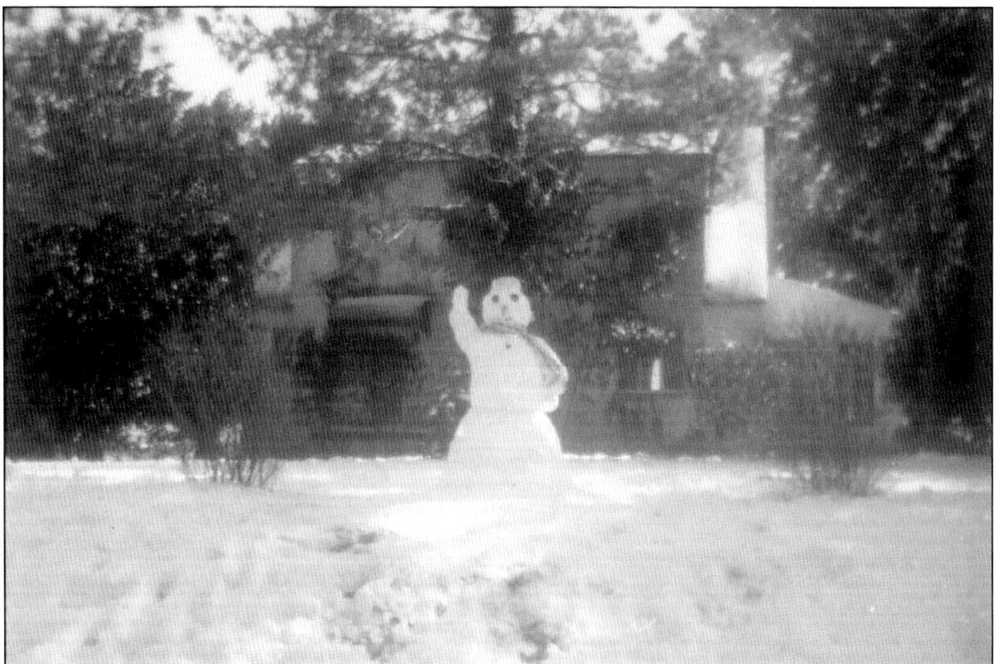

Occasionally enough snow falls to make a snowman. This snowman wears a cheerful scarf and waves at a passerby. The big snow of 1973 had its lighter moments although it paralyzed traffic all over the state.

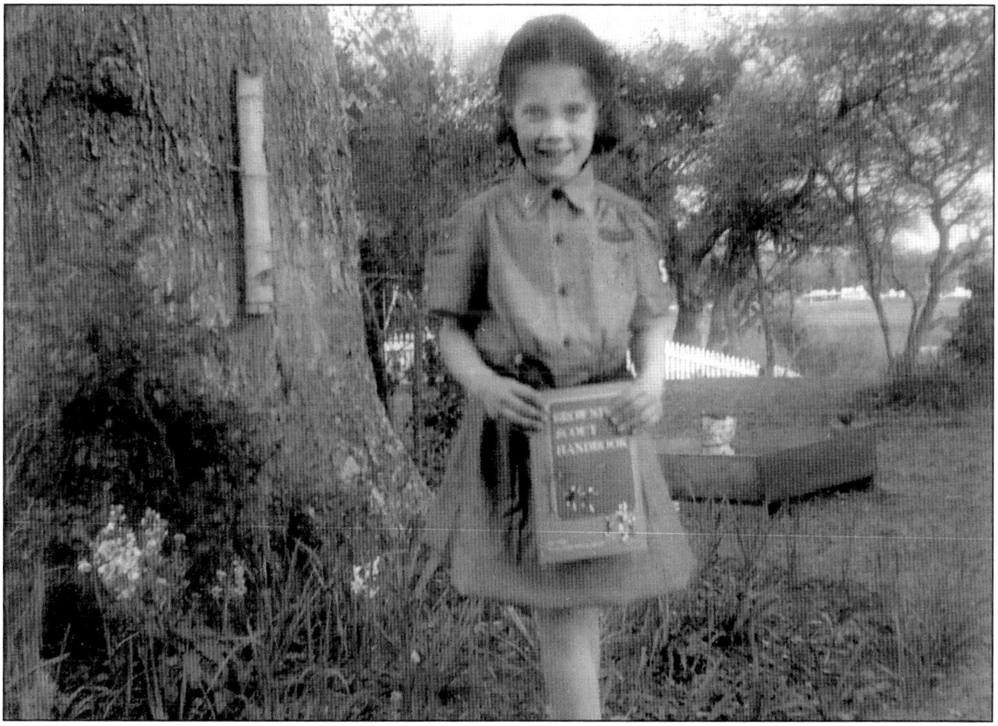

Scouting has been important to youngsters in Mount Pleasant for many years. Pride in becoming a Brownie is obvious on this young lady's face. Her Brownie Handbook is a prized possession.

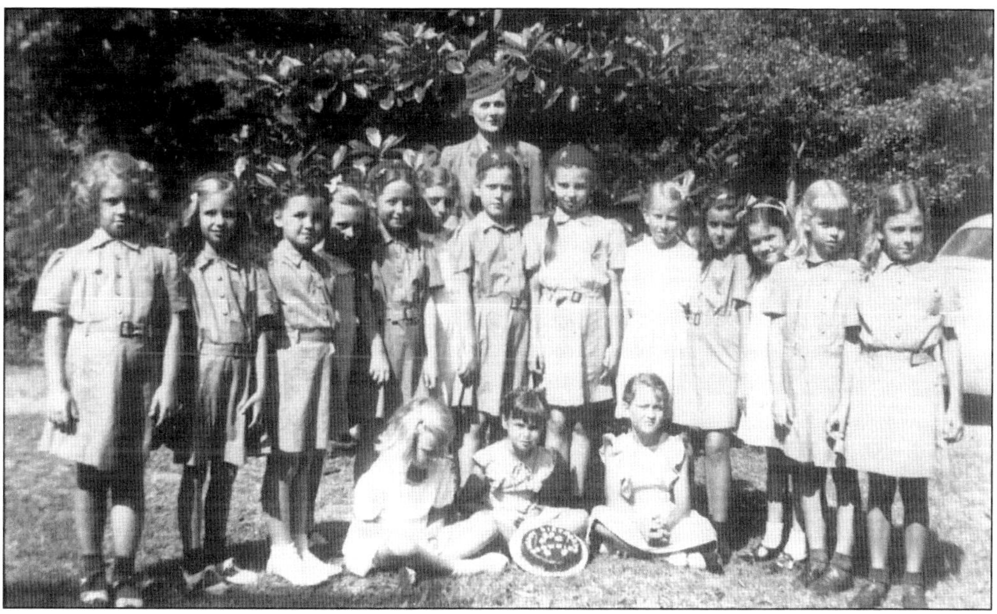

This Scout Troop's group picture dates from around 1946. Many of these girls still live in the area. Annual ceremonies involving all the troops in the area were held on the Jasper Green ball field next to Moultrie School. The stands were filled with relatives and friends of the girls.

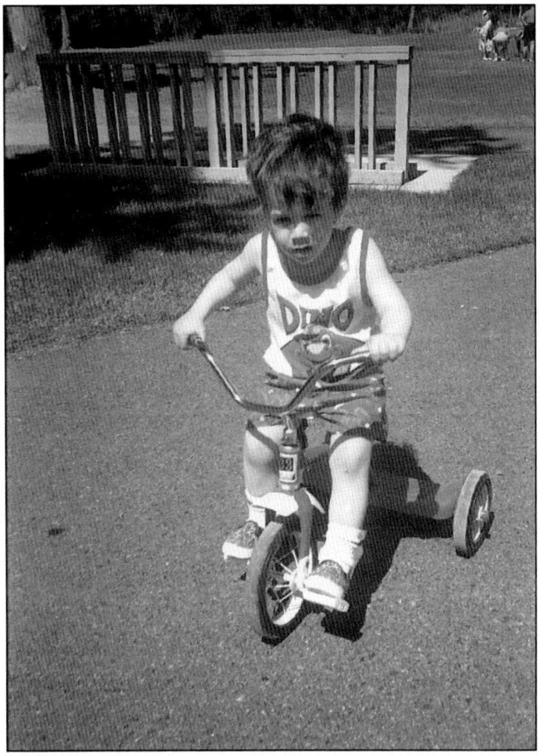

This little boy pedals fiercely as he goes down the path at the park. Charleston County in the latter part of the 20th century purchased land in various areas for parks. In the Mount Pleasant area, it was part of an old plantation known as Palmetto Grove. The park commission wisely kept part of the old name and called it Palmetto Islands Park. The islands are connected by boardwalks and are wonderfully accessible in this nature-oriented park.

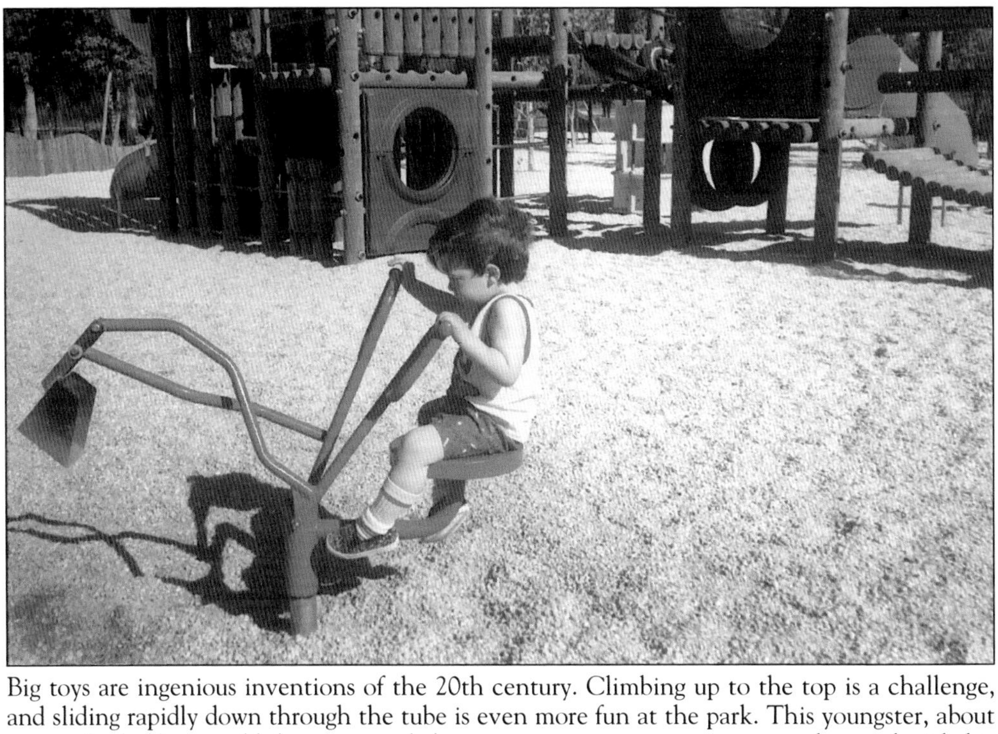

Big toys are ingenious inventions of the 20th century. Climbing up to the top is a challenge, and sliding rapidly down through the tube is even more fun at the park. This youngster, about two-and-a-half-years old, has mastered the movements necessary to scoop the sand with his shovel, although his feet barely reach the controls.

Ten

BRIDGES

Mount Pleasant, although a peninsula, relies heavily on bridges. The 1929 bridge to Charleston was a most important link. For 37 years, the Grace Memorial Bridge was used by cars going to and from Charleston. As narrow as it seems today, that is the way it was. Sometimes tourists panicked and had to be driven over by local police. It was a toll bridge until June 29, 1946.

In 1966 a second bridge parallel to the Grace was opened for traffic. Named for Highway Commissioner Silas Pearman, it was designed with three lanes. At the time of its construction, it was noted that access would be inadequate from the Charleston side. Other bridges from the town span Shem Creek and the Intra Coastal Waterway. The latter to Sullivan's Island, the Ben Sawyer Bridge, replaced the one now used as a fishing pier at the end of Pitt Street. In most recent times, two bridges some distance from the original town bridge the Isle of Palms and North Charleston.

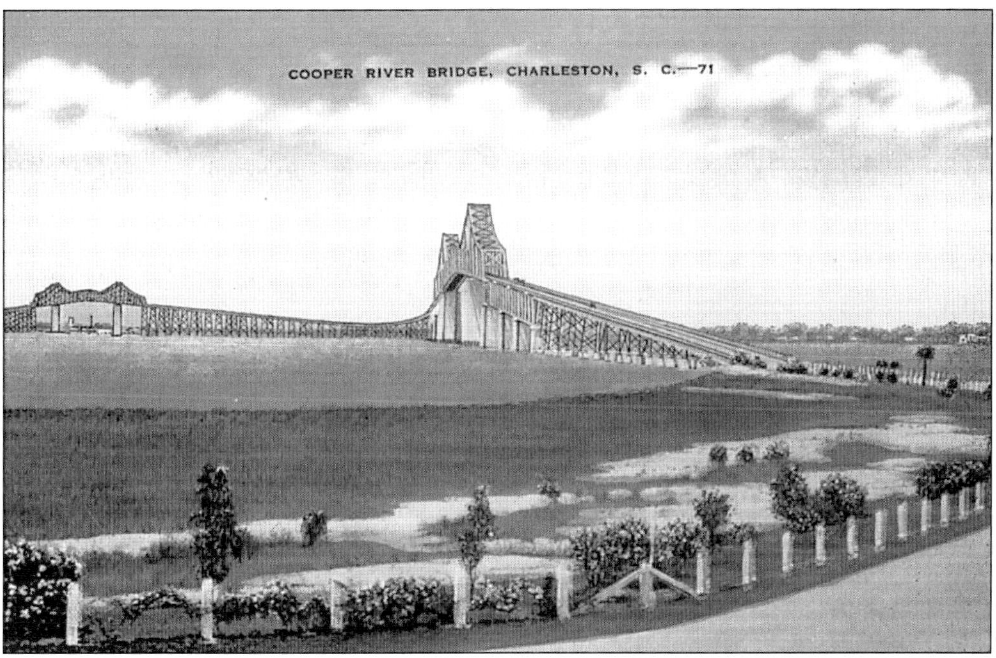

This representation on a contemporary postcard shows the majestic spans crossing the Cooper River and Town Creek. Each spanned the waterway at right angles, hence the curve in the middle. It cost $6,000,000 to build and was basically two connected cantilever bridges.

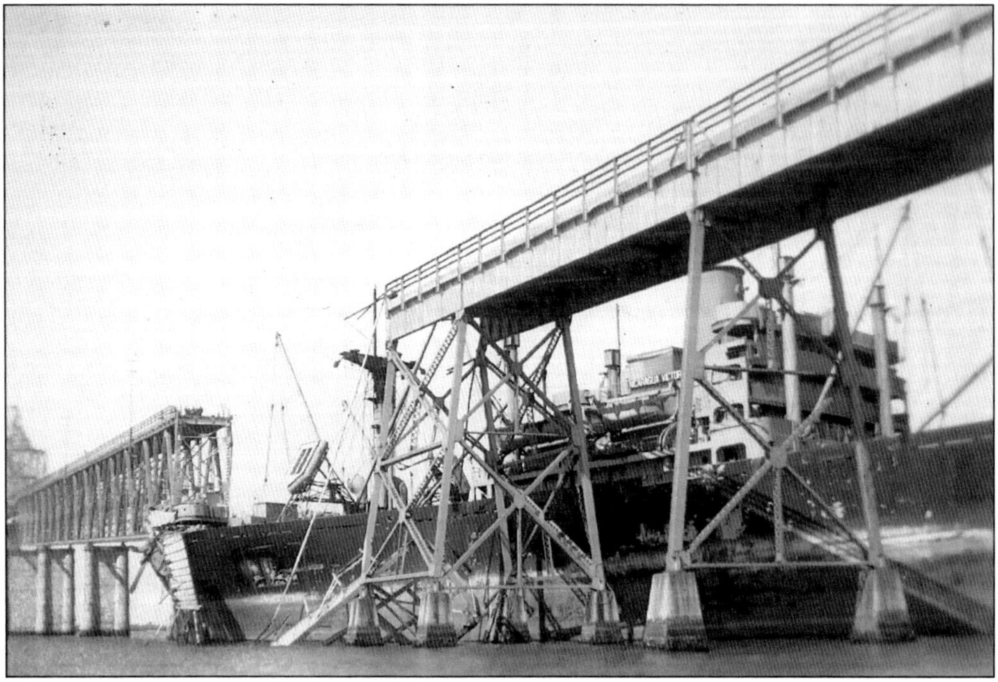

During a sudden squall on Sunday afternoon February 24, 1946, a ship, the *Nicaragua Victory*, dragged anchor in the Wando River and plowed into the Grace Bridge. The impact tore away a 240-foot section on the Mount Pleasant side some distance from the main shipping channel. Local photographers shot many pictures from their boats before the ship was removed. These are from Lee Royall and Robert Coleman.

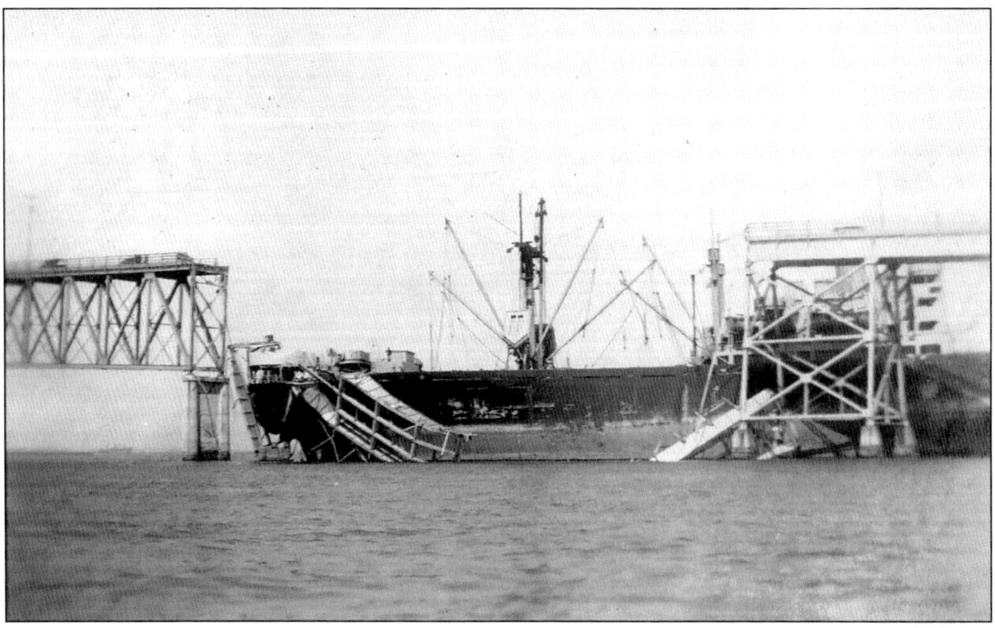

The ship and the broken bridge are seen in this close-up. A family of five were in the only car that plunged into the water. Others narrowly escaped a similar fate. Ships such as this one, known as "the Victory ships," were the work horses during World War II.

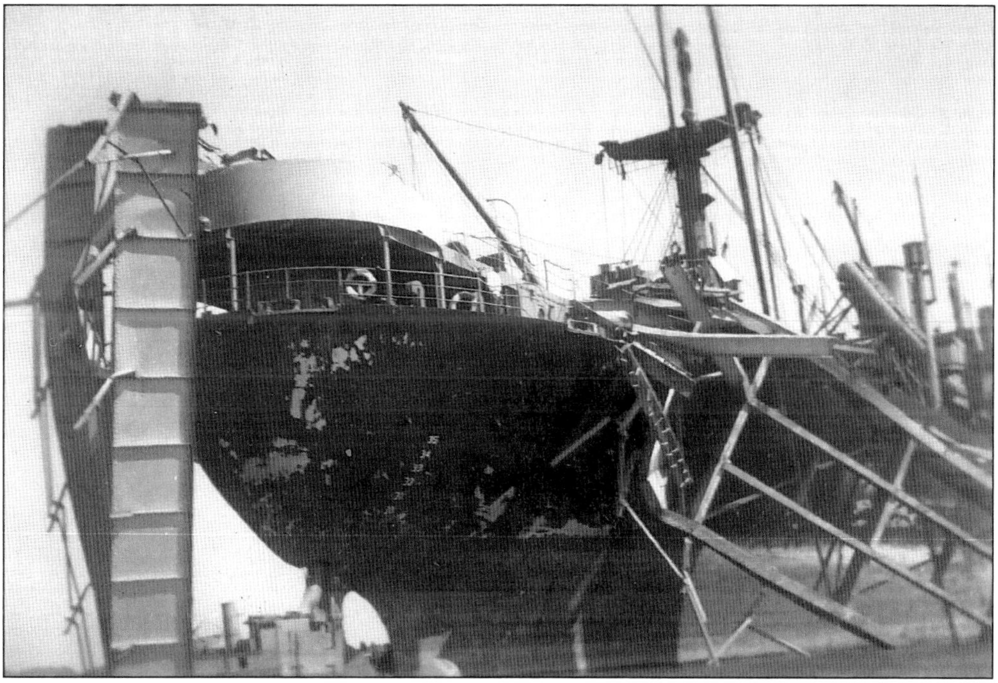

Two other views show the ship wedged between piers of the Grace bridge in the 1946 accident. The photographers moved from one side to the other to get both bow and stern.

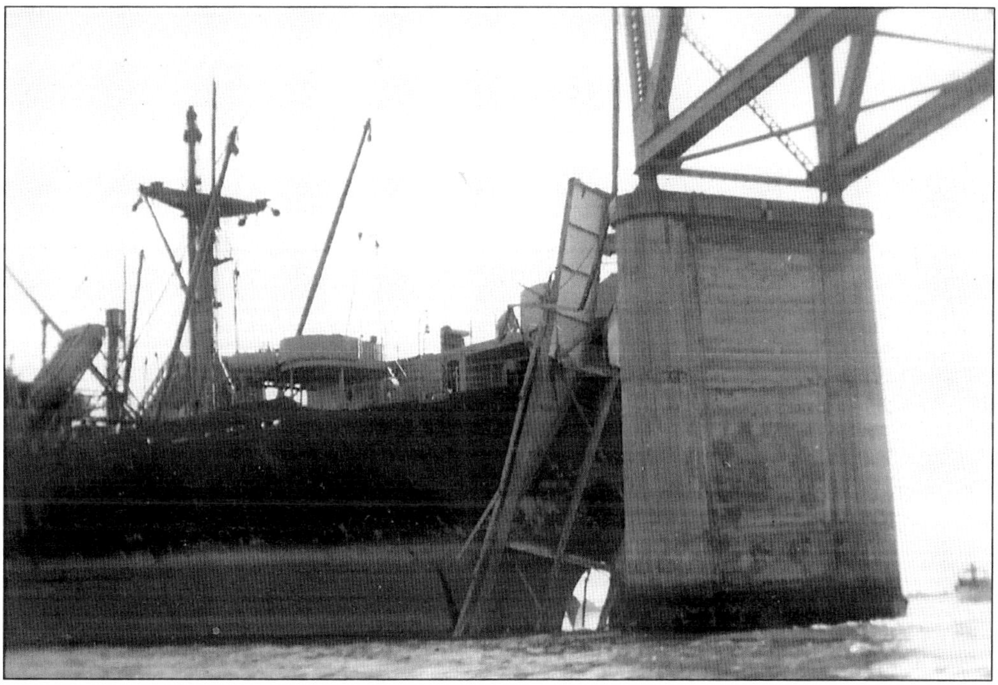

The 10,000-ton freighter dragged anchor in the squall, while the ebbing tide further wedged the ship. Traffic resumed April 4 with a parade and great rejoicing. Repairs were completed in June.

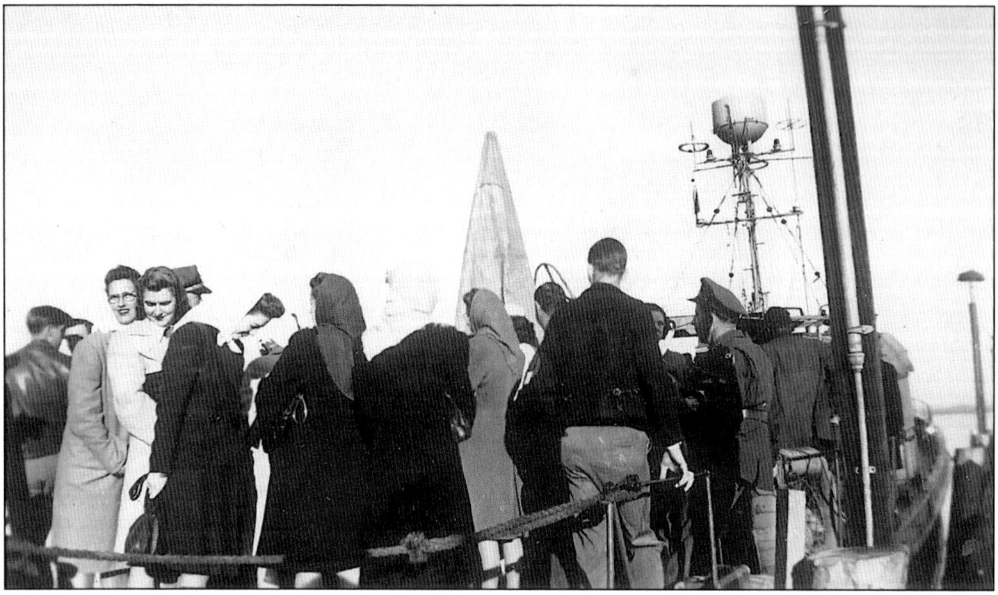

During the interval before the bridge was repaired, the Coast Guard boat ferried passengers between Charleston and Mount Pleasant.

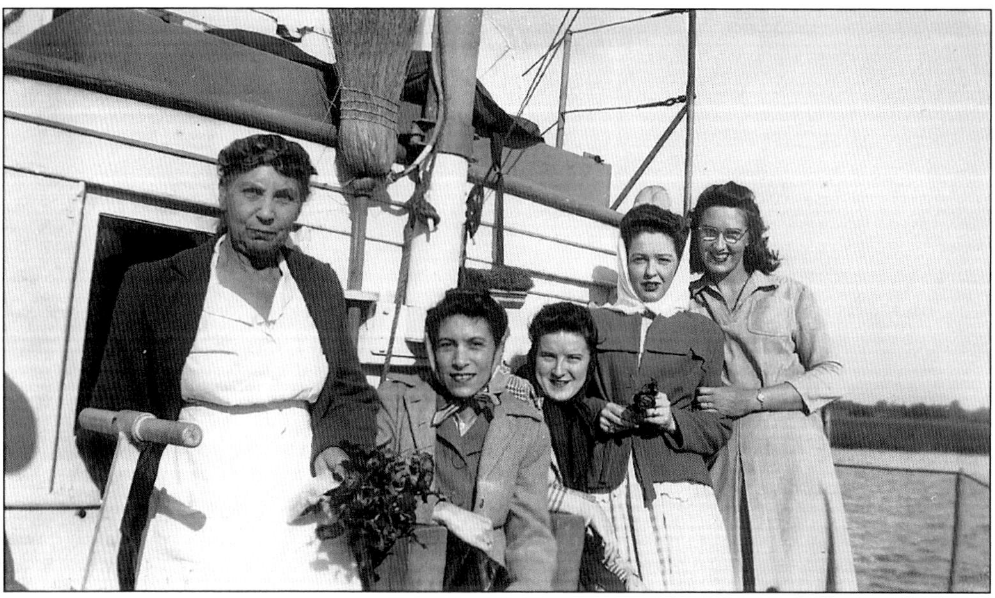

Because it was an 80-mile trip from Mount Pleasant to Charleston via Moncks Corner, the coast guard offered water transportation until April 4 when a Bailey bridge was put in place. Permanent repairs were completed in June and cost more than $300,000. Since the ship that damaged the bridge had been chartered by the federal government, the state collected almost all the cost of the repairs when it sued. This group of workers on their way to Charleston seem pleased that transportation by the Coast Guard is available.

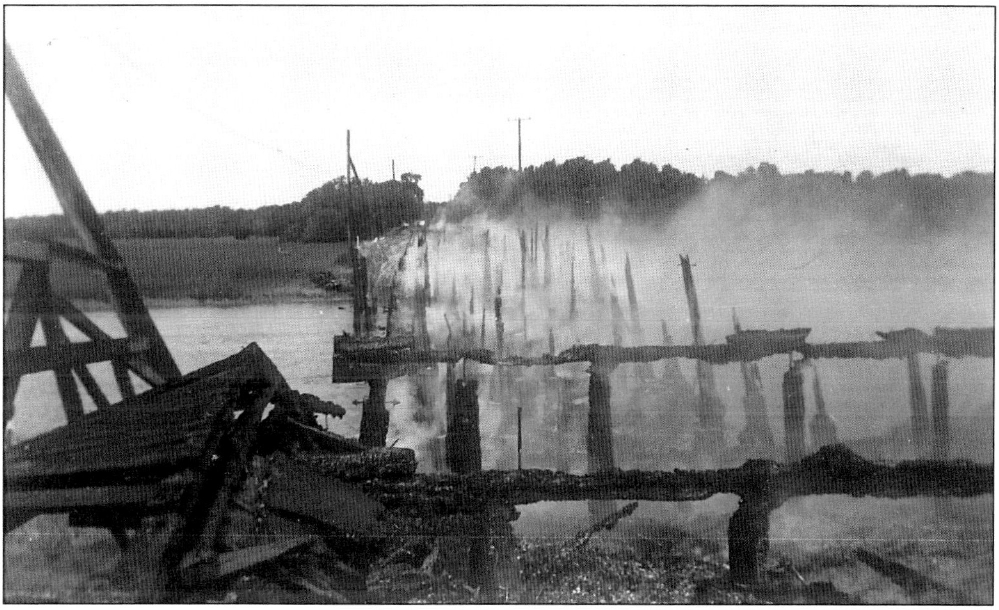

In the early 1940s the wooden bridge over Shem Creek was destroyed when a two-car collision started a fire. As seen in the image, it was totally engulfed in flames. Without a way to cross the creek, people on their way to Charleston from Mount Pleasant had to drive around the headwaters of Shem Creek by going north on Highway 17 to Bowman Road, left onto Mathis Ferry Road, then to the foot of the Cooper River Bridge. It was a trip of some seven miles; part of it was not paved. Arthur Ravenel's efforts resulted in the new bridge being built.

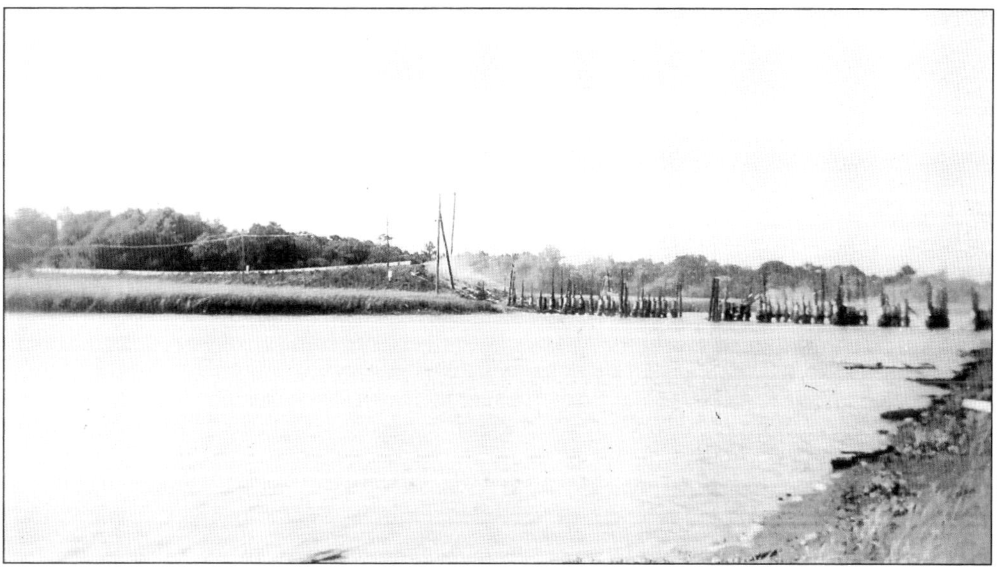

This distant view of the bridge on fire shows it being consumed to the approaches. The replacement bridge was constructed of steel and concrete and is still in use. This World War II Memorial Bridge honors the four young men from Mount Pleasant who lost their lives—Lt. Col. Hampden E. Montgomery, 1st Lt. William G. Daniels, 2nd Lt. Robert F. Lancaster, and Boatswain. James M. Deer.

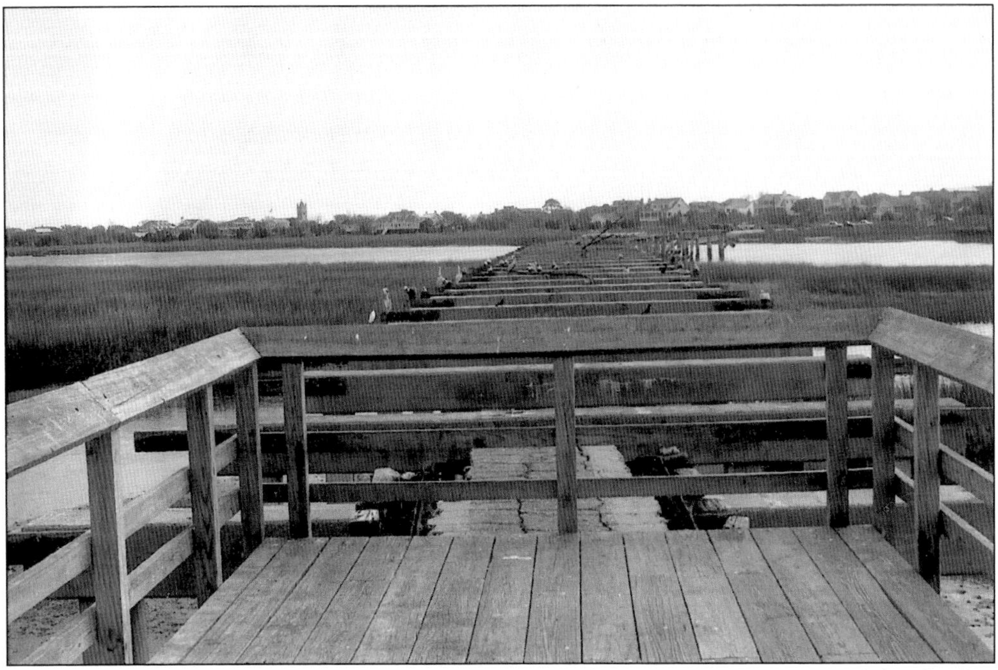

The old bridge, as it is known today, located at the end of Pitt Street was a steel drawbridge. It crossed Cove Inlet from Mount Pleasant to Sullivan's Island. When the Ben Sawyer bridge opened June 18, 1945 it was closed and partially dismantled. The Town of Mount Pleasant has made a fishing pier out of the remaining part.

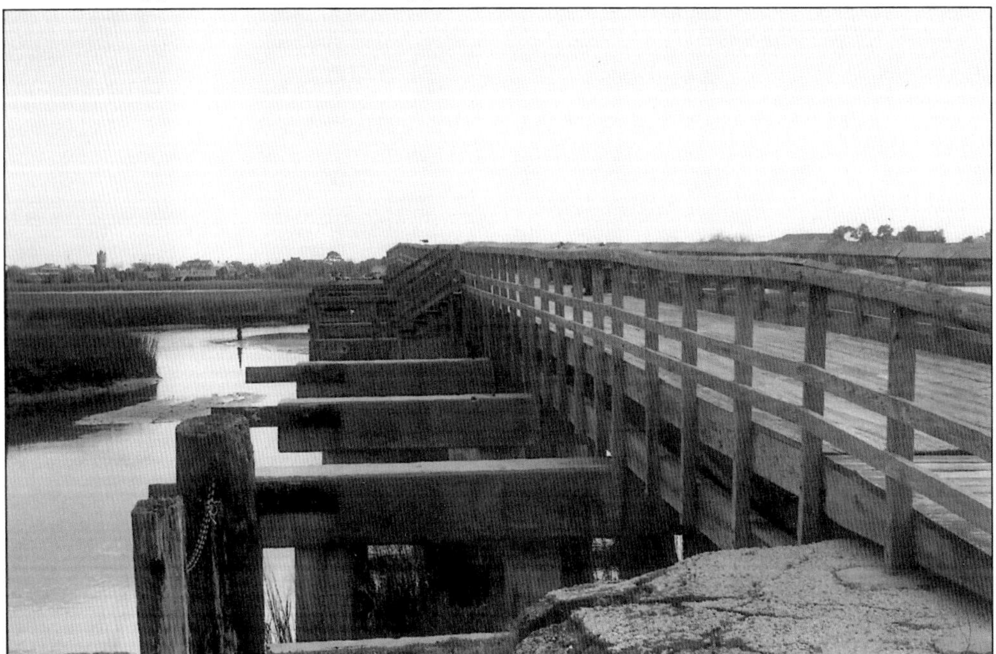

The old bridge extends through marsh, and is a great bird watching spot. Places to the left still indicate the trestle used by the trolleys in the early years of the 1900s as they rattled their way to Sullivan's Island from the Hibben Street ferry wharf.

Eleven

The War Years

Headlines in the Charleston News and Courier *of December 7, 1941, declared "U.S. and Japan at War" after the attack on Pearl Harbor. Tire rationing began January 5, 1942 with only vehicles in essential public service being eligible for tubes and tires. Food stamps allotted scarce items on the home front. Lookouts were posted on the Cooper River Bridge. Surveillance of the waters was carried on for the appearance of enemy submarines. The Charleston Naval Shipyard went into high gear to provide needed ships and supplies. With the draft taking the young men, girls became welders and did other critical work. Mount Pleasant was doing its share in the war effort. This chapter highlights some of the activities both at home and abroad during the war years and 50 years later.*

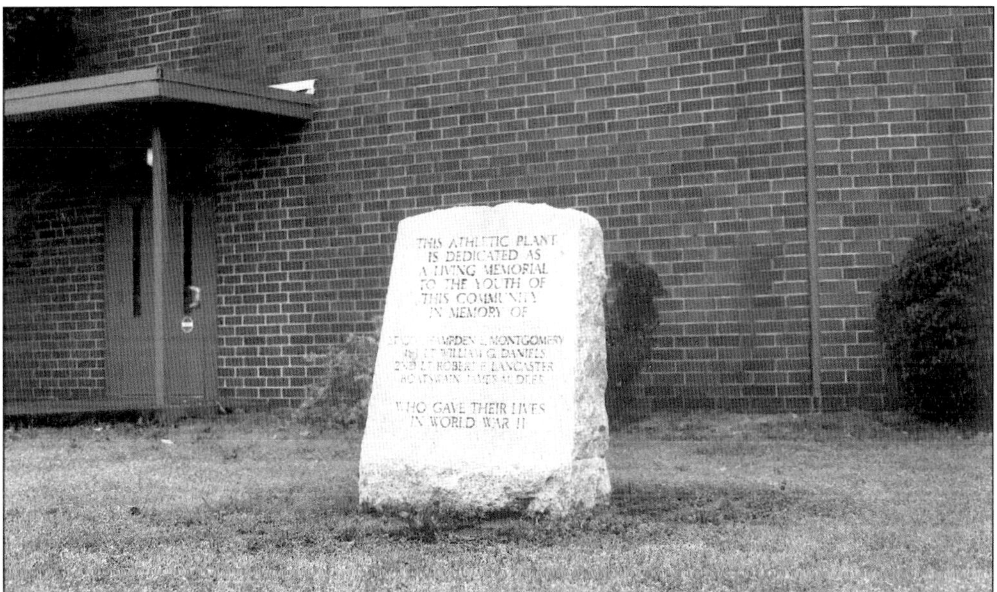

The granite monument in front of the Moultrie school gymnasium pictured here states "This athletic plant is dedicated as a living memorial to the youth of the community in memory of Lt. Col. Hampden E. Montgomery, 1st Lt. William G. Daniels, 2nd Lt. Robert F. Lancaster, and Boatswain. James M. Deer," the four young men who gave their lives in World War II and for whom the bridge over Shem Creek is also named. The Museum on the Common in 1995 hosted a traveling exhibit and also paid tribute with a rose garden in the shape of a star, with the fifth rose being a Peace variety.

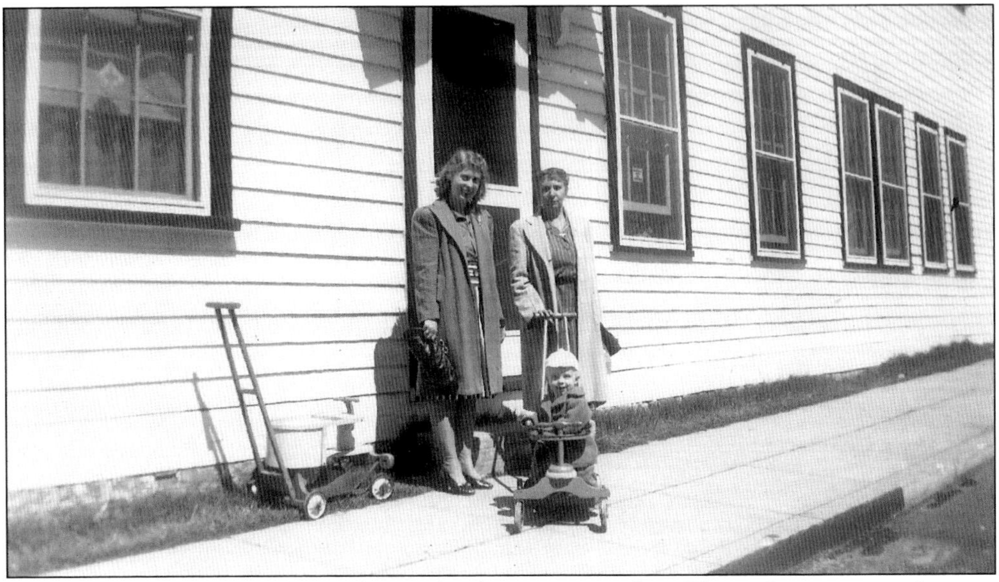

With the men away on both war fronts, families came together. The multigenerational groups found help by having each other nearby. These family members stand in front of the Doughty Apartments on Venning at Pitt Streets. Note the design of the stroller, a far cry from the elegant ones of today.

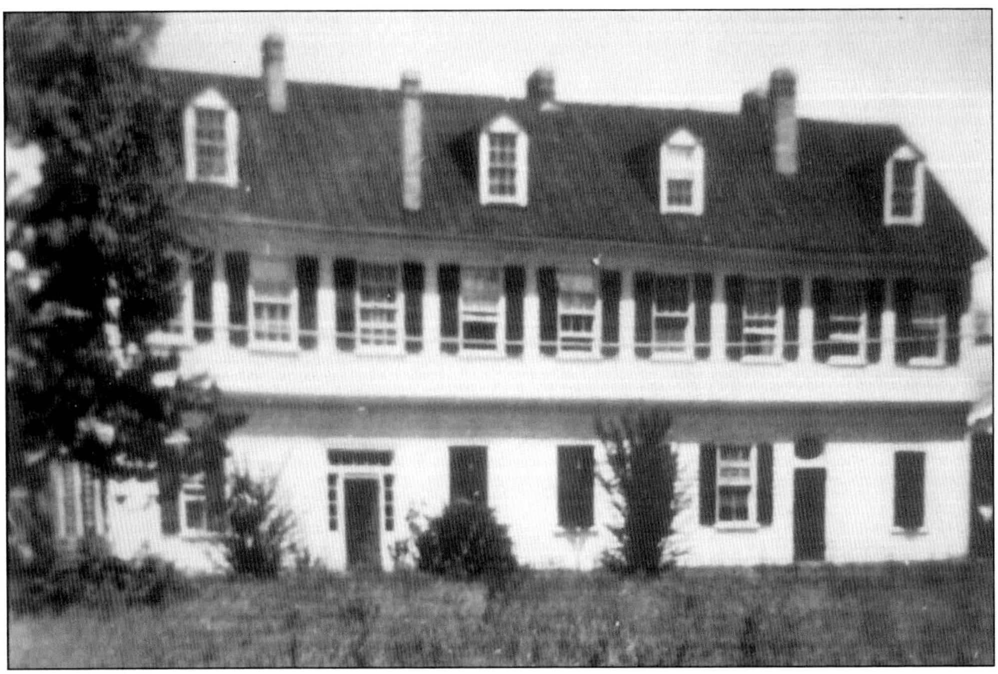

Demand for housing increased as the war continued and work at the Charleston Naval Shipyard expanded. Patjens store on Church Street was converted into apartments, as were various other houses.

Sewing clubs were organized to provide items of clothing for the servicemen. Knitting needles clicked as members produced wool socks, scarves, sweaters, and other items. Sewing machines worked overtime on shirts and pants. Ladies rolled thousands of yards of material into bandages. The ten ladies shown here formed one of the sewing clubs.

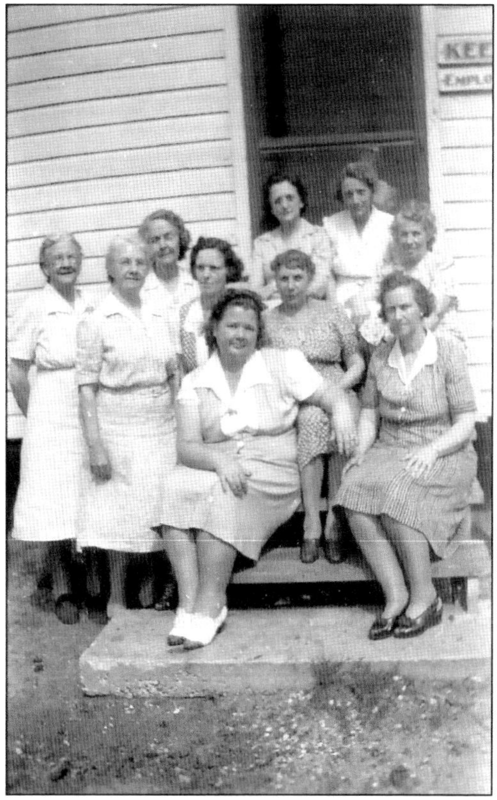

Christmas came as usual, but with the boys away in the war, things were quite subdued. Pictures were so important, both from the home front and from overseas. Letters from her three sons were read and re-read, then saved. All three returned safely. A number of Mount Pleasant families had several sons in the war. The following pages illustrate where two bothers served their country in the South Pacific and in India.

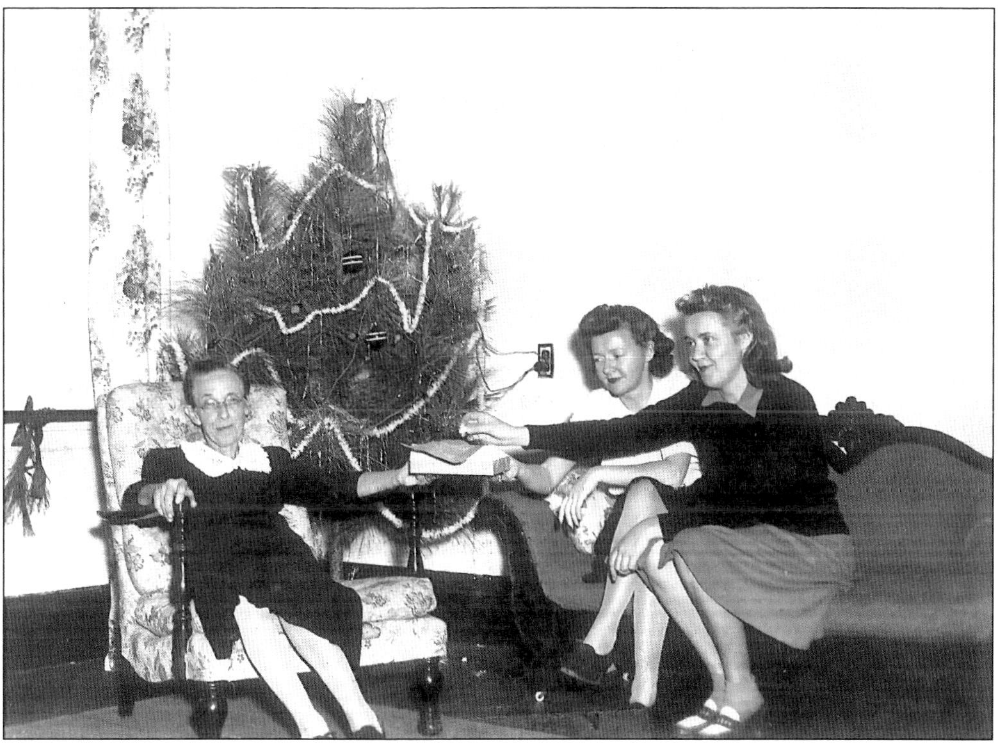

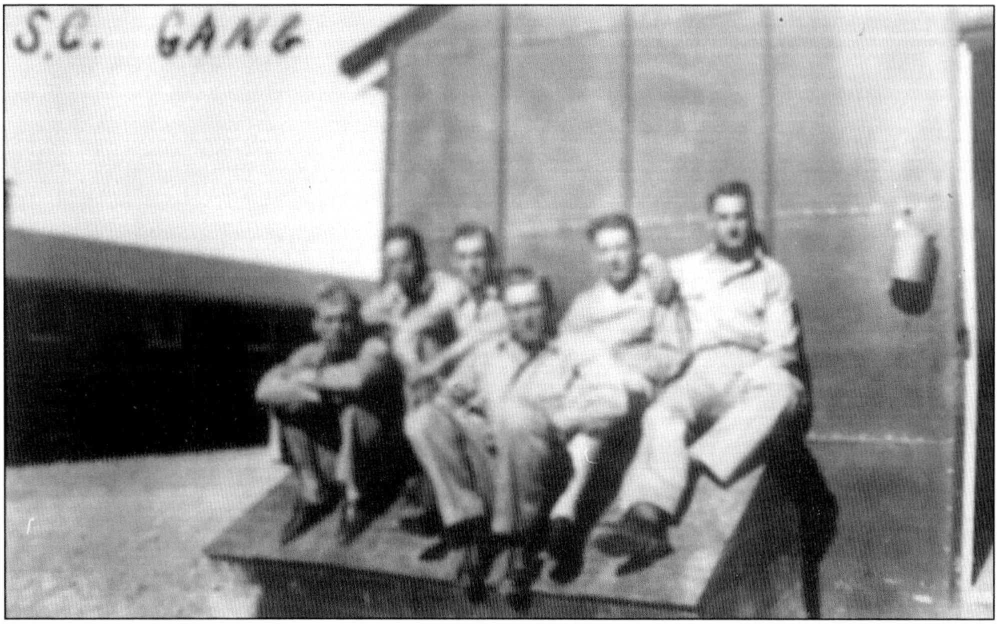

Friendship in far away places is always possible when you locate others from your own state as these young men at boot camp have discovered. Utah's landscape, climate, and vegetation was all quite different from South Carolina, but finding something in common and pleasant appeared to cheer the boys far from home.

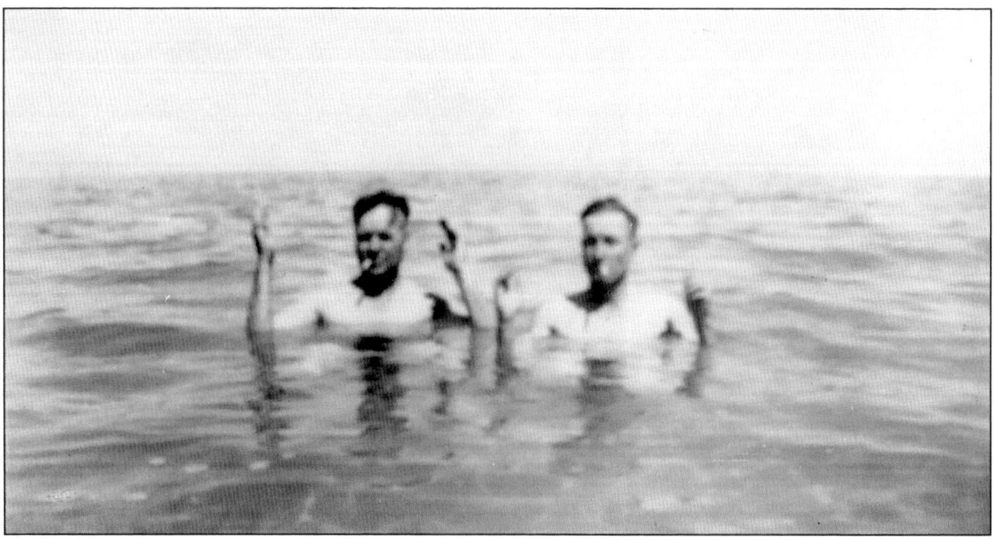

Swimming in the Great Salt Lake was quite an experience as you can see. It was quite different from the Atlantic Ocean back home, but it still provided a bit of recreation. Salt Lake City was not too far from camp and was a place to go when leave was granted for these boys from Mount Pleasant.

After training in Utah, the Mount Pleasant young man was sent to the other side of the world, to Guadalcanal. Again everything was different from the Lowcountry of South Carolina. The sign noted that the Red Cross provided a service club. Another picture he took captured the "Mosquito Bowl," which was something he felt he knew something about.

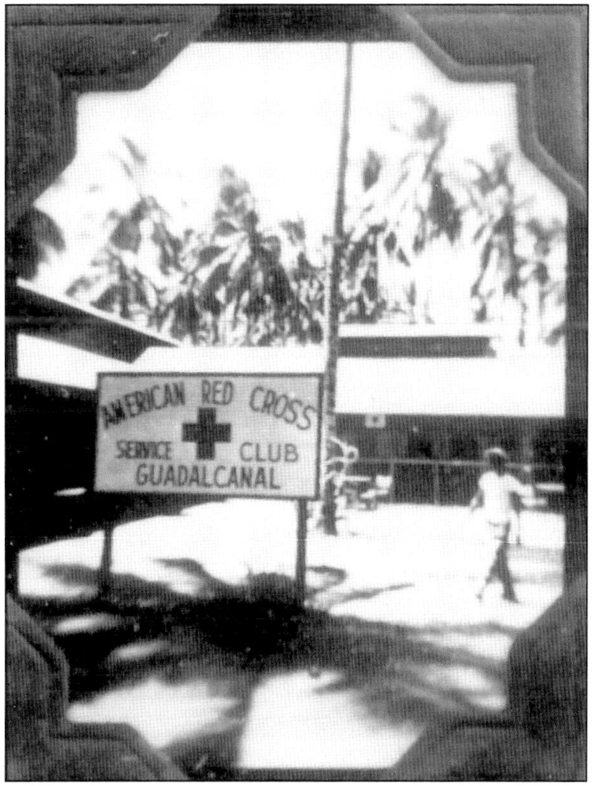

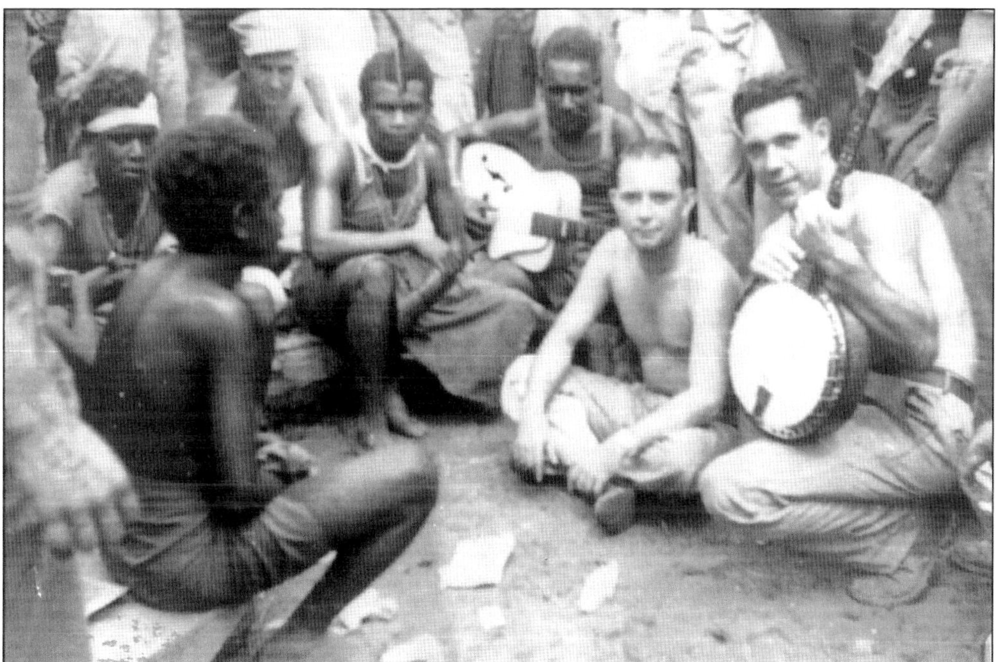

Again friends are where you find them. A series of pictures with the Guadalcanal natives being entertained and entertaining with banjo and guitar music was sent home to Mount Pleasant.

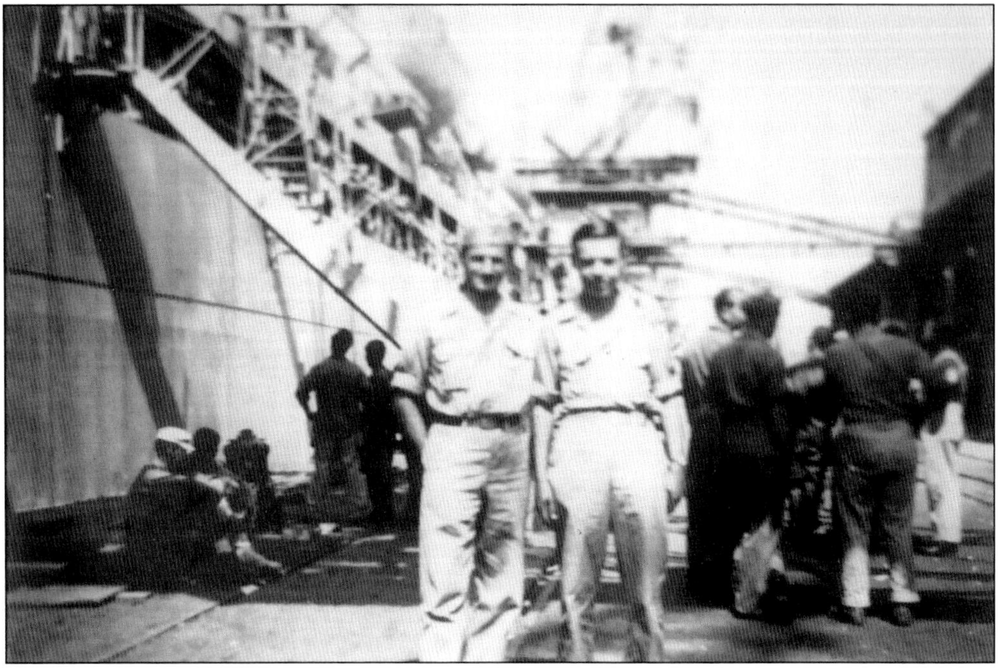

The young man from Mount Pleasant (right) went around the world in his tour with the United States Army. From a camp in Louisiana, he was sent to Pennsylvania, then Norfolk where a transport ship carried him to Casa Blanca. The trip continued to Oran, Port Said, the Red Sea, Bombay, and finally by train to Calcutta. After a year and a half in India his journey continued eastward until he was again in the United States—but this time, on the West Coast.

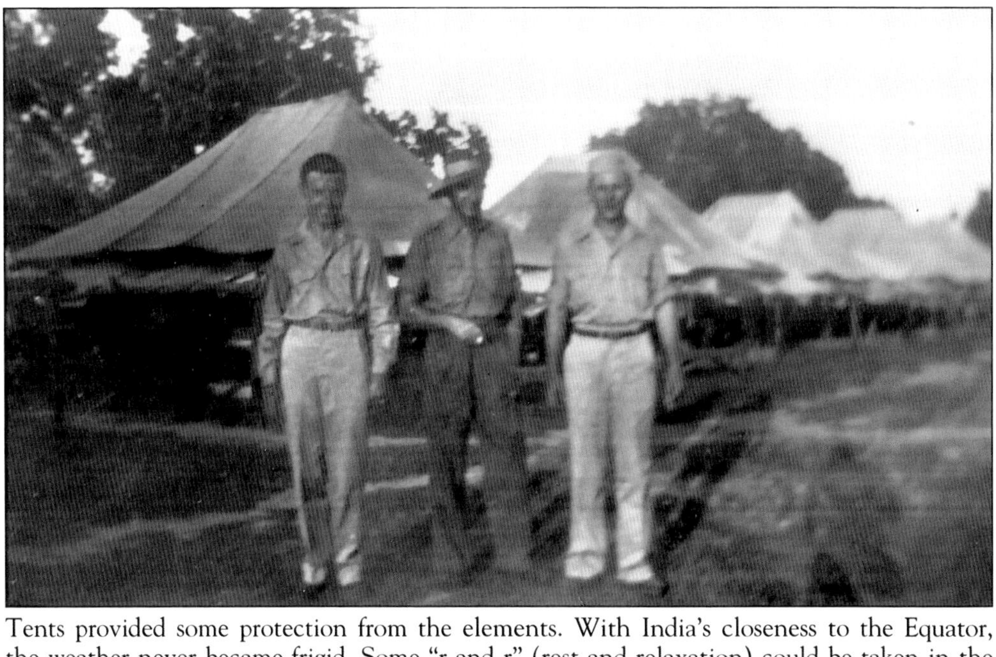

Tents provided some protection from the elements. With India's closeness to the Equator, the weather never became frigid. Some "r and r" (rest and relaxation) could be taken in the mountains. The man on the left was from Mount Pleasant.

The Indian bearer named Samnaryan smiles as he holds up a copy of the Charleston *News and Courier*. The Soldier is reading a copy of *Life* magazine.

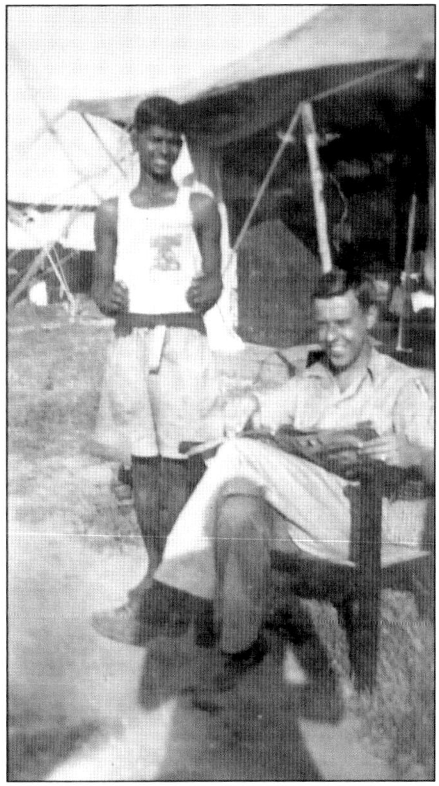

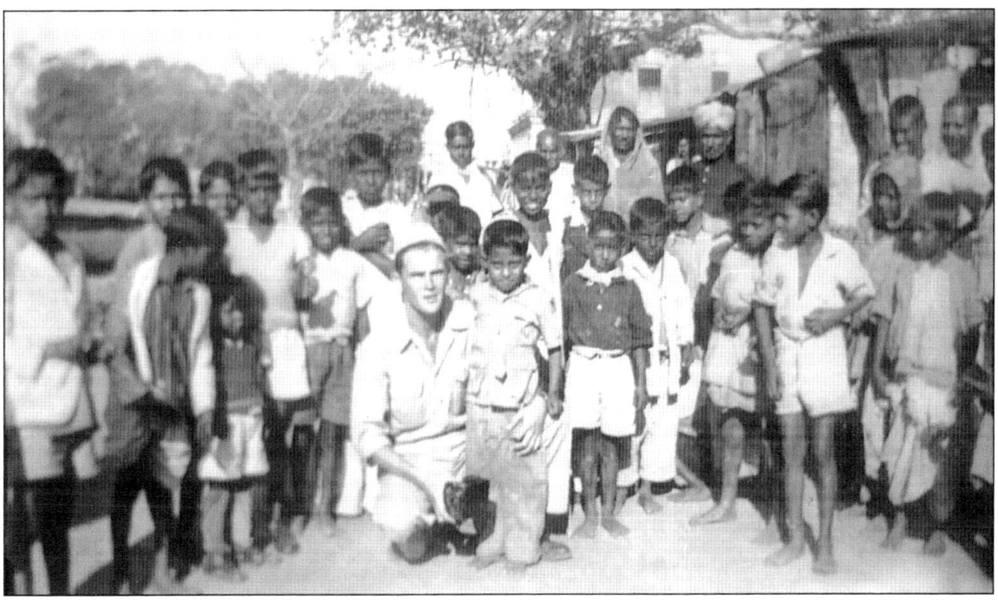

Some of the villagers of Kanchrapara pose with their new friend from America.

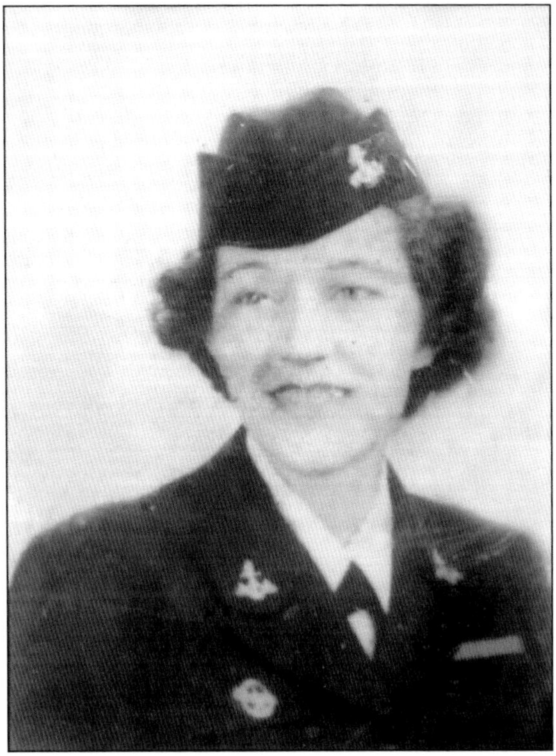

Young ladies also served their country in the military during the war. Stationed at Hunter College in New York, this Mount Pleasant girl worked in personnel. She had enlisted in the WAVES in the summer of 1943 and served until the end of the war. When the war was over she returned to South Carolina and worked in several responsible positions at the VA (Veteran's Administration) and later at the *News and Courier* in personnel.

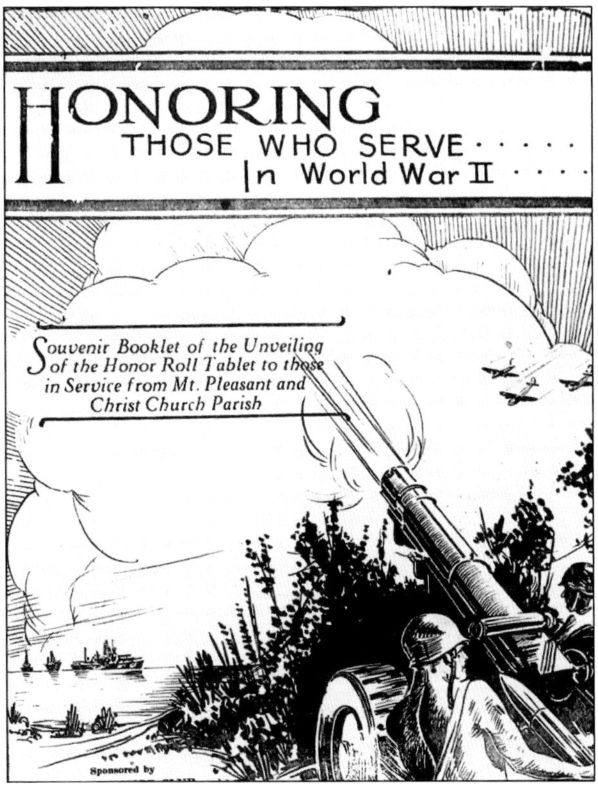

This 40-page booklet honoring those who served in World War II was compiled by the Exchange Club. On July 22, 1944, a year after the club had been chartered a program was held that included patriotic music, pledge to the flag, address by Mayor Erckmann, and a reading of the 143 names of those who were serving their country. The invocation and the benediction were pronounced by local ministers. Articles covered the history of Christ Church Parish, future of East Charleston County, the schools, the yacht club, and basket weaving. Advertisements were from establishments in Charleston and Mount Pleasant.

Major W.W. North was a veteran airman. His little airstrip was on Remley's Point just outside the town. As a member of the Civil Air Patrol he aided the Coast Guard in tracking submarines. He flew many search operations trying to locate the clear trail of oils from the exhaust in the water that indicated their presence. If they raised the periscope it left a straight line. The picture and article by *News and Courier* reporter Pertuit shows North at age 73 in 1961.

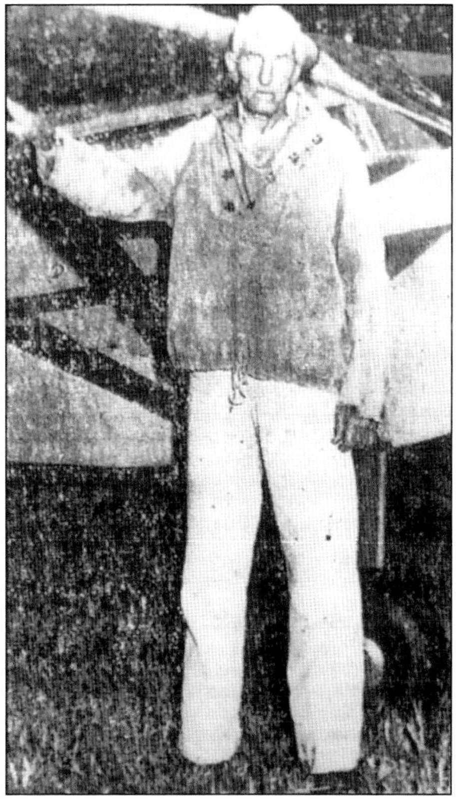

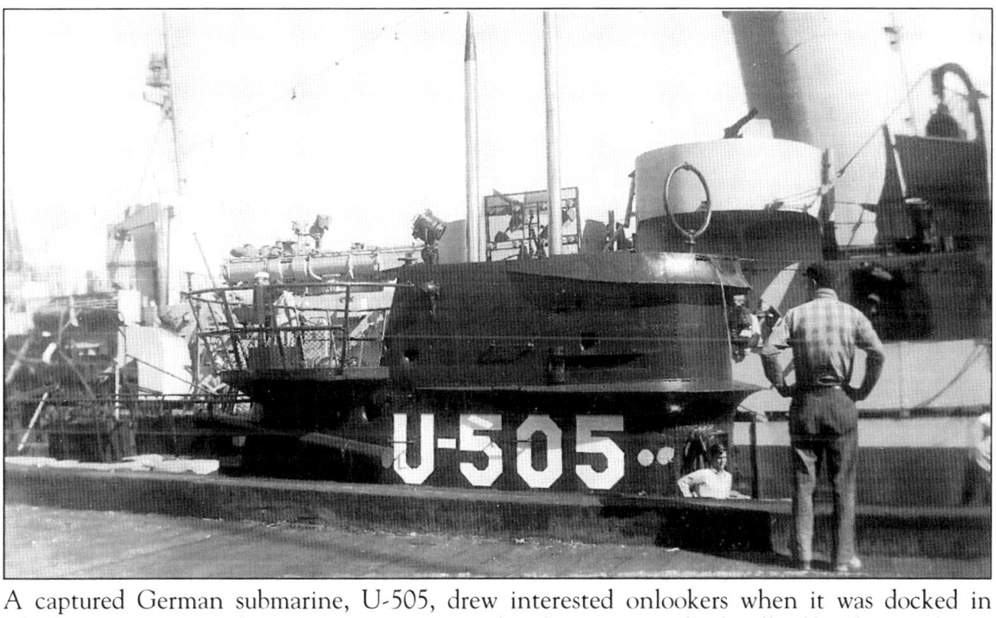

A captured German submarine, U-505, drew interested onlookers when it was docked in Charleston on November 3, 1945. Stories circulated concerning foodstuffs of local origin being found aboard.

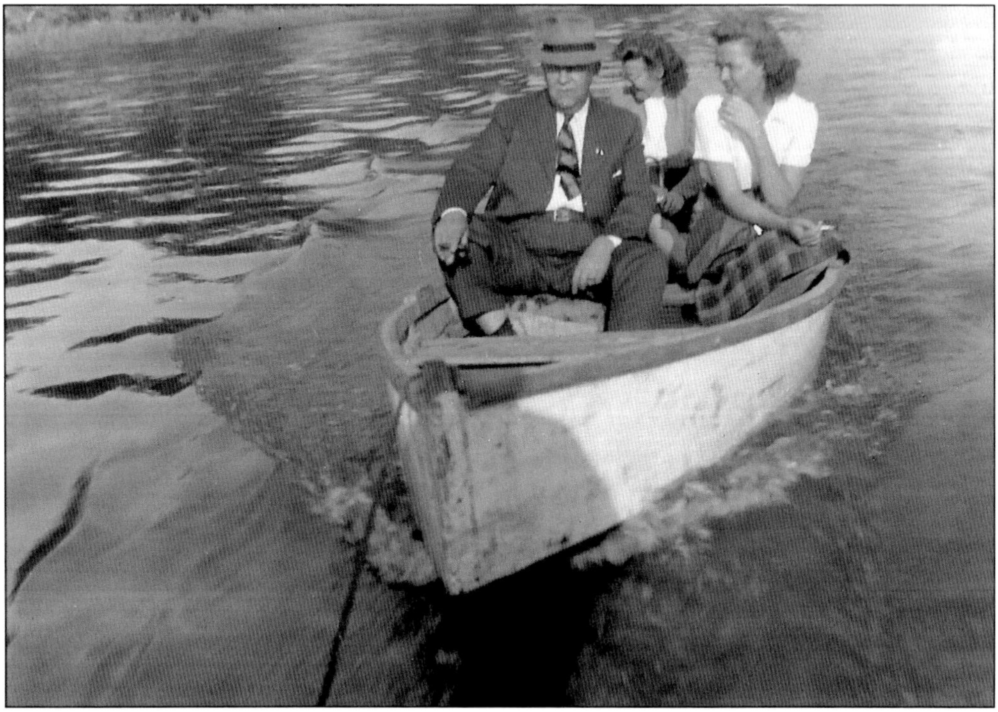

After the war ended, the Navy mothballed many ships in the Wando River. Whatever was in them was dumped into the water. A favorite Sunday afternoon excursion for the local people was to search the water for whatever could be found, as these three friends are doing.

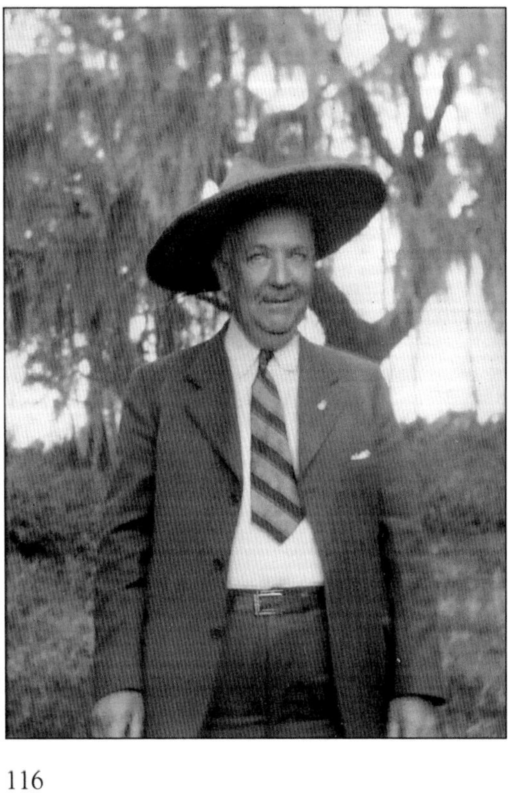

The gentleman models a hat that he found in the Wando River, which may have come from the Orient. During the week he worked as a bookkeeper at Bay Fruit Company on Market Street.

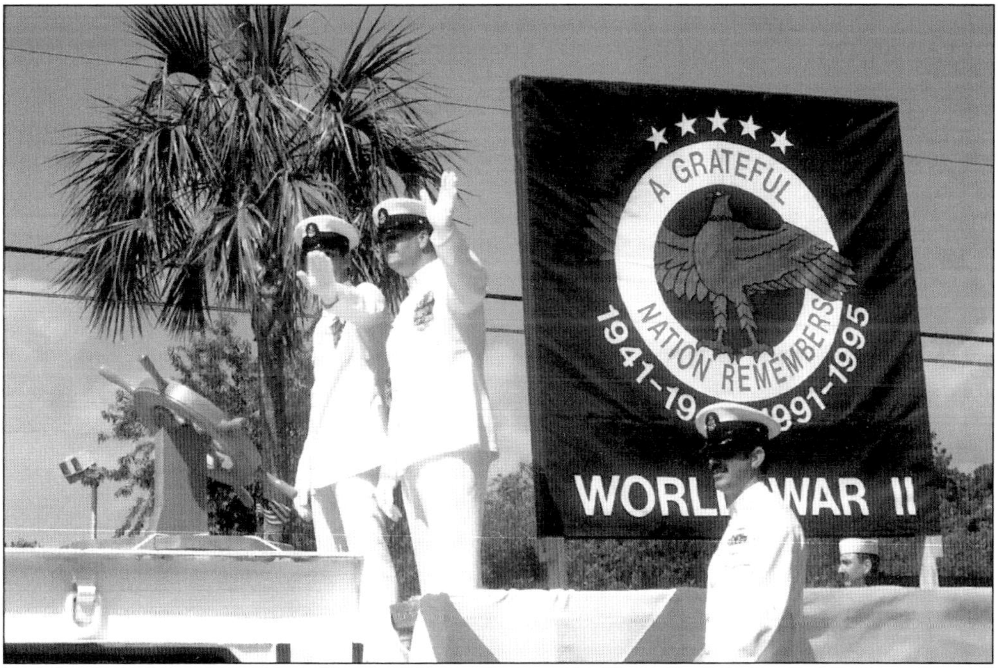

World War II was over in 1945. Fifty years later Mount Pleasant celebrated the event with exhibits, parades, and concerts. The Museum on the Common had a special traveling exhibit called "The World in Flames, World War II," with documents from the National Archives. It filled one of the adjacent suites with memorabilia. The words on the float shown above—"A Grateful Nation Remembers"—capture the essence of the parade.

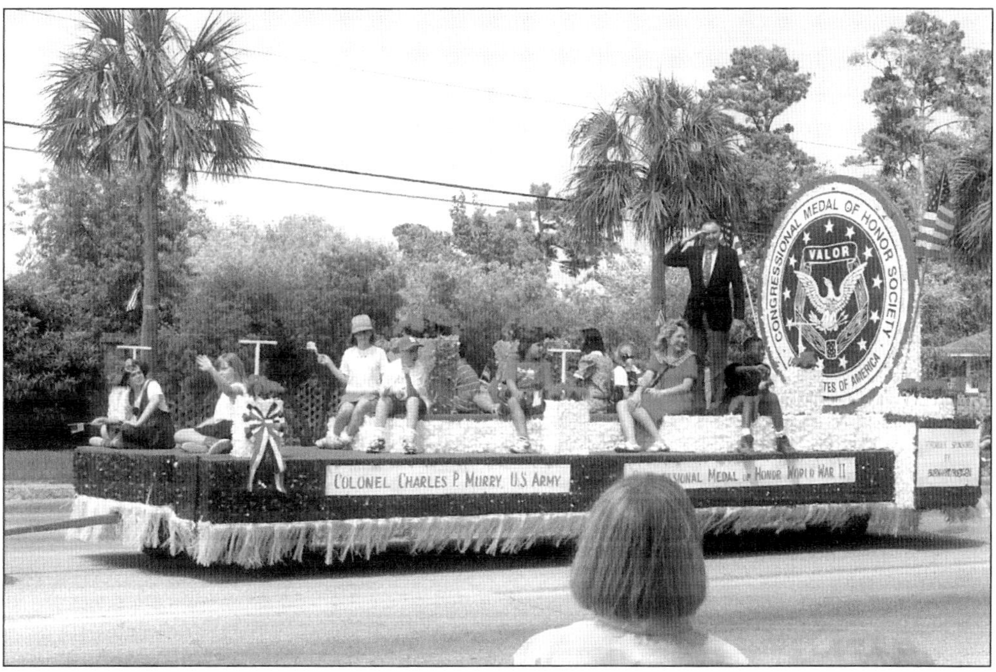

The Congressional Medal of Honor exhibit arrived at Patriots Point and was added to the permanent displays there.

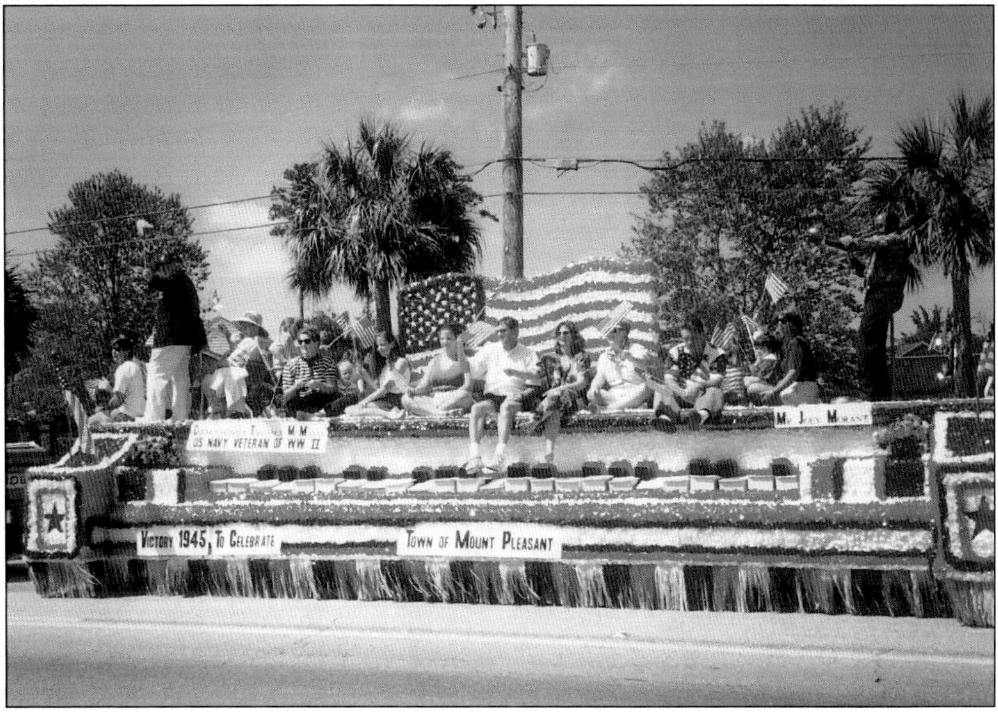

The "Victory '45" parade included many floats, like the one shown above. It was sponsored by the Town of Mount Pleasant and featured an American flag with various dignitaries aboard.

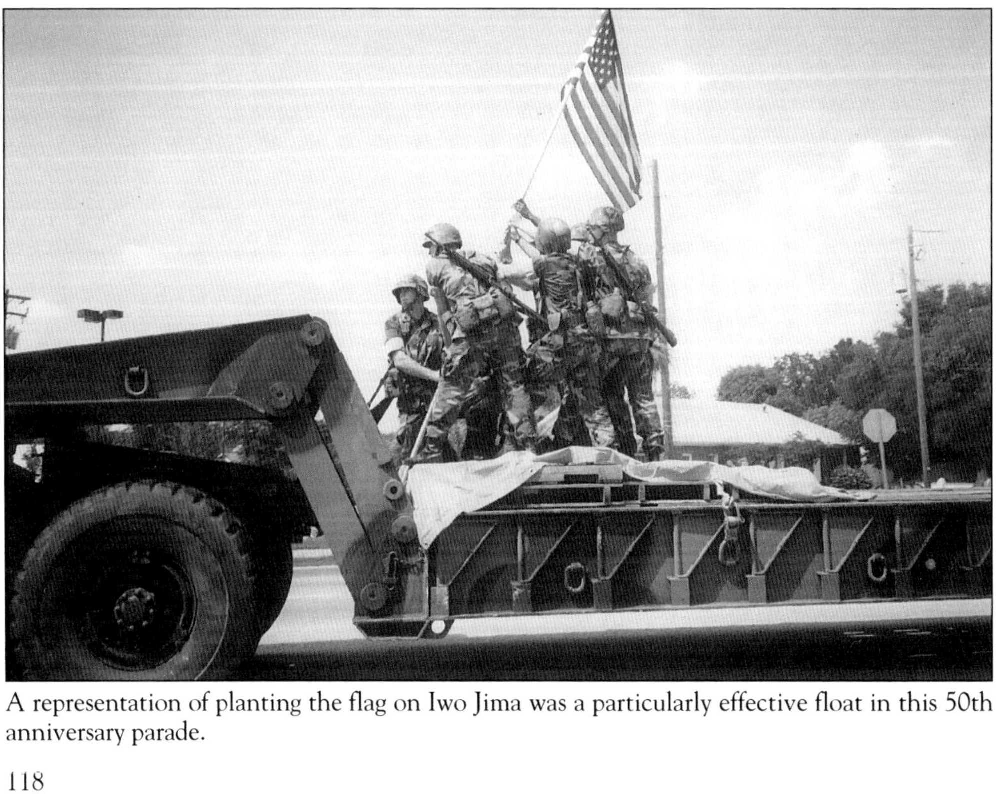

A representation of planting the flag on Iwo Jima was a particularly effective float in this 50th anniversary parade.

Twelve

EVENTS

At the end of the 20th century many events were taking place as the town expanded rapidly. A brief mention of three will conclude this story of the Friendly Town: the 1975 arrival of the aircraft carrier Yorktown *for the naval museum at Patriots Point, the 1987 celebration of the town's sesquicentennial, and the 1989 devastation by Hurricane Hugo. Other events of interest at century' s conclusion include the Scottish Games at Boone Hall, the Cooper River Bridge Run, the Children's Festival, the Blessing of the Fleet, the Parade of Boats, and the development of the Wando Terminal.*

Mention needs to be made of the work of archaeologists who document areas before they are developed. They trace ownership records as well as discover what secrets the land holds of past habitations. They are literally our historians today.

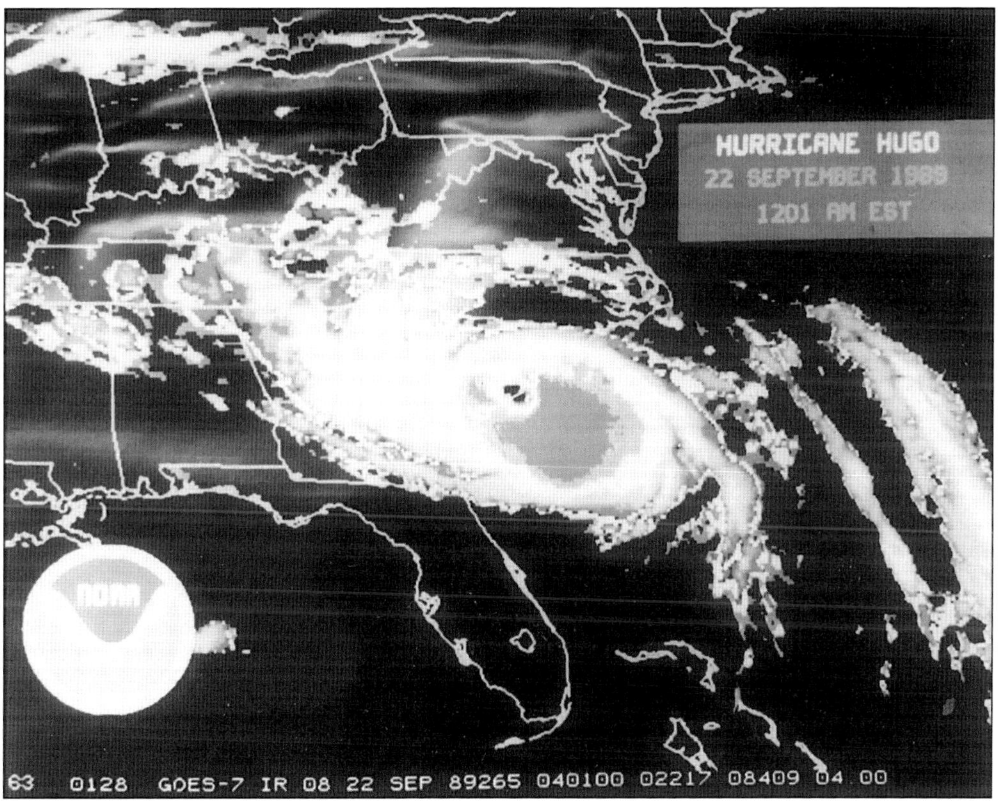

The image here is the NOAA picture of the immense storm named Hugo of September 21, 1989 that changed the landscape of the Lowcountry.

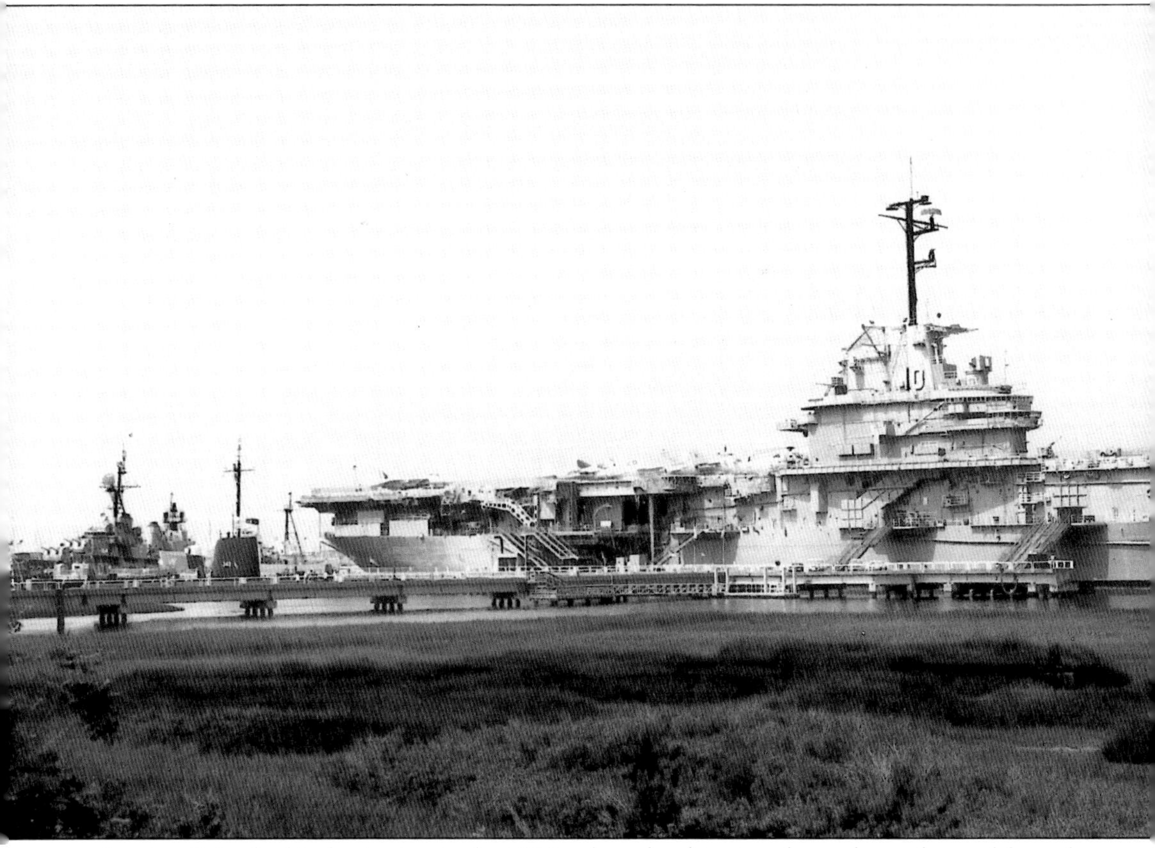

Patriots Point had its beginning in the 1950s when the shipping channel was changed from the James Island side of Charleston harbor to the Mount Pleasant side and tons of dredged material (called spoil) were deposited on the marsh in an area known as Hog Island. The resulting infestation of mosquitoes from the cracked mud flats caused the Mosquito Abatement Program to be established. Part of the 500 acres, which was a splendid place to find sharks' teeth and fossils, became a Naval Museum Complex. After years of planning the World War II aircraft carrier the *Yorktown* arrived in 1975. On its first day opened to the public, January 3, 1976, over 2,500 visitors came. A ceremony was led by Gov. James B. Edwards and Mount Pleasant Mayor G. Magrath Darby. The image above shows the complex with the Destroyer Laffey, Coast Guard Cutter Ingham, Submarine Clamagore, and #10 the "Fighting Lady" aircraft carrier with about 25 aircraft on her deck. A golf course, hotel complex, marina, and ball field are located on the rest of the acreage.

Mount Pleasant observed its sesquicentennial of incorporation with a week-long celebration in October 1987. Pictured is the cover of the souvenir booklet that contained a history of the town as well as the program of events, which included regattas, dances, drama, band and choir concerts, art exhibits, Civil War reenactment, fireworks, and a gala ball aboard the Yorktown. The festivities ended with a parade on Sunday, October 18. A video, "A Journey Through Time," was made, which portrayed the town's history as told by various residents and was narrated by Dean Swanson of local television.

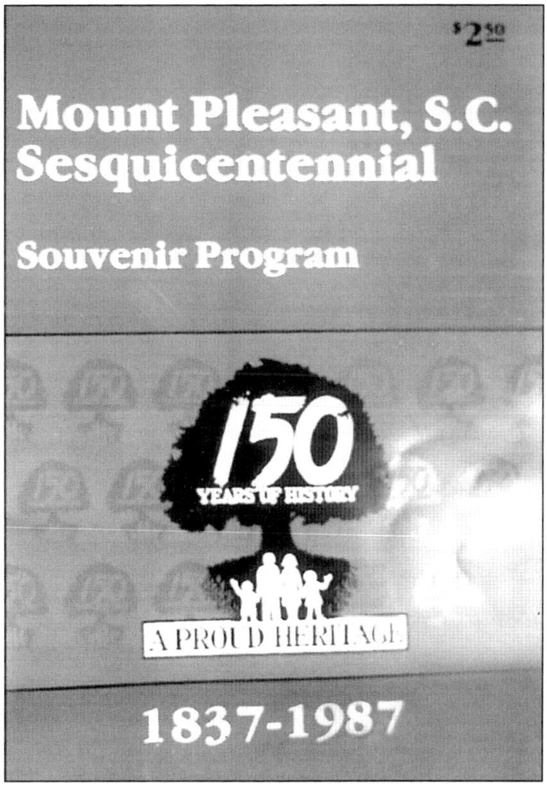

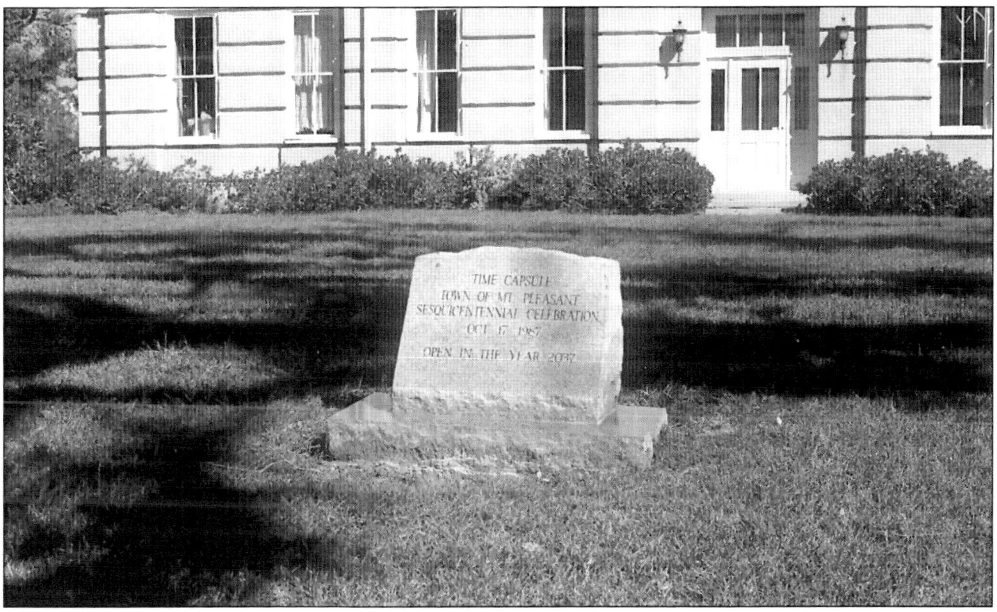

One of the events was the placing of a time capsule on the grounds of the town hall as seen here. The inscription indicated it was to be opened in 2037, the year Mount Pleasant will turn 200. Richard L. Jones was the mayor; R. Mac Burdette, administrator; and James B. Bagwell III, chairman of the sesquicentennial committee. The theme was "150 Years of History, a Proud Heritage."

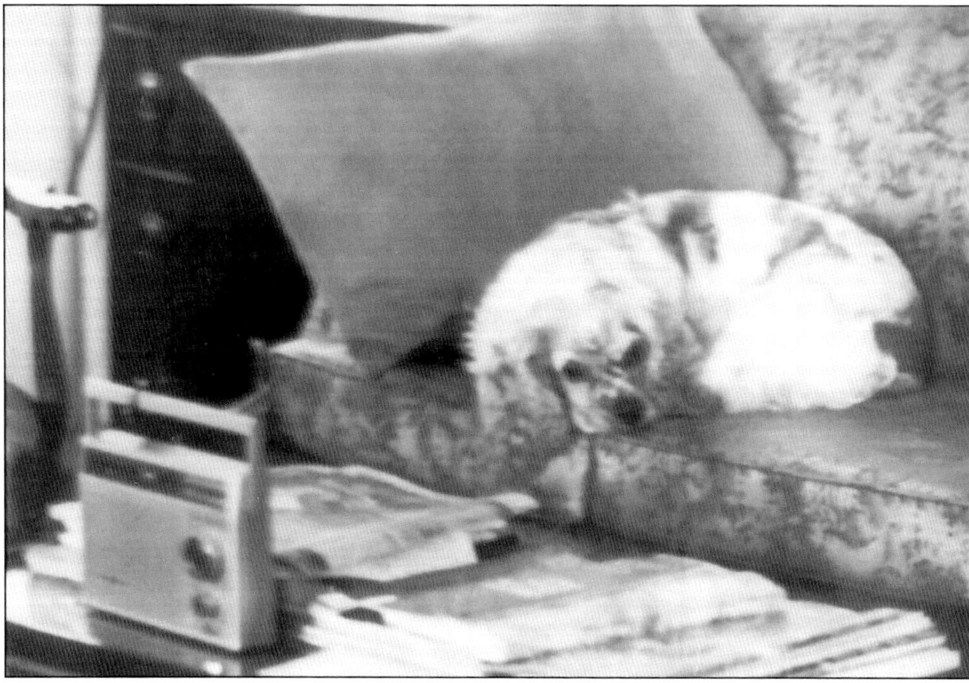

After spending days off shore, the hurricane was taking direct aim at the Charleston coast. Like other animals, this cocker spaniel sensed that something strange was about to take place. By 10:30 p.m., the electricity was gone. By 1:00 a.m. the eye had passed with a deceptive calmness. By 4:30 a.m. the storm had roared northward cutting a swath 50 miles wide throughout the whole state and into the next, some 200 miles in some 500 minutes. The damage it did to the forest was more than the combined disasters of Mount St. Helens, Hurricane Camille, and fires at Yellowstone.

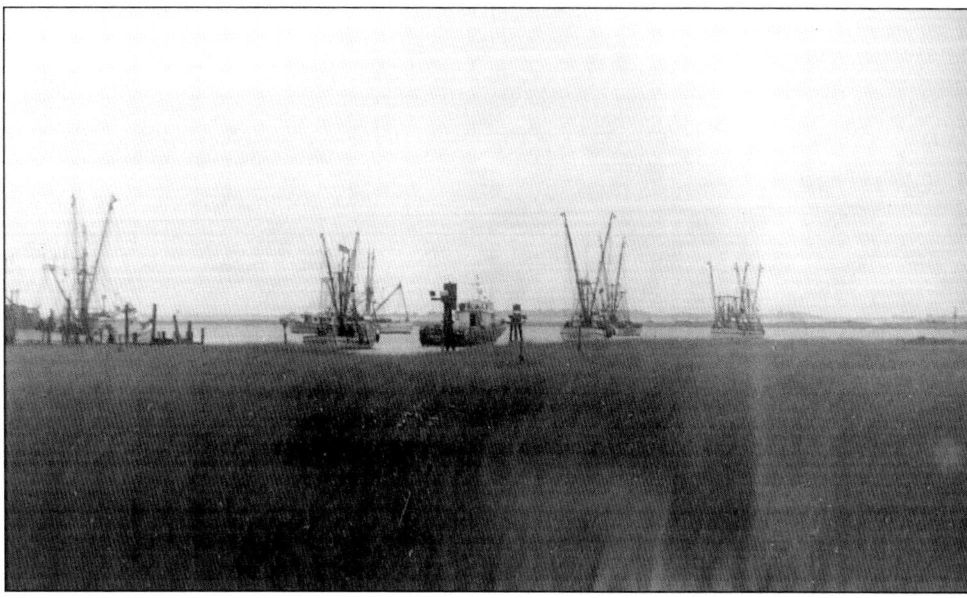

The trawlers on Shem Creek decided to leave and seek a safer place away from the harbor area. The storm found them and one by one they sank as reported by their captains.

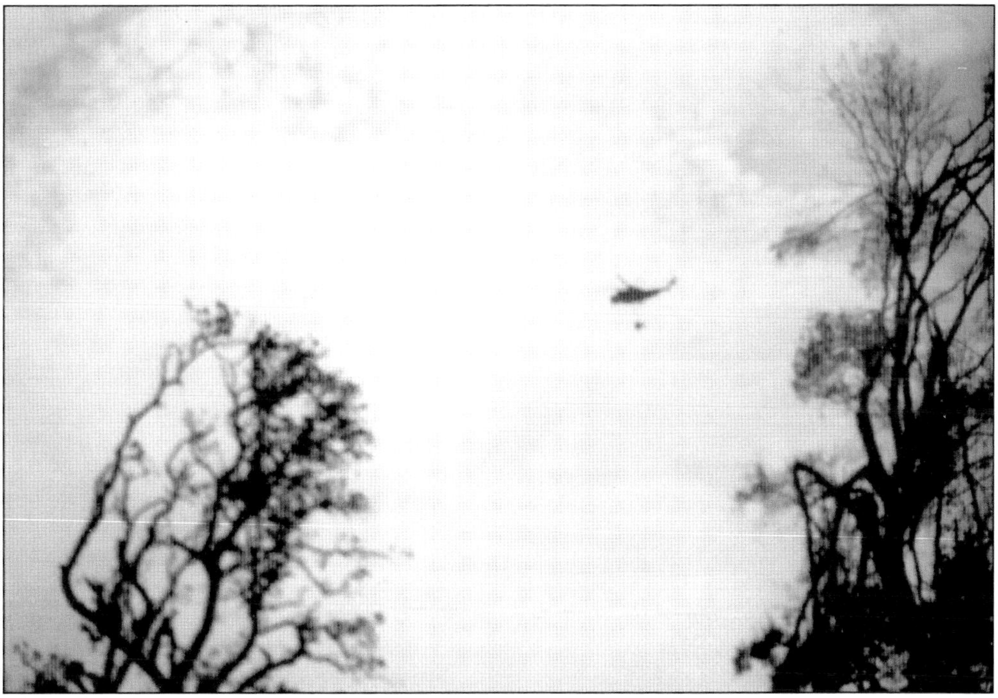

Planes flew mercy missions, and helicopters carried supplies to the islands. Noise filled the days with clean-up operations, and the islands were off limits. The Ben Sawyer bridge broke, while for some, the electricity did not come on for eleven days. Those with gas stoves were able to prepare food. Mount Pleasant Waterworks continued in operation because of the flow of the artesian wells, while telephones worked spasmodically. The newspaper was printed and delivered.

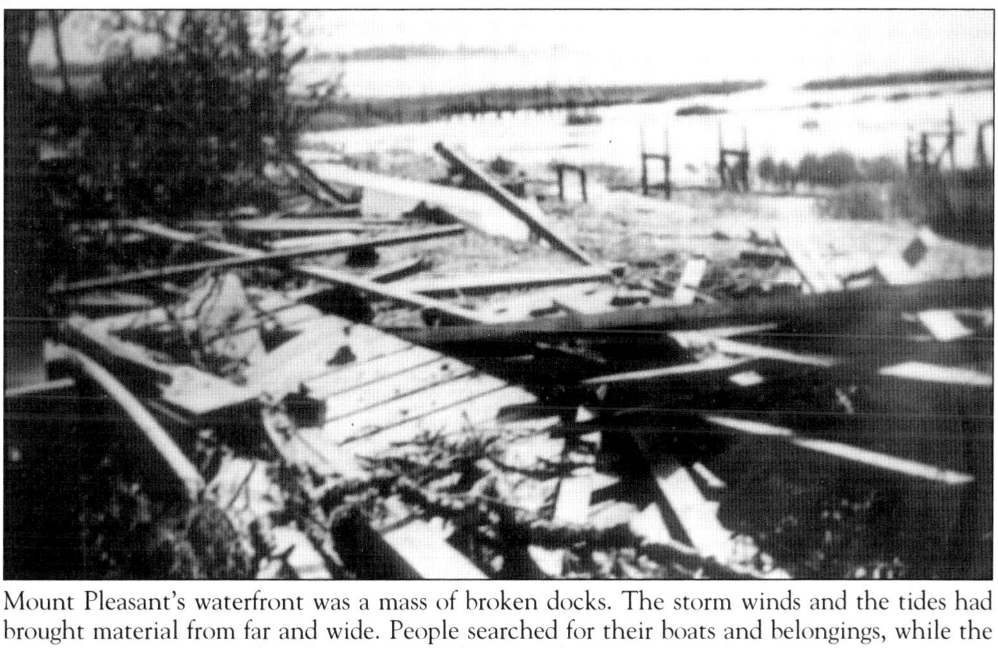

Mount Pleasant's waterfront was a mass of broken docks. The storm winds and the tides had brought material from far and wide. People searched for their boats and belongings, while the curious came in to see what devastation had occurred.

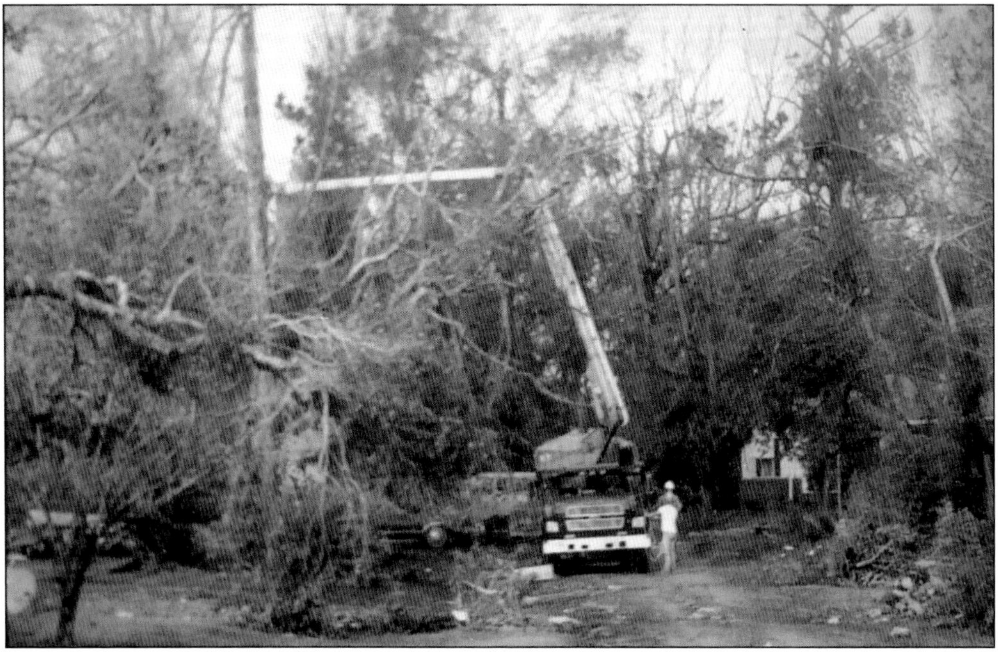

It is hard to believe, but a street is really under all the debris in this image. Even more unbelievable is the speed with which help came from all over the country. Convoys of power companies' trucks came from everywhere to untangle the mass of wires and restore electricity. In addition to food, ice was a precious commodity. Lines formed as the grocery stores opened.

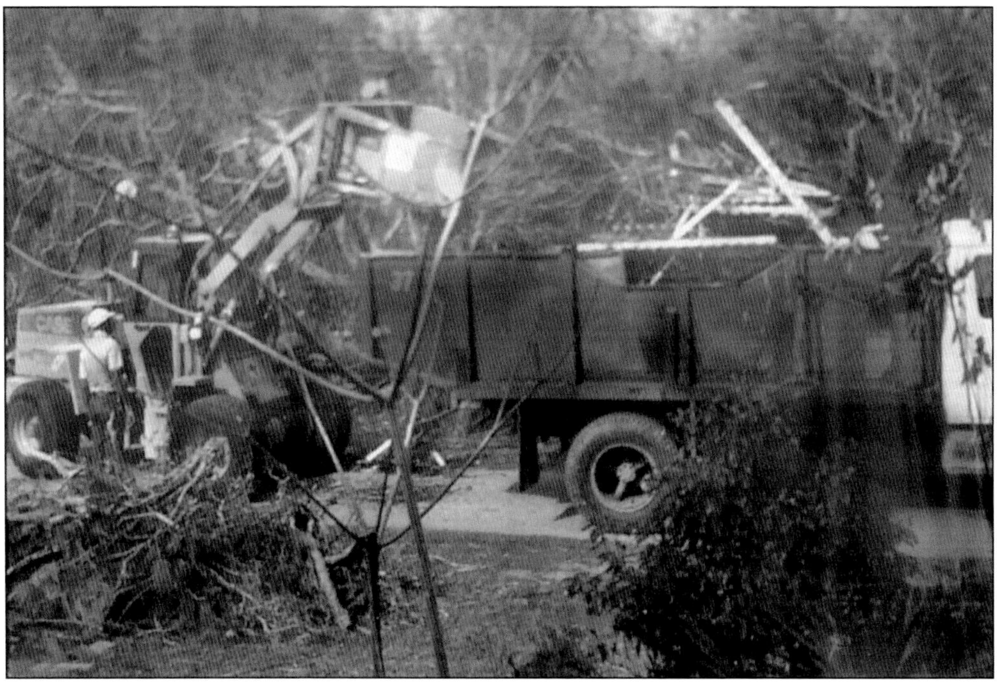

Manpower with huge trucks moved mountains of broken trees as well as household items strewn all over the area. Huge disposal sites burned continually in the north area. The National Guard was on duty, and curfews kept the people inside. Gradually life returned to "almost normal."

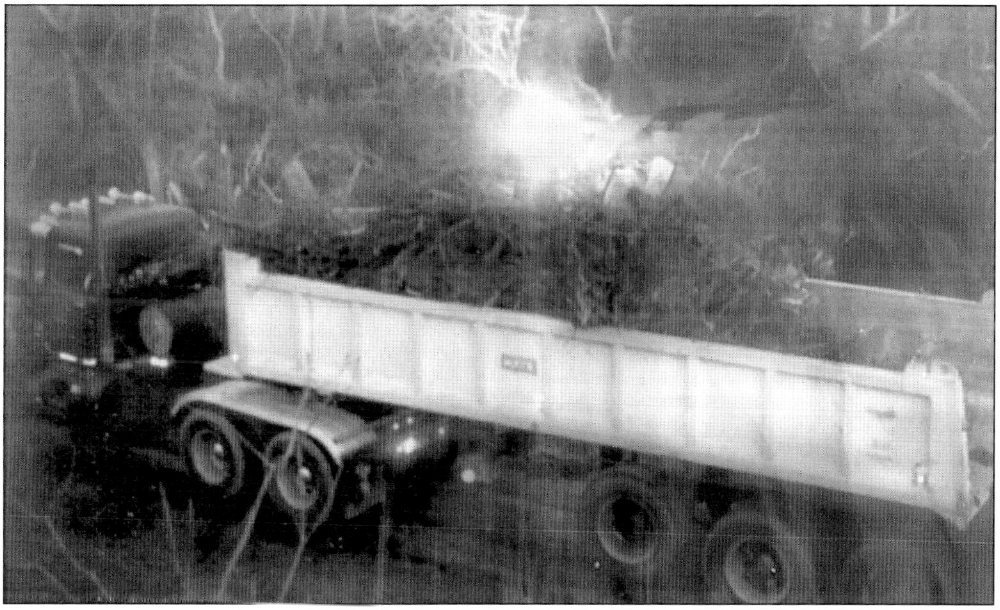

Trucks provided by FEMA worked around the clock to clear what nature had destroyed in a matter of hours. Weeks of clearing finally returned the landscape to the point where rebuilding could take place. Along Highway 17 tops of pines were sheared off at the same height as if a giant cutter had been at work. Stories of freak happenings included those of cabinets filled with fragile china and glass being moved out of the house by the storm and set down without anything being damaged. Other places, complete devastation had occurred from wind and water.

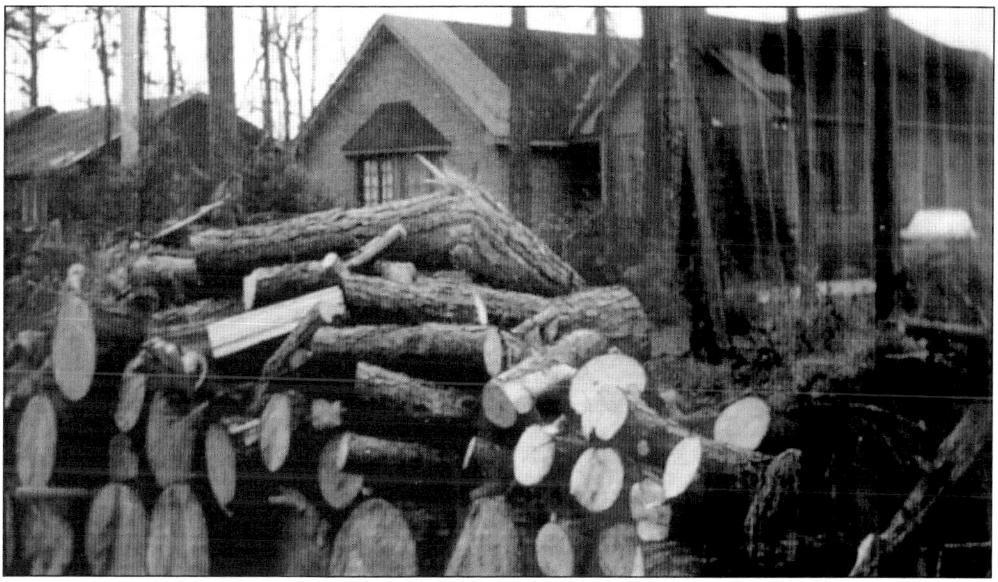

Tree trimmers appeared from everywhere. Some were out to make a buck; others were intent on helping people. The town tried to keep everything legal with licensed people doing the work. Piles of cut-up trees appeared along every street, as shown in this image. Roofs were covered with blue tarps to shield from the rain. Noise of chain saws and construction hammers filled the air.

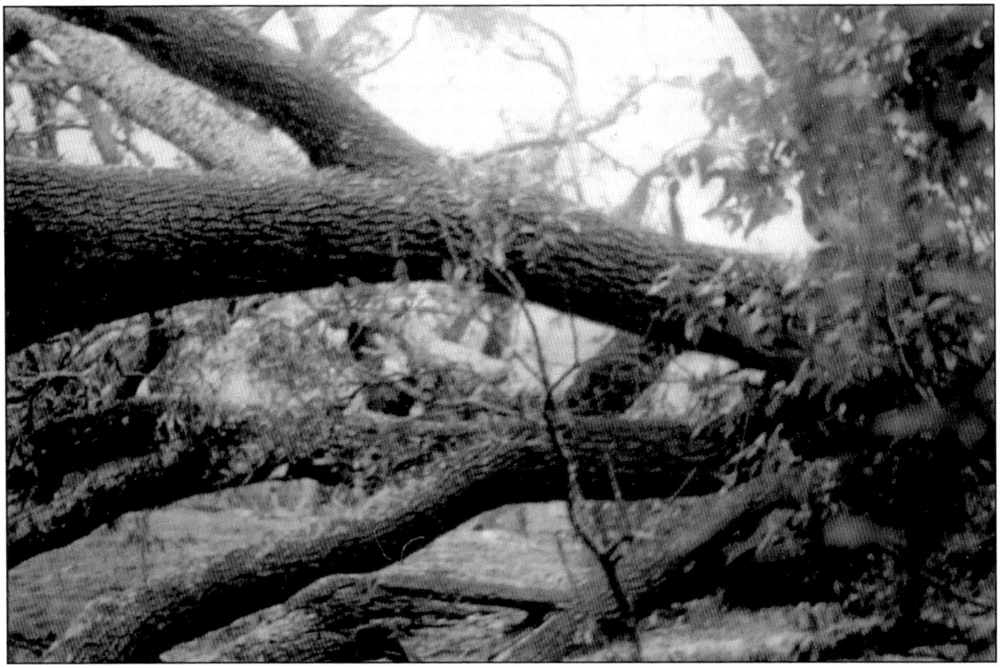

Yes, the photo is printed correctly. Massive oaks were downed by the hurricane. The area looked like a war zone. Even leaves were stripped from the trees left standing. Strange grasses and weeds came in with the blast of the storm that had probably been carried from the islands where the hurricane had passed through before striking the Carolina coast.

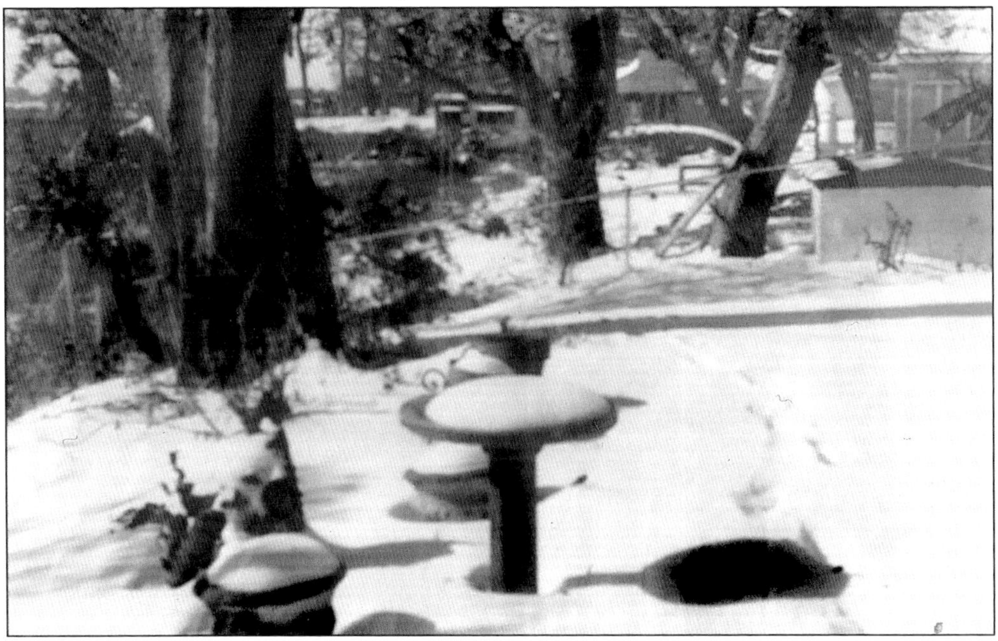

In December, just before Christmas, nature blanketed all the ugly of the storm's aftermath with beautiful snow. Small birds needing food came near houses. They had obviously weathered the storm just months before and their survival was remarkable. Many animals had died, however, and it was some years before their populations returned to normal.

"Captain Hugo" was created from a storm-felled oak tree by sculptor Stanley Wayman, artist-in-residence at the Museum on the Common. Creating it took away some of his frustrations after the storm. It has been recognized by the Smithsonian Institute as a National Folk Art Treasure, and by the National Museum of American Art and the National Institute for the Conservation of Cultural property, 1994. Some years later, a woodpecker family enlarged a knot hole and built a nest in Hugo's midriff.

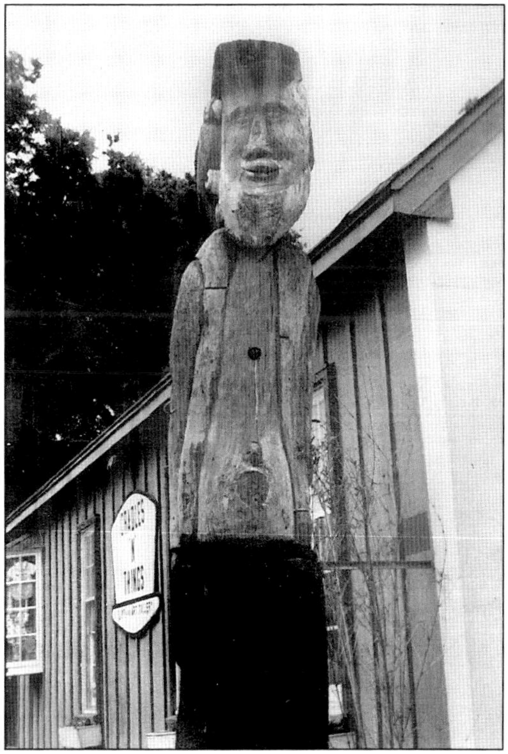

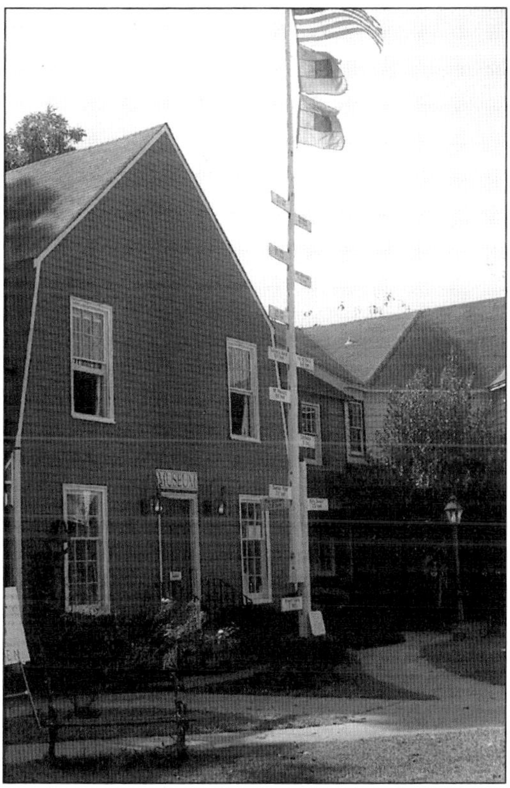

In front of the Museum on the Common is a tall post with many cross bars on it. Each depicts how high the tide and surge rose in various places between here and Georgetown. The genesis of the museum was the exhibit "Hugo Revisited," originally displayed at the state museum in Columbia. In 1994, the MOC presented "Phoenix from the Wind," an observance of the fifth anniversary of the hurricane.

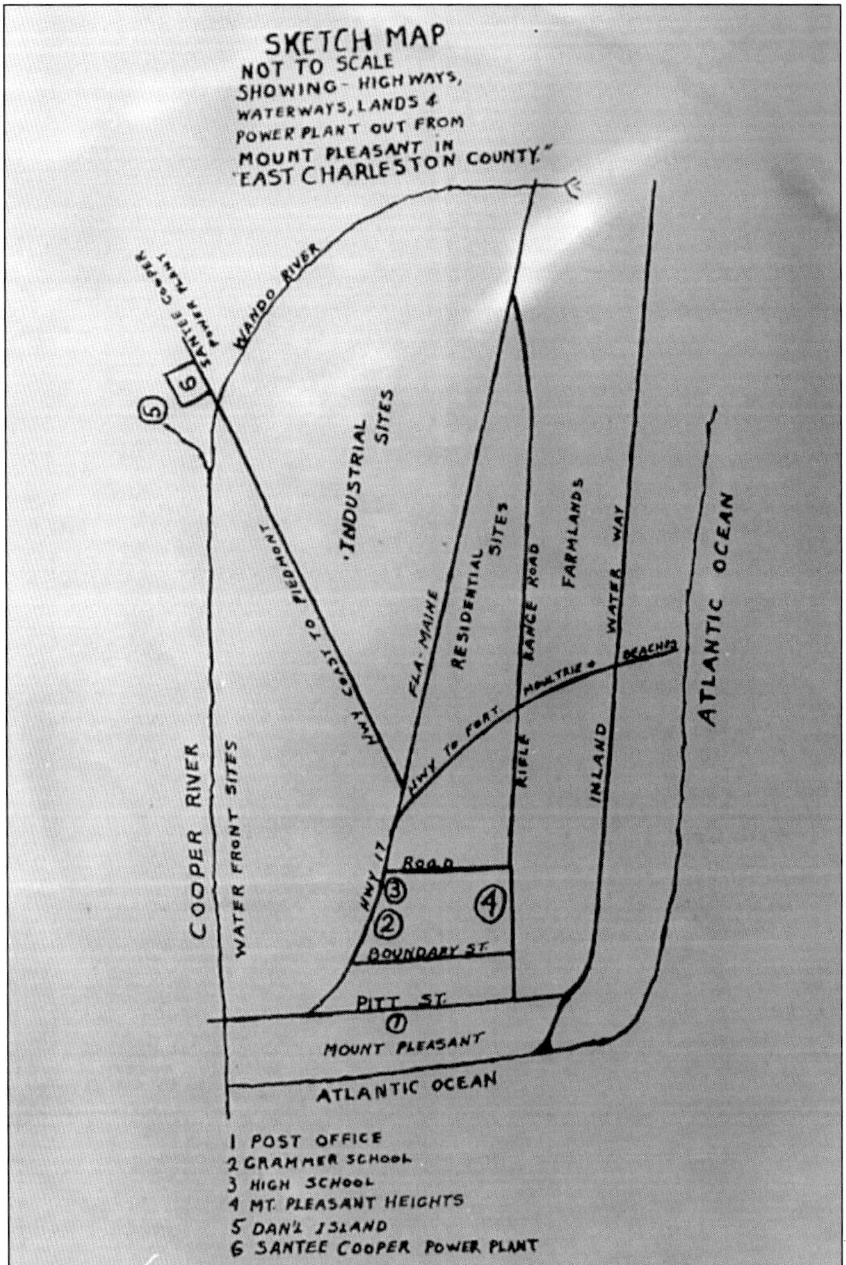

Over 50 years ago a sketch map in the booklet honoring World War II personnel indicated potential growth for the area. It has certainly taken place. This growth may be compared with the circles that emerge when a stone is thrown into a pond, ever widening as the boundaries of the town have done until the area around the little villages has become a metropolitan municipality of the 21st century.

The Friendly Town has attempted to delineate various customs and memories since the 1937 celebration of a century of incorporation with which the *Victorian Village* ended. Ever building on the past, the town looks forward to the future.